the names of all the flowers

the names of all the flowers

a memoir by melissa valentine

THE FEMINIST PRESS
AT THE CITY UNIVERSITY OF NEW YORK
NEW YORK CITY

Published in 2020 by the Feminist Press
at the City University of New York
The Graduate Center
365 Fifth Avenue, Suite 5406
New York, NY 10016

feministpress.org

First Feminist Press edition 2020

This book is supported in part by an award from the
National Endowment for the Arts.

This book was made possible thanks to a grant
from New York State Council on the Arts
with the support of Governor Andrew M. Cuomo
and the New York State Legislature.

This book was published with financial support from the
Jerome Foundation.

First printing July 2020

Cover photograph: *Untitled (For Jr.)* by Sadie Barnette, 2019
Cover and text design by Drew Stevens

Library of Congress Cataloging-in-Publication Data is available for this title.
ISBN: 9781936932856

PRINTED IN THE UNITED STATES OF AMERICA

For Junior

AUTHOR'S NOTE

With the understanding that the nature of memory is ephemeral, the following is true and factual based on my knowledge and memory. In the name of narrative flow, I have in some instances re-created dialogue, collapsed time, and reimagined certain details and conversations, but the story and all events herein are true. Some names have been changed to protect the identities of individuals.

"all these years of death later
I search through the index
of each new book on magic
hoping to find a new spelling
of your name"

AUDRE LORDE, "Alvin"

"I know what the world has done to my brother
and how narrowly he has survived it. And I
know, which is much worse, and this is the crime
which I accuse my country and countrymen, and
for which I nor time nor history will ever forgive
them, that they have destroyed and are destroying hundreds of thousands of lives and do not
know it and do not want to know it."

JAMES BALDWIN, *The Fire Next Time*

INTRODUCTION

Oakland, CA & Selma, AL
2016–2017

When I move back to Oakland around 2012, after being away for six years, I reach out to a childhood friend and we decide to reconnect over dinner. Her brother Corey has passed the threshold into adulthood. He has lived to become a man in his early twenties, and when we decide to have a drink at a bar after dinner, we are both surprised when he walks in with their cousin. We haven't seen each other in a long time. I remember him as a boy perpetually in the back seat of my friend's car because he was undersupervised and grief-stricken. They'd both lost their father back then, and we all gravitated to one another because of our common loss; they were fatherless, I was brotherless. The boys, now, don't smell clean, their clothes are a bit dingy, their faces greasy. Corey's hair is wild, long, and frizzy around the edges as if he's slept on it for days, and in both of them, him and his cousin, I see my brother Junior as if he were alive before me. I see him everywhere. We drink and we clink our glasses of Hennessy together again and again in celebration of our reunion. How good it is to see the boys all grown up and living.

When we were teenagers, my brother used to come home late. His hair looked like Corey's—long, frizzy, and unkempt, face slick with oil. He would look dirty and he would smell like the old smoke and alcohol that oozed from his greasy pores. But I'd be so happy to see him. Like the wild man he was, he would turn on the light no matter if it was midnight or three o'clock in the morning. "Hey," he'd announce himself in the dark. He was probably high or drunk or both, or a zombie from not sleeping for days, or he just wanted someone to talk to. "What time is it?" I'd ask, but I would not protest, would not ask him to leave, would not ask him to turn the light off. I just wanted a time stamp: he's home now. I would sleep while he ate his burrito on my bedroom floor. Maybe I'd wake up occasionally if he said something, asked me a question. He would finish eating and leave me, go downstairs to his bedroom, or sometimes he'd stay there, sleep on the floor of my bedroom and drift out in the morning. He was safe. He was home. That's what mattered.

After a few drinks, we decide to continue the reunion at my apartment not too far away. "You live in Funktown!" The boys lament about the east Lake Merritt neighborhood they'd grown up in, now hip and expensive, quickly whitening. "It's crazy over here," they say. They perceive the new neighborhood with wide eyes, completely shut out. Unemployable, without much education or experience, they cannot afford to live anywhere, let alone in the neighborhood they grew up in. It is an us-and-them kind of conversation. We the Oakland natives, they the white gentrifiers. I tell them that every year my building gets whiter and I see more and more license plates from places like Idaho, Oregon, Ohio. And then I change the subject and tell them how excited I am that they're here. What I don't say is how happy I am that they're still alive. We walk up to the door of my apartment and I am jubilant. I am with my brother. We are in one of those dreams where he's alive and I tell him, "I knew you weren't dead. I knew it."

I switch on the lights, put on some music, and open a bottle of wine. My friend grabs the wine glasses. I see that the boys have found the only kind of entertainment I have: a set of pink tarot cards. Slightly embarrassed, I feel the need to apologize. "Sorry," I say. "I don't have a TV." Because most people have them, but all I have are books and tarot cards. They surprise me by wanting readings. I chuckle to myself and agree. My friend pours the wine and I burn a stick of palo santo. I begin smudging the room and the cards, having them believe I'm some kind of diviner.

A total amateur, and drunk, I pull some cards for them. They are cards I am never excited to receive: the Moon, Death. I don't know if it's true, but I try and say something meaningful. I tell them they will be all right. I tell them they may go through a dark time. I tell them they will undergo a transformation and it will be difficult but they can survive. I give them the bad but inevitable advice I'd received when I myself had gone through a dark time. I tell them to survive. I explain that there is an *other side* to whatever is going on, but they'll have to work very hard to see it. I don't

3

really know what I'm saying but I say it with confidence. They nod. "Okay," they say. They hear it. They listen to each other's readings and offer commentary. At one point I cry. Maybe I've had too much wine. It is Junior I am talking to. "Do you have any questions?" I ask the cousin after his reading. He is very tall but his giant T-shirt that looks like a nightgown makes him look boyish. In his manner of speaking that muffles any sign of vulnerability, he says he does have a question.

"Okay." I look at him and wait for it.

"Well," he begins, shyly, "what I really want to know is . . ." He pauses for a moment. "Am I special?"

Corey provides the commentary during his reading. "Yeah!" he exclaims, as if that was the question for which he, too, had always longed to know the answer. I am confronted with my aliveness and theirs, both the improbability and the hope of it. I look at the men.

"Oh my goodness," I say in a sisterly if not motherly tone. The question is shocking and painful. My friend covers her mouth, feeling devastated like I do. "You are absolutely special." I say it matter-of-factly, without any doubt. I am talking to Junior now. "You are so deeply special. I need you to know how special you are."

GROWING UP, EVERYWHERE around me there was death. In Oakland, where I'm from, it was daily news. In fact, in 1991, around the time this story begins, a story headlined in the *Oakland Tribune* calling it "Oakland's Bloodiest Year." The city saw the most homicides it had ever seen that year, but that was only the beginning. In the years following, those numbers would increase. These crimes happen overwhelmingly in black communities. We are left to make sense of the losses, pick our communities back up, and go on living after each one with no tools, no resources, and, because it is so normalized, no discussion.

This book is an ode to our collective grief and trauma. It deserves to have a name. It deserves discussion. When I gave mine a name, it began to heal. And though it will always be with me, I can say now, without shame: I have been traumatized. Each time there is a death in the news, I am retraumatized. Especially a young black person. Remembering is not just about honoring our trauma, it is about honoring life and speaking truth to injustice. Death should not be such a normal part of our lives. Burying young people should not be so normal. And yet, we all touch it. We are deeply hurt by it. This book is for all who have touched this and all who suffer in silent trauma and grief either directly or indirectly. Therefore, this book is for all of us.

My brother Junior ran for his life and was finally murdered on the side of a freeway in West Oakland in 2000. He was shot in the head and left bleeding on the street. He had been released from prison just a week before. He was nineteen and had spent the first year of his adult life in prison. Before that he'd spent time in a jail, and before that, in juvenile detention centers in Oakland, as well as a group home. He graduated from boy jail to adult jail just as soon as he turned eighteen. He was killed weeks before his twentieth birthday. His killer was never found and his murder most likely not even investigated, because his was one of eighty homicides that year. He was the school-to-prison pipeline in effect, black-on-black crime, a statistic, a flash on the nightly news, a nobody, a thug, just another homicide—a person.

This book is my love letter to those who mourn every day.

We ready black boys for prison, not life. We ready black boys for death, not life. One in three of all black babies born today will spend time in prison. The American criminal justice system holds more than 2.3 million people in approximately 1,719 state prisons, 102 federal prisons, 942 juvenile correctional facilities, and 3,283 local jails. These facilities are overwhelmingly filled with black bodies.

These are statistics. But real life doesn't happen in perfect percentages. In my family there were two black boys and both spent time in the system. My brother didn't grow up in what we might imagine when we think of disadvantage, when we conjure the picture and story of a black felon. He came from a two-parent household on the good side of the city. So, what happened? What happened to my family? What happened to my brother? What went wrong? The city happened. The system happened. Survival happened.

THIS STORY STARTS in Oakland, California. I was born in 1984 to a white landscaper father and a black postal-clerk mother. An odd match, my parents found each other in San Francisco in the late sixties. They'd both escaped something, and perhaps that is what bound them. My father, a white Quaker from Allentown, Pennsylvania, a landscaper like his own father, hitchhiked to California after a difficult semi-imprisonment to the United States for his decision to conscientiously object to the Vietnam War. Working in fields outside of San Francisco for pennies, picking strawberries with undocumented workers, he paid his dues and escaped the war.

My mother, a black woman of the Deep South, the eighth of fourteen siblings in Selma, Alabama, boarded a Greyhound bus for San Francisco in 1965. One of her sisters was already there with a house in the Fillmore District of San Francisco, where she'd started a family. My mother would follow suit, with many dreams in tow—dreams as lofty as becoming a singer, and dreams as practical and urgent as saving enough money to build her parents in rural Selma a bathroom. She did both, taking singing classes at the City College of San Francisco in between long hours working as a nanny for wealthy white families of Nob Hill. She escaped the South. Her South was rural life, it was Jim Crow: sharecropping, segregation, no opportunity. San Francisco might as well have been another country.

They married in Marin County in 1972—an interracial marriage, still illegal in Alabama—overlooking the San Francisco Bay, and then moved across that same bay to Oakland to buy a home and start a family. I am the fifth of six children. Cornelius, the firstborn, arrived in 1973; then Claire in 1975; Vivian in 1978; Christopher Jr. in 1980; and me in 1984. We split off into little groups. Junior and I were the closest for a very long time. Then Angelica arrived in 1992, and suddenly our clan had a baby to look after.

Junior and I were both young enough to have the 1990s

in Oakland as the backdrop for our childhood—hip hop, R&B, absolute pride in blackness and our culture, and also a crack epidemic, a war on drugs, the three-strikes laws, and pervasive violence in our communities. We didn't have the word *gentrification* yet. It was segregation then, stark class division and more often than not, race division. There were entire sides of town you didn't want to find yourself in during day or night—the entire west side, the vast east side, and many parts of the north. Those were places that instilled fear. We lived in one of the nicer parts of North Oakland. Our neighborhood was wedged in between three distinct areas: West Oakland on the worst side; Piedmont, a wealthy enclave, on another; and Rockridge, an affluent hillside neighborhood of North Oakland. Depending on which direction we walked, we could find crime, unsupervised and bored city kids, drugs, and police, or we could find European cheese samples, quaint antique shops, and independent bookstores. Our neighborhood was right there, on the edge of prosperity and desolation. We were somewhere in that middle—some of us crossing back and forth in both directions, fluidly affiliating with all sides of Oakland; some of us educated in private schools, making code-switching awkward; and others of us matriculated into Oakland public schools, making the street our familiar friend.

Junior and I went to public school, me always ambling a few years behind him, watching and learning how to protect ourselves from our city, which seemed to lure kids like us—kids with busy, stressed parents, little money, and little attention—into the street where we could find what we sought: money, entertainment, attention, social status, and power. It is a setup perfectly designed for our failure, for our demise. Surviving the power and lure of the street all around you is the exception, not the rule.

The place you are from summons you. Like the trauma of grief, you start to know it as if it's part of you. It travels; wherever you go, there it is. However old you get, there it is. Whatever progress you think you make, there it is. Even if you leave and it dissipates for a while, there it always is when you return: home, grief. I made it out by what felt like the skin of my teeth. I moved to New York for college, and when I returned to Oakland, there it was, waiting for me.

It shape-shifts. It becomes people. It becomes substances. For many years I attempted to subdue it. I drugged it. I fed it lots of liquor. I spoke mean to it. Sometimes trauma is loud: *Who do you think you are?* it yells. Sometimes it's so quiet you mistake it for yourself: *Who do I think I am?*

Every year I inevitably become older than he was when he died. Older and older and older I become. He remains nineteen while I grow old. When I moved back to Oakland after being away for college, for a very long time I couldn't take the freeway exit that he'd died on. After the shooting, my family had gone back to the site and written poetry all over the wall he died in front of. Our words were immediately covered by the state—we had defaced state property, they said. Ivy covers the wall now, and each time I am in a car with someone and they take that exit, because how could they know, my breathing speeds up and it gets loud: *Who do you think you are?* Every time I pass by the place, I feel the need to say how much time has passed. "Gosh, Junior, I can't believe I'm twenty-five now." Twenty-six, twenty-seven, twenty-eight, twenty-nine, thirty . . . I keep getting older and you're still dead. My life is always in relation to it.

It is hard to enter this story because it is not past tense; this story is alive and ongoing. Its aliveness is exhibited in the constant rate at which murders of black men are committed, in the grief- and trauma-informed lives of the people left behind in the aftermath. We are all witness and therefore no one is spared from this loss. This state of grief—personal and collective—is our shared consciousness.

SIXTEEN YEARS AFTER he's gone, I find myself in Selma, Alabama, alone with my mother. No dad, no siblings, just us that year. Mom has pleaded with me, begged me to accompany her to our now shrinking family reunion, and so I do. She doesn't drive and so she needs a chauffeur and I think she wants my company. Dad has taken a new gardening job with the city and all my siblings are either busy or no longer interested in these nostalgic trips back home. I take the opportunity to write in the quiet country and be with Mom in her happiest state. Even though nearly everyone has died, she is still most peaceful on the red dirt of the land down home.

It's been a while since I've been back and I don't know which relatives I'll find. That year, there is a boy there who is Junior. Some cousin of some cousin or other has come with his little sister to be with their grandma-in-law who is married to my uncle. I can't really understand who the children are or why they're there, but immediately I feel they are there for me to witness; they are me and Junior. They are both sweet and innocent but he's older and the change he's about to endure is so visible to me. He's about to become a teenager—that tragic time when blackness takes on new and unwanted power, from something you just innocently, even joyously *are* into something others both fear in you and for you. It is during this transition that you must learn to protect yourself by any means necessary. This boy is about to become a black man.

It is July. We board the plane to Alabama with the news that Alton Sterling has been killed by a police officer. When we land, Philando Castile has just been killed by a police officer. This news feels constant and every time someone dies like this, Junior dies again. These deaths are distinct, of course. Police brutality victims and homicide victims on the street are distinct, let's be very clear, but what echoes through my body and triggers my own trauma is the loss of young black life, again and again; we have become used to it both in the news and in our neighborhoods. I thought this country house without internet, surrounded by nature, would be a good place to get writing done, but when I open my document, the cursor blinks at me: *death, death, death*. Nothing I write can make sense of all the death, connect it on the page the way it's connected so intricately in my mind and heart. I'm in the place where it all started. I'm in the Deep South where murder was not only permitted but celebrated; I'm in the land where Jim Crow was born. I'm in the heart of America. I'm home.

I open my laptop, but I can't focus and I can't keep my eyes off those two kids. The whole time, they remain in the corner of my eye. I think I remain in theirs too. They beg me to take them behind the house to see the creek Junior and I once played in. They want to be near me, ask me questions about my life. I'm the youngest adult there. I watch them as they run around and chase each other, while they sit on the porch and catch their breath.

When they leave I squeeze them both and tell them how sweet they are. I have become some kind of old auntie person, unrecognizable even to myself. I barely know these kids. They're not even kin to me. "Do you know how sweet you are?" I ask them. They politely nod yes. "Will you promise to stay sweet?" They smile fidgety smiles and wrinkle their noses awkwardly under my attention. I release them once they've promised. We both know they are lying, that they might try, but that every system in existence will try and steal their sweetness, make them tough so they can protect themselves and each other, so they might survive. But, however futile my demand is, it is imperative that they know.

When they leave and the festivities of the family reunion are over, the quiet is acute. Unlike all the summers we'd come as children, when Junior and I were there together with our cousins to run free in the wild woods, now all the elders have almost gone and the children, too—grown up, uninterested, estranged, or dead. There are no big meals left to prepare, there are no grandparents, there is no Junior. It is just me and the remaining old ladies now. My oldest aunt occupies the trailer behind my late grandparents' house. My other aunt, who used to live in the house, died some years before from diabetes complications and so it is empty, a guest house for relatives in the summer. This house was my grandmother's good house. After the Jim Crow era, they were able to move from the one-room shack into this house. They could farm their own land and not have to sharecrop on the white man's land in exchange for almost nothing. They could grow their own food for a few more cents and save up to build this house. It wasn't a far move. It was just down the road, under a mile away.

Now, the absence of life is absolute. How old I've become, how many people have died while I live, how long they've all been gone. My own life echoes loudly out of the ringing silence: *Who has come before you? Why are you here? What have you come to do?*

On one of the last days of our trip, I drive myself into town to work at the Selma Public Library. I intend to use the Wi-Fi there to get some work done, but when I find a seat in the research area upstairs, I become too distracted by the files of family records surrounding me. Where were our people from? Here. But where exactly? I find myself rummaging through files, searching for the surnames I know. Finally I find the oldest census records for Perry County. I look under my mother's maiden name and there we are, the property of one of the richest men in town, classified by color: 119 slaves. 103 of them black. 16 of them mulatto. Living in 25 houses.

When I leave the library I am in a daze. The sun is so hot, my skin instantly becomes wet. I get in the car and turn on the AC full blast. While the car starts to cool off, I begin to catch my breath and look around. There is nothing. It's just rows of dilapidated buildings, one gorgeous but empty antebellum hotel overlooking the Edmund Pettus Bridge and the Alabama River, and, eerily, no people walking around because it's too hot and because there's nothing to see. Relatively unchanged since the 1960s, it is not hard to imagine White Only signs in every window. No one wants to come here.

Just beyond downtown, just one or two streets over, out of view, are the projects, youth, many people without work. The Wal-Mart and fast food economy is not nearly enough to sustain people and so instead a poverty cycle is firmly in place. You can see it just as soon as you step away from the downtown, beyond the perimeter of the city where there are empty houses in which families squat, streets where drugs necessarily supplement incomes, and fatal bullets are shot.

This city, like so many cities, was built by its black citizens and now what? No generational wealth to speak of, no nothing. Just our stories. Our records. I drive down one of these streets in a daze, on my way back home to the country. The plantation-style homes I pass aren't quaint; they are opulent white supremacy with nice bows around them. All I can think is 119 slaves, 103 black, 16 mulatto, 25 houses. I slow down for the first person I've seen in a while: a black man with long sagging denim shorts and no shirt, who crosses the street before me. I am struck by the beauty of the glistening skin of his back, and by the contrast of his tough exterior against the softness of this landscape. I sit with my hands clenching the wheel. I become angry. Sad. This is a slave town. This is an African town. Even after the man has disappeared into the green distance, I include him in my vision. I marvel at the beauty surrounding us. It's so lush out here. You can grow anything on these rolling hills, these peaceful pastures, in this thick, intoxicating air. This is slave country. I step on the gas. I'm still so hot despite the AC, and it matches the clashing in my mind. All this beauty and all this ugly. *Damn.* I drive back home oscillating between the two, holding both.

The next day I go into Selma again. I need to escape the blinking cursor on my laptop. The trauma of grief is loud today. I find a place to get my nails done. In the salon chair I let my body be limp like it wants to be. Someone moves my feet and hands in and out of warm water. I sit in a long row of black women in salon chairs. CNN blares on every television in the shop, and no one can stop looking. Black murder is the news of the day. Everyone is mourning. We watch as black murder is sensationalized, made to matter for one moment in the world the way it matters for us every single day. Surely each one of us women in this shop has lost someone in a similar manner. We watch as reporters interview the sisters of the victims, the mothers.

For one moment they are asked what they think.

PART ONE
INNOCENCE

Oakland, CA & Selma, AL
1990–1993

ONE

Junior is walking ahead of me, his curls bouncing on the back of his head. He's bigger than me, his legs longer and faster. He stops and points at the ground below him: a wet block of cement. He grins his mischievous grin, and I know it means we are going to do something we shouldn't. I watch him as I always do. *Go first. Show me.* He turns to our neighbor's yard and finds a thin stick in a patch of sour grass; he shows me his weapon, and I watch as he etches his name into the wet cement, a crust forming around each letter as he scrapes. *C.C.V.* He offers me his stick, and I quickly etch my name before the sun dries the cement and it's too late. *M.C.V.* We look down at our work, proud, hands on hips, sun scorching the backs of our necks. Now we are permanently here.

There seem to be two seasons here in Oakland: fog or sun; winter or spring. No in-between. The in-between is the life we must decipher, the life that hangs in the air like the thing you cannot say. I am seven years old, standing at three feet tall. My biggest fear is speaking. My brother is eleven years old. If I had to guess, his biggest fear would be running out of space. He is fast and big, and he needs a lot of space to feel free. Maybe his biggest fear would be not being free. When I grow up, I want to be big and free like him.

I have only been to three places in my life: Oakland, Alabama, Pennsylvania. Oakland is home. It is where I was born. It is where I live. Home is where you live and where your heart is supposed to be. Oakland is graffiti and blood-stained cement; it is redwoods and eucalyptus trees; it is rolling hills and the silver, undulating San Francisco Bay that reminds you that you are on the edge, that you are small.

Alabama is mythical. It is the home of my mother and the home of snakes, ghosts, sounds of the night. The night is alive in Alabama; it sings or groans or warns. I can never tell, so I turn the air conditioner on full blast to make it stop. In the morning it's safe again. No one around for miles, just us and the kudzu. Mom is awake in Alabama. I remember what her face looks like, her smile. There is only one season there: summer, July. A violent, wet heat. The dirt is red like the under-color of my mother's brown skin.

Pennsylvania is the home of my father. I imagine my father as a child, sitting quiet and still in his Pennsylvania Quaker meeting house, restless and bored between his older siblings, my grandparents shushing him the way he does us when Junior and I make too much noise every Sunday at the Berkeley Friends Meeting. In my only memory of the place he is from, the season is fall. The wood is dry, the creek is cold, the people are white, the land is flat, the grass is still green. There is no wind to blow the red and orange leaves, but they fall anyway, as if the giant oaks lean over and place them gently on the ground themselves. The houses are pretty, the air smells like the batter of something sweet; I make believe I am inside of a painting hanging on a wall in a museum, an observer of a pleasant scene.

Our house in Oakland is in the in-between. In between the hills and the flats. In between Oakland and Piedmont. In between rich and poor. It is a border and I am without shape, like liquid, or like wind, forming myself against walls. I am the roses that someone planted around the edges in between. I am the weeds that won't die.

Our house is surrounded by life: vegetation, children, all out of control, growing inside and out of the house in varying shapes and colors. Mom comes from farmers; she has thirteen siblings, she is familiar with the growing of things. She was a sharecropper, but she also grew food: black-eyed peas, collard greens, and her favorite, okra. The sight of fresh okra makes her beam like no other material thing can. Inside the house is the wildlife we created—all the children and the objects that make up a life.

My bare feet are round and ashy. My chubby knees are full of scars. I've waited all morning for the sun to come out and am celebrating its arrival on the front steps with my dolls. The front door to our house bursts open. A gap-toothed, oversunned Junior fires from it.

"Look what I got," he says, shaking a set of keys, bouncing as if his feet are made of rubber. His little body works hard to contain his wildness, but always, it wants to be elsewhere, to go, go. In his face I see the male version of my own: buoyant curls around soft, sun-splotched cheeks.

I look up from my naked, starving Barbies. With their blank, blue-eyed stares, they await the soft magnolia petal skirts and bowls of poisonous berries I prepare for them at the top of our front steps. I look down at Junior, who has made his way to me and is seated on the step below. He visors the sun with his hand and looks back at me.

"What're the keys to?" I ask, pushing aside my pile of berries.

"Julia and Josh went on vacation." He grins. "Josh gave me the house key, c'mon." He motions for me to follow.

"But Mom said not to leave the house."

"C'mon!" Junior is already at the bottom of the stairs.

I don't want to miss out. I am the baby after all, and to be invited along makes me feel like I have been chosen. I push my dolls and their things to the side near the iron railing and follow. Mom is deep asleep and probably won't even notice. I don't know what we'll do, but whatever it is, it'll be worth the trouble we get in. My bare feet consider going inside first to get shoes, but I quickly decide against it— better not to risk waking Mom. The walk is short, and I like feeling the prickly, hot cement on my feet.

The streets on our block are lined with decorative pear trees in bloom and some giant trees that Dad planted way before we were born. Some of them have gotten so big their roots have begun to lift the sidewalk. Every home on our street has a well-kept garden and a new car in the driveway except for ours. The front of our old craftsman house has two carob trees, exploding with edible, dark-chocolate-colored pods. There is a patch of garden in between them that is the resting place for Dad's big plant pots and an over-growth of poor man's orchids.

The sidewalk is busy with traffic. Neighbors walk their dogs and stroll their children. There is a hospital two blocks down, and often nurses in scrubs power walk by on their breaks. They all inevitably stop in front of our house, lift the stroller or guide their dogs over a knotted water hose that litters the front sidewalk, around the rusted black Camaro whose nose protrudes out from the driveway. These are the people who crane their necks up toward the front window, trying to catch a glimpse of who lives in this house.

Mom is asleep most days. Her night shift as a sorting clerk at the San Francisco Post Office leaves her on a vam-pire schedule. Dad makes other people's homes beautiful for a living, drawing out fancy plans of their backyards on giant paper scrolls and drawing in blue ink where he will put this or that shrub or vine around the premises.

In the summertime, we must occupy ourselves. Our older siblings are too busy, too far away to watch us. Junior's lithe body is the one I'd rather have, and so I follow him around wherever he'll allow, my legs thumping inelegantly after him like a small giant. I try desperately to keep up as though we share one body. We are often left alone, in the wilderness of childhood. We often take long bike rides through Piedmont, the wealthy neighboring town. While he muscles up the hills, I walk my bike, taking deep plea-sure in looking into the homes of rich people, the soft light from the lamps and chandeliers providing a perfect view into luxurious and comfortable lives. I want to feel that kind of comfort, any kind. I want to sit on a plush white couch and watch Nickelodeon while Mom makes macaroni and cheese from a box. Something like that. When I finally catch up to Junior, we both coast downhill toward home, screaming gleefully in fear and joy as we ride the wind on our BMXs.

Sometimes we visit Bee up the street in the yellow apartments. She is very old and lives alone. She fixes us ice cream and ginger ale when it's hot, and watches us eat. Her wrinkled leather lips smile at us, pleased, as she puffs away on her Benson & Hedges. I ask if I can use the bathroom just so I can sit on her cushioned pink toilet seat, take off my moccasins, let my toes sink into the fluffy pink bathmat, drink in the smell of her potpourri, and wash my hands with silky floral soap. It is best to stay out as long as possible each day to avoid the darkness of our own house, the weight of objects.

Today I follow Junior up the street to Josh and Julia's house. It is yet another attempt to entertain ourselves while school is out. This act of breaking in seems benign; we have nothing and they have everything. It is an act of justice. And as the smallest person in my family, I am thrilled just to be invited—to be in the presence of my cool big brother who does not consider authority or consequence, who knows only desire. We walk past Mr. Kramer's, the old World War II vet who yells curse words at Dad when his things spill over into his side yard: ladders, hoses, plants, empty pots, rusty cans of fertilizers, bags of soil, garbage, and smelly bags of compost. Some mornings you can hear crashing and Mr. Kramer out there yelling, "Fucking asshole Chris," and "Goddamn you, Chris."

Julia and Josh's house is covered in wooden shingles. Their garden is neat with a lawn and manicured camellia bushes; purple wisteria drape the front porch and a brand-new blue Volvo is parked in the driveway.

Junior heads straight for the side yard that's blocked by a white fence we'll have to climb. Junior makes it look easy. He takes a running start and then, like some kind of ninja, boosts himself up and over the fence.

"C'mon," he says from the other side.

I place one of my bare feet on the water spigot on the side of the house, the one their neatly coiled garden hose is attached to. I get a grip on the fence and hurl the other leg over, leaving my body teetering at the top. I don't ask for help. The last thing I want is to be a nuisance and no longer be asked to accompany him on adventures like this, but before I get the chance to struggle, Junior's warm hands pull at my leg, guiding me down to the ground. By the time I can dust myself off, he's already ahead of me, trying the key in the back door.

What if someone is home? What if an alarm goes off and the police come? My mind moves to these places quickly, but the door opens easily because we have the key. But for me, the little one, the Goody Two-shoes, the budding voyeur, I both am afraid of getting in trouble and can't look away. The blinds that cover the glass door shiver as we race inside the house. The kitchen is the first room. I half expect their fluffy poodle to come running up to us like she always does, but then I remember we are alone. Once inside, we immediately start looking for treasures. I am struck by the absence of my friend. No one is home, just the humming presence of their objects, neatly placed and cared for. I follow Junior to the pantry. "Jackpot!" he yells, and we fill our arms with as many Squeezits and Fruit Roll-Ups as we can hold. After we've ransacked the pantry for junk food, we search the rest of the house. My adrenaline is rushing from the feeling of emptiness around us, from the potential risk of being caught—but the possibility of all this being ours is even more intoxicating.

We skip over the living room and dining room, head upstairs to the kids' rooms, and split up. Romantic paintings of female silhouettes with red lips and kohl-lined eyes cover the walls of the stairwell and seem to watch me as I make my way to Julia's room. I look down for tracks made by my potentially dirty feet; I am careful not to leave a trace of myself.

Julia's room is at the top of the stairs and to the left. Junior goes to Josh's, on the right. Julia's room is full of light. A skylight on the ceiling of her loft bedroom brings in a beam of light filled with sparkling, magical dust particles. The room smells plastic, and a faint smell of sunscreen hangs in the air. It feels strange without her there. I climb the wooden ladder that leads to the loft where I know all of the Barbie stuff is put away in storage bins. The heat has risen and it feels as if I'm floating in a warm spaceship. I look out the side window and peer into the backyard, imagining this is my bedroom, this is my garden.

I think of Julia, her pale, freckled nose and feline face. This is the room where we play. I open the container of Barbie clothes. I've seen them all before, and I lay out the ones I want: the cheerleading outfit, the ball gown, the nurse uniform. They lie there on the carpet next to her pink princess bed. The sun from the skylight envelops me. Sitting on my knees, I study the outfits I've chosen. The silence makes itself known; I can't even hear Junior in the other room, only my thoughts. What must he be doing? Has he found anything good? What does it mean to be people who steal from their friends? I become aware that we are stealing. My homemade Barbie clothes await me on the front steps and these beautiful ones stare at me, asking me to take them, but I no longer want them. For a moment longer, I stay in the warmth, surrounded by the nice outfits and the frilly floral bed and the soft carpet; I like it here, and I let myself enjoy being in the space before putting the clothes back and heading down the ladder to find Junior.

Junior is excitedly looking at baseball cards. I turn my back to him and look out the glass door that opens to a balcony and overlooks the garden and swing set. I stand near the glass door wanting to be in the presence of this luxury; I attempt to inhabit it until Junior is ready to go. We finally head back downstairs, both empty-handed, to where the real goodies wait for us in the kitchen. We are done here.

One after the other—me trailing behind, of course— we hop back over the fence, tossing our treats over first. With our arms full, we make our way across the street to the Catholic church and sit on the steps between two giant statues of white lions. We make ourselves sick eating Fruit Roll-Ups and Gushers filled with berry-flavored slime, and wash it all down with sugary Squeezits. I cannot imagine anything more fantastic.

People walk by licking massive ice cream cones from the nearby ice creamery.

"Yuppies," I snicker as a group passes us. It's what I've heard Dad call them. I am being provocative, practicing what I think might be a bad word.

Junior gives me a look, squinting his eyes a little, which I recognize as affirming his status as older and more knowledgeable than me. "They're just white people," he informs me.

We watch more white people pass by as we laugh, telling jokes to each other and desperately stuffing the last sweets in our mouths, saving none for later. There are so many of us at home that we have learned to eat competitively if we want any. We head back home. All of my Barbie things are where I left them on the steps. We go in and I feel instantly repelled.

The house feels cool, as if shaded. The curtains are drawn; no sun comes in. No one is home except for Mom in the back room sleeping, her distant snoring the only sound. My feet are covered in an ashy-brown dust from the hot ground and the fence I climbed. As I approach the bedroom I share with Junior and my big sister Vivian, a knock on the front door makes me jump. I stop cold and listen for a moment to the terror racing in my chest, waiting for whomever it is to disappear. Another series of soft knocks repeats. I move toward the door like a gunman. When I am a safe distance from the closed door, I draw up the courage to ask who is there like Mom taught me.

"Can Melissa come out and play?" It's Natalie, a girl my age from up the street.

I let myself relax a little, but I do not open the door. I open the mail slot in the middle of the door and peek out so she can see my lips move.

"Hi," I say, tight-lipped.

"Can you play?"

I am filled with dread, hoping she doesn't ask to come inside. In an act of protection, I put my back to the door and spread my arms before answering. I take a deep breath and crouch back down to the mail slot. "I'll be out in a few minutes."

"Can you make us butter tortillas?" Sometimes I come outside with concoctions I've made in the house while Mom is asleep and Dad is at work. Vanilla cinnamon milk or tortillas cooked in butter.

"Okay," I say, relieved I didn't have to open the door. "Come back in five minutes."

I'm happy to have something else to do besides sit in the dark house. In the kitchen, I light the stove, listening to it click a few times before the flame finally catches. There's a pan already there, thick with some previous meal's slick grease. I smear butter onto it anyway and add a flour tortilla until it's bubbling and ready. All of the dishes are dirty and too difficult to wash, so I pick it up with my hands and deliver it to the soft knocks that have returned at the door. My hand reaches through the mail slot to the outside where the kids grab it on the other side.

"Are you coming?"

"I'll be right there."

At Natalie's house we play Barbies. Natalie's uncle has just come back from a place called Brazil, and from her room where we play we overhear him going on about his trip. A glittering mobile of the solar system hangs from the ceiling. Brazil and outer space may as well be the same.

"Where do we live?" Natalie asks. It's my turn to choose where our dolls live in their make-believe lives.

I space out for a moment; my head shifts back up at the spinning planets on the ceiling of her tidy room.

"Brazil," I say, still looking up.

I spend most of the day out of the house even though Mom told me not to. The sun is still bright in the sky but going down. I overhear Natalie's mom tell her from the other room that I should probably go home to have dinner with my family. As I march down the street, I look into the houses of my neighbors: the soft light of lamps illuminates cozy scenes—relaxation, dinner preparations. A heaviness enters my legs; my walk becomes labored.

My sister Vivian greets me from her post on the couch. "Hey. Where have you been?" *The Maury Povich Show* is blasting, which means Dad's not home yet.

"Mommy's mad at you," Vivian says idly. "She wants you."

I take a deep breath and walk toward Mom's room through the sliver of a path in between a dining table and a piano, both erupting with papers and garden tools, wine boxes filled with more of the same, disfiguring the shapes of the furniture they live on. Mom's door is ajar. I open it to find her asleep and snoring loudly. Junior is sitting at the foot of the bed, pouting with his arms crossed. She wakes to the slightest noise, the tiniest movement. She's heard me, and without opening her eyes, she knows I'm there.

"Sit down," she says.

I join my brother at the foot of her bed, the place of punishment.

"I thought I told you two not to leave the house."

I try and defend myself. "But Mommy, I was bored and I just went to—"

"Shh! Sit. And be quiet. I don't want to hear it. You kids will be the death of me." Junior lets out a loud grunt of protest.

Her voice is impressively awake, and then as quickly as she disciplines us, she is back asleep, only able to hear us in her unconscious. My mother has been asleep my whole life. This is what it feels like to me. Every night Dad drives her over the Bay Bridge and into San Francisco where she stays all night. Her title at the post office, as I understand it, is Goddess of Zip Codes. She is proud of the specialized knowledge she possesses about San Francisco, all the numbers, borders, and maps she has memorized. She comes home to a house full of energetic children and a teenager who want her attention, who want her homemade lunches and hot breakfasts of grits or oatmeal, who want her eyes on them. I want her attention. I like being at her side, like when she calls me her right-hand man. Just like she is the Goddess of Zip Codes, in our big, messy, chaotic house, she is the Goddess of All Things, and when she's not happy, she blames Dad and Dad blames us and then no one is happy. Most mornings, though, she helps us out the door and off to school, then makes herself breakfast, watches a soap opera or two, and sleeps for the rest of the day.

Being at the foot of her bed is something like attention, but not the kind I want. I think of an escape. The curtains are all pulled tight so light can't get in. On one side of the brass bed is a mountain of clothes packed to the ceiling, and on the other is a vanity stacked with pay stubs from the post office, an arrangement of Mother's Day cards, an anniversary card from Dad, a bouquet of dying honeysuckle clippings, a photo of Grandma Annie looking small next to a big cactus plant, trinkets and bills—all covering the vanity so that its surface can't be seen. Next to all these objects are the only things in the room that really interest me: perfumes in bottles that resemble diamonds and crystals. Beautiful by Estée Lauder, a dark purple bottle of Poison by Dior, and a red bottle of Opium by Yves Saint-Laurent.

When she is awake, Mom is the kind of woman who wears perfume. Behind me, she snores rhythmically; her faint and not unpleasant garlic breath fills the room. She is also the kind of woman who eats whole sections of raw garlic to ward off a cold. Her hair is wound up in rollers beneath a pair of holey underwear. She is the kind of woman who thinks they are as good as silk for setting her curls. I long for the smell of perfume, the smell of my awake mother. During the summer when school is out, since Mom can't watch us during the day, she forbids us to leave the house. When she finds out I've left, she punishes me by making me sit at the foot of her bed for as long as I can stand it: discipline and childcare in her sleep.

All I can think of is getting out of this room and taking

a bottle of perfume with me. I want to touch the bottles, spray them on my neck and wrists the way she does. If I can't have her I will wear her, have a part of her with me all the time. Just as I adjust my body so I can reach for the vanity, the bed creaks and her snoring stops. Back down I go. She snorts a few times, and I can hear her breath adjust to my movements, getting deeper the longer I sit still. Junior is onto me. On her exhale, I try again and he joins, both of us trying to escape. She stops snoring, snorts. We play this game for what feels like eternity.

When a big rolling snore comes like thunder, I take a deep breath and go for it again. I very carefully slide myself off the bed, imagining I am small and light. On her next exhale, I tiptoe very slowly toward the door. Junior has also made it to the floor successfully and is behind me. Under my foot the floor creaks and she snaps awake.

"Get back!" she roars.

As fast as we can, we sit down at the foot of the bed. She is back asleep, snoring deeply. There is nothing to do but surrender to the rhythm of her breath. Without looking at her, I visualize her belly inflating and deflating on each breath, filling the air with her essence, watching me without seeing me. She teaches me how to live with my eyes closed. I stare at myself in the vanity mirror, my two-day-old pigtails blending into the rest of my face. My brother looks at me, tries to telepathically ask how we'll get out of here. The little slivers of light coming in from the windows start to fade as it becomes night. We take on a sepia quality along with the rest of the room—unidentifiable shapes of grays and browns in the dark. The mirror reflects to me a strange and shapeless glob of little girl and her big brother, antsy, both working against all of their natural inclinations in order to be the silent and still children Mom needs us to be. Behind us, she is a seal or a mermaid—some large fish in repose—occupying the worlds of land and sleep. I learn to wait and I learn to long.

The summer days bleed into one another. Every day the outside calls to me, and I am left to decide: Will I be good or will I be bad? Will I stay or will I leave? Will I be able to move between the outside world and the inside one of my family, of Mom's orders from bed or bath?

Today, like all days, Mom calls for me (I am the baby, the right-hand man). Her voice was meant to sing opera, not call for little girls and boys. It warms the corners of the bathroom and spreads out to find me: *Me-lis-sa*, it sings. I don't want to help. I am not ready to be seen or found. But her voice reaches me, and I have no choice but to obey. And helping her bathe is something like attention.

She is lying in the bathtub with her eyes closed. I know she's called to me because the water has gotten tepid and she wants me to run it hot again. There is all manner of junk surrounding her, but the bath is just a bath—just her body soaking in water. She is serene, possibly asleep. I study her, from her long, pale breasts all the way up to her jaw, her mouth, her eyes; she is so still. She startles awake from a dream or from the cold water. She looks disoriented, grimaces, and adjusts her body.

"It's cold." She looks at me. "Close the door," she says. "There's a giraffe coming in." I think she must be dreaming still, talking about giraffes, must be half-crazy or half-asleep. "Close the door," she says again, looking directly at me as if to say, *Didn't you hear me the first time?* "There's a giraffe coming in." I close the door so a giraffe won't come in. I don't yet know the word *draft*.

"Turn the hot on." Her orders are harsh without being mean. "Wash my back." It is routine. There is no please or thank you or other formality. I always wash her back; I always come when she calls. I feel pride knowing that she relies on me and I can make her happy. If she is the Goddess of All Things, I am the Angel of Peace, hypersensitive to the emotions of others, seeing sadness or chaos or anger that goes unnoticed and wanting to resolve it, heal it, wanting them to be happy until it creates disturbance in me. Is it possible for everyone to be okay? Who will make sure I'm okay? Who will be sensitive to my emotions and try and make me happy? Surely that is someone's job in this family. I wash her back because she can't reach, and then I end up washing her hair, too, since I am already back there. I don't like this job, but I've grown accustomed. I have spent hours of my short life looking at the hair follicles of her back, counting the rolls of her back; I am careful not to rub too hard on the parts where her bra has chafed her skin raw. When I get to her hair I start to enjoy it. I like the way it curls up under the soap and water, forms tiny black-and-gray spirals that stretch in my hands. I massage her scalp and she falls asleep again, sinking slowly down into the tub.

"Mommy," I say to wake her up when her mouth is almost touching the water. She silently sits back up. As if giving a baby a bath, I take an empty container lying around, fill it with water, tell her to put her head back, and rinse her curls. She doesn't mind if some gets in her face; I think she likes to be touched, by me and by the water.

"You can go now," she says, dismissing me when I'm done. And I know she will begin the laborious process of standing, drying herself off, and getting into bed for the day. She will fade into sleep, and I will be released into the day to entertain myself, see what the neighbors are doing, or find my brother and go on an adventure.

TWO

In the evenings, the house takes on a different energy. Instead of feeling like prisoners, as it is easy to feel during the day, we—me, 7; Junior, 11; Vivian, 13; Claire, 15; and Cornelius, 17—become focused on squeezing out as much pleasure as we can from the TV before Dad gets home from work. Like much of the furniture in the house, the TV is secondhand, either given to us by someone, bought at a thrift store, or found on the street. Because we didn't have one until now, we are transfixed by the gray machine with fake wood panels and a crooked antenna. Dad never leaves valuable things in the street, so even though he despises the *boob tube* and thinks it kills brain cells—and even worse, you have to *sit on your ass* to watch it—he rescued the old, oversize 1980s machine and it ended up in our living room. We have to get up and manually click an ancient knob to change the channel. It sits on top of one of the dining chairs that doesn't match our dining set in front of the fireplace and mantel. Mom likes the TV there because it deters Dad from building out-of-control fires with brush he's rescued from his landscaping jobs. Though it was never officially discussed, once the TV arrived from the street, we figured out quickly from Dad's commentary that KQED was acceptable and all other channels were not. The worst is a sitcom because it has mechanical laugh tracks that make Dad want to yank out what hair he has left.

Dad's sole focus when he arrives home at night is getting Mom out of bed and ready for work—a thirty-minute countdown to departure. This process is a game of Dad easing his own anxiety (like me, he also wants her to be happy and proud of him) while we observe, hiding our excitement that the moment they leave, we will be in position to press the power button on the boob tube. I am giddy to be part of this sibling family, my little feet kicking on the couch. All I know about life is this family.

One night, Dad bursts through the front door at 8:10 p.m. with a sigh and begins unloading tools from his truck. He moves slowly and leaves the door open. If the door is open, it means Dad is home. He has so many things loaded onto and inside of his truck, he's got to make room for Mom and make sure nothing falls off on the freeway on the way to the city.

"Daddy, do you have to leave the door open? It's cold," I grumble from the couch.

"What's it to you?" he says harshly, walking right back out. When he comes back in, he says, "Little fresh air won't kill you." And back out he goes. "I'm getting the truck ready," his fading voice says, which means he is relocating his work tools from the front seat of the truck to the floor of the living room so Mom can sit there instead. He places a large rusty machete on the floor next to the front door, a stack of five-gallon cans that leave a trail of dirt, and a rake.

"Why are you putting all that stuff there, Daddy?" Vivian asks.

"Peck, peck, peck," he says. Henpecking, that is.

"Someone could kill themselves on that machete," Vivian says.

He squawks like a bird to show us how we sound to him, and out the door he disappears. Vivian and Junior look at each other and roll their eyes. I stare at the dark TV and hold my breath, patiently waiting for the moment the truck will pull away, when the smell of Mom's perfume is all that's left of them.

When Dad comes back in, he puts more tools down in the living room and then addresses us. "Can one of you lazy women please go help your mom?" he asks, even though Junior is sitting there too.

"Mommy doesn't need help," I say.

"Did you ask her?"

"Chris!" Mom calls from her room.

"Will one of you go and help your mom?" he asks again, quietly this time.

"But she's calling you . . ." Vivian says.

"Chris!" Mom calls again, operatically.

He storms through the living room to find Mom.

"Oh good," I hear her say. "I just wanted to make sure you were here. I'll be ready to go in five minutes. Are you ready?"

"Did one of the girls make you a lunch?" he asks.

"Damn!" Mom yells. That means she's forgotten about lunch. "Melissa!" she sings. "Fix me a lunch, will you?"

I look at Junior and Vivian, not understanding why I am being punished and not them. They sneer at me. I feel I must make Mom happy.

"Ha ha," Junior mocks me. I shove him as I unglue my lazy, henpecking self from the couch and drag myself to the kitchen.

I open the fridge and try to think creatively. Black bananas fill the refrigerator. We had rabbits out back that kept having babies, and when Dad discovered that the neighborhood market threw out their wilted produce at the end of the week, he volunteered to take everything, including the black bananas. The freezer is full of them too. The idea was that, since rabbits don't eat bananas, we would. "We'll make smoothies," he said, smiling brightly. Except that no one had. Beyond the bananas, there are multiples of everything: several bags of tortillas, several half-empty gallons of milk, a bundle of fresh spinach and its rotten counterpart, fresh apples and spotted ones, fresh cheeses and cheeses growing green mold, fresh lettuce and rotten lettuce, fresh tomatoes as well as bruised ones.

I find a Tupperware container on the floor, and maneuver around the sink full of dishes to wash it out. I place it on a pile of phone books stacked atop a kitchen chair, and bend over this makeshift counter to get to work on Mom's lunch. I want to finish as quickly as possible. I break lettuce up with my fingers and slice the tomato using my hand as a hard surface and a butter knife to slice. When I'm done, the pieces are rough and uneven. What else can I put in this salad? Dad stomps past me toward the back door. "Great!" he says. "Being a help." And he is out the door before I can respond, leaving the back door open. I can't wait for them to leave for the city. The faster I finish this project the better.

On the kitchen counter, I pick through a pile of bags containing various kinds of bread. I peek in some of the bags and find rock-hard baguette pieces. We can't throw them away because Dad revives them by soaking them in water and cooking them on the stove and leaving them there for days because even he can't bring himself to eat the soggy twice-cooked bread. It is the act of saving it that matters most. Beneath the hard bread, I find some sliced wheat bread that looks okay, so I go for it. I use my hand as a surface again, slice one of the fresh cheeses, stuff it between the bread, and pour some ranch dressing on the lettuce. I'm free.

"Your lunch is ready, Mommy!"

She pokes her head out from the bathroom, toothpaste oozing from her mouth. She's nearly transformed in jeans, a fresh purple blouse, and pressed curls. The only thing missing is her post-office apron and her perfume.

"Thank you." She nods. "Thank you," she says again, winking at me. I am her right-hand man after all, but I feel like a fraud. I look at her and smile. I hope that when she opens up her lunch at work and sees what I've done she'll be happy. I hope she won't be able to taste my carelessness.

Back in the living room, we wait. Mom saunters through the dining room and into the living room wearing her denim apron with USPS stamped on it in white letters, her badge pinned to the front pocket. She is ready. Dad honks the horn outside. Just a few more seconds before we can watch TV.

Mom flashes a smile, a little burgundy lipstick on her front teeth. This is her morning; she is full of energy and out the door.

"You kids be good."

"Bye, Mommy," we sing in sync.

And the door closes. That's not good enough, though. We need to see the truck drive down the street. Sometimes they forget things. You never know. They might run back in for her lunch or a letter that needs to be urgently postmarked with yesterday's date. I watch as the truck disappears into the night. When I think it's safe, I yell, "They're gone!" and Junior jumps up to turn on the TV.

We relax momentarily into *The Simpsons*, but we're careful to watch the time. Dad sometimes returns and presses his palm against the TV to see if it's warm, to see if it's been watched, so we must allow a few minutes to let it cool off.

Junior takes up almost the whole couch with his legs. I sit next to him on a chair—the good, crimson velvet one with fancy wooden Victorian legs and arms.

"Stop being an asshole, move over," Vivian demands. He doesn't move—in fact, he keeps inching his feet closer to her until they're touching her thighs. "Get your nasty, smelly feet off me!" she screams in disgust.

"Stop, Junior," I plead. I can barely hear the TV over all the shouting. Junior smiles deviously. He enjoys picking on Vivian; she is usually the victim of his bullying, while, as the little sister, he seems interested in protecting me. He picks a piece of calloused skin off one of his feet and dangles it over her face. She screams and makes spitting noises as the skin approaches her mouth. Then, in a matter of seconds, their bodies become a blur of punching arms, a rolling mass, determined to get a good hit in, hopefully the last, leaving the other crying or pleading for time-out. They don't care what or whom they roll into. When they come rolling toward me I jump out of the way.

"Stop it!" I yell with my arms held out like a crossing guard. My fear escalates along with Vivian and Junior's fight. They fall into the good velvet chair with their combined body weight. One of the fancy arms collapses with a snap. They stop only briefly to assess the damage. "Mommy's going to be mad," I scold, shaking my head. My siblings can be beasts.

Junior takes the moment of his opponent's shock to gain an advantage. He grabs a mechanical pencil from the coffee table and goes to stab her in the shoulder. Vivian cries out in pain. She grabs her arm and flees to the bedroom in tears. I look at Junior and then at the arm of Mom's good chair and shake my head. "Mommy's going to be so mad at you guys."

"Who cares?" Junior says.

"Why did you do that?"

Junior shrugs and doesn't answer.

"Apologize."

"Man, shut up." He shoos me away like I'm a pest, and I feel like one, with nowhere to go, the youngest of the herd. After the fight, the mood has dimmed and we all disperse and become our own islands. Me with my dolls and Vivian staring up at the top of her bunk across from me, we listen to slow jams on the radio, both of us passively singing along to "Silly" by Deniece Williams and "Angel Baby" by Rosie and the Originals. We are Quaker, and I am told that means we don't believe in war, don't believe in violence, but sometimes it feels like there are wars going on at home.

Doing bad things gets you something like attention. Junior had always been recalcitrant—it is his way—but there had been a subtle shift in him since he started middle school. Perhaps whatever he is doing to survive there—talking back to teachers, refusing to do schoolwork, stealing Mercedes emblems in the surrounding neighborhood, avoiding being jumped—doesn't leave him when he enters this house. Recently he came home crying to Mom that some kids stole from him on the bus. What he didn't tell her was that what they'd taken from him was jewelry he'd stolen at their request, as some kind of initiation, bullying, or both. They'd convinced him to steal jewelry from a shop near the school because they said the attendant didn't pay attention; it was easy. To win these boys' respect he did it, and they stole it from him immediately, threatening to beat him up if he didn't give it up. That day he came home in tears, deflated and humiliated, and since then he had been forgetting to leave his outside self out there, at school or on the bus. His trouble progressed and as his little sister, it did not surprise me to find out that Junior had been expelled for talking back to a teacher at the end of the school year. After several meetings with the teacher and the principal, and then downtown with the school district, the verdict was firm: he would not be allowed to return in the fall for the seventh grade. So Mom and Dad have been looking for a new school for Junior: one in the hills where rich kids go, one they believe will keep him safe from trouble and safe from troublesome boys—other black boys and their ways of survival.

He stays in the living room by himself—enjoying his own space because none of us have any or maybe feeling bad about hurting Vivian, about ruining the chair—until after I fall asleep. Eventually I hear him open the door to our room and climb up to his top bunk in the dark. At least when Dad comes home the TV screen won't be warm.

Some variation of this happens every night when Mom and Dad leave for the city. When I was a baby, and Cornelius and Claire lived at home (now Claire is away at boarding school and Cornelius is living in a dorm at UC Berkeley), we had a name for the fun—and sometimes brutality—that occurred during that hour of freedom. Battle Ram positions were assumed the moment the truck pulled away. "They're gone!" someone would shout, and down the hall we'd run: Claire and Junior on one side of the bedroom door; Vivian, Cornelius, and I on the other. Since I was a baby, I participated from Cornelius's shoulders. Battle Ram was a simple game of ramming your body and all of your power into either side of the opened door to see who was strongest. Physical and loving, competitive but one, this was how we entertained ourselves and expressed our hearts: *I love you! I will protect you! I am strong! I matter!* I mostly yelled and cheered from Cornelius's shoulders while they furiously pushed. Cornelius was so much stronger than the rest of us that whoever had him on their team always won.

Television, a previously foreign object, is now in our home and I have to study it. Many mornings I wake up before everyone to watch *Sesame Street* alone. I squeeze myself into my miniature chair and pull it up so close I can see each individual pixel. I can see there are things to learn. There are places to go. I meet little boys and girls from places called New York where autumn dumps heaps of leaves in the streets just for jumping in. On TV it snows in the winter. The houses where these children live are clean and their parents hug and kiss them, make them dinner at the same time every night, tuck them into beds inside bedrooms that they do not share with their siblings. These parents stroke their children's heads, get down on their knees and say I love you.

One night, when Dad gets home, a little after eight o'clock as usual, I can tell he's flustered by the way he throws things onto the floor. "Shit!" he yells as he bursts through the door. He slams down some tools and leaves the door open to go out for more. We sit anxiously, unable to enjoy the TV, but not motivated enough to turn it off. He comes back in and this time slams the door.

"Shit on a goddamn brick!" He stomps toward us. "Who's going to help your mother?" He often speaks through Mom. *Who will help me?*, he really wants to ask, but cannot, does not understand he needs help. Always her.

"Mom doesn't need help," I say, not looking at him, hoping he'll go away.

"How would you know if you've been sitting on your lard asses in front of the TV the whole time?"

"Don't call us lard asses," Vivian says, cussing defiantly because he has.

"Sorry," he says. "*Lazy* asses! Go help your mother!"

"Mom doesn't need help," I say again, staring at the TV.

"You like rotting your brains out?" We say nothing. The laugh track starts and my body gets tense. "Ha ha!" he imitates the laughter in a booming voice that makes me jump. "This is oppressive!" he screams as he walks out the front door.

Vivian gets up and turns the volume down, a compromise. He comes back in and slams the door again.

"Hey!" Mom shouts from their bedroom. "What's the meaning of all that slamming?"

"This oppressive garbage is disturbing your mother." Jaw clenched, he bangs his fist down on the closest table. A vase of wilted flowers and a stack of papers quiver.

"I need quiet!" He brings his hands to his head and pretends to pull out his hair. "Gah!"

"We turned it down," Junior points out.

"This is a really good episode, Daddy. Don't make us turn it off. Please?" I whimper.

He paces behind us for a moment. It sounds like he's rearranging tools. I let myself settle again, eyes glued to the TV.

He walks in front of the couch with a tool in his hand.

"Man, I can't see," Junior says.

Dad approaches the TV set. "This is the last night you'll be able to rot your brains out." As he moves toward the light of the TV, I can see that in his hand is a pair of hedge clippers. "You see this?" he asks, holding up the TV cord. "No more." And he snips the cord in half. The TV dies in front of us like there's been a power outage.

We look at one another with open mouths. Junior huffs to our room with his arms crossed. "Man," he mutters on his way out. Vivian and I sit in the dark living room, watching as Dad goes deeper into the house. I can see him at the dining room table looking under piles of papers. Then he moves to the bookshelf and shuffles some papers that are wedged between books. "Damn it to hell," he says as he walks into the kitchen, where cabinets begin to slam and objects crash to the floor.

"What in god's name is happening in there?" Mom yells from her room.

Dad clears his throat, embarrassed by his behavior in front of her.

"Nothing, Theolia." He is calm with her. "Is your lunch made?"

Before he can hear her answer, he is back in the living room, where Vivian and I are still sitting in the dark, mourning the loss of the TV. He stands over the couch and looks at us, takes a deep breath, and whispers, "I've misplaced the truck key . . . Could you please help me locate it before your mother finds out?" Dad loses things every day and becomes flustered, blames other people, will go to great lengths to pretend the thing isn't lost and try and recover it on his own, but he can't hide it now. Mom is depending on him to take her to work.

"Psh." Vivian pushes out the sound for *no way* and follows Junior to our room, leaving me alone. The last thing I want to do is help him. I watch her walk away and reluctantly agree to sneak around Mom and try not to look suspicious as I search.

I turn the front-porch light on. I have a sense for Dad's tracks. If we were animals in the wild, I'd be able to hunt him down. I spot a hat he had been wearing earlier that day sitting in the far corner of the top step. It sits upside down, acting as a makeshift container for seeds, pods, and receipts. He must have been walking up the stairs to come in and then, when he got to the top step, thought he should probably check the mail first. So he set down the hat, went to the mailbox, then probably decided not to go into the house just yet. I instinctively look in strange places when helping Dad find keys. He loses them at least once a week. I open the mailbox and there they are.

Dad is hovering over the dining room table, moving things around, berating himself quietly. I walk up to him and tap him. "Found them," I say. He exhales and smiles, laughs a little, embarrassed.

"How in the—" He takes them from me. "Where in the—" And before he can hear my answer, he is heading toward their bedroom, to Mom, so he can show her that he has things in order.

"Theolia," he says. "The truck is ready, I've got the keys. I'm ready to go when you are." He chuckles as he heads outside to prepare the truck for Mom. "Holy cow," he says to himself like I'm not there. "Oh boy."

"In the mailbox," I say, but he doesn't hear me.

ONE DAY I find Mom sitting in the kitchen distractedly watching an afternoon soap opera, holding a knife, a skinned apple, and a bowl of freshly peeled garlic cloves. In the fading afternoon light, juggling all of these items, she carefully slices bite-size pieces of apple and pops them into her mouth, followed by a whole piece of garlic, which she chews and grimaces. This is what she does to ward off a cold: apple and garlic, which she swears is an ancient remedy learned from her great-great-grandfather, who may or may not have been Cherokee. Sickness is not an option for Mom, nor is relaxation of any kind. She took a full year of maternal leave each time one of her children was born. That was not rest, but a kind of work she enjoyed. A year of maternity leave for each baby, equaling five total years of not-rest. She loves caring for babies; she loves them easily. It is the grown-up children she has trouble with.

I am fascinated with her garlic eating, the determination with which she prevents illness. I would rather be sick than eat raw garlic. I turn up my nose in awe watching her. She does it before her bedtime, after she's had a chance to change into her stained nightgown, eat breakfast, and fuss and complain about the bad shape of the house. It is late morning, and soon she'll be asleep for the rest of the day.

"I wish a tornado would come and just blow it all away," she often says. I have no response because, even though I agree, the thing that no one will say is that the tornado, in order to be successful, must also blow away Dad because all of the mess seems to be his. And I wonder if she means blow all of *us* away too.

In the minutes before Mom must get out of bed, I lie with her. Sometimes Junior joins me. She is always asking the time, scared she'll run out of it. She is a mound in the center of the bed; Junior and I lie on either side of her. The bed is the only functional furniture in the room. The vintage writing desk we inherited from our Pennsylvania grandfather, with its glossy, dark finish, is covered in papers. *Papers* is the universal word in our house for *mess*. Dad's papers. No one knows what the papers actually are, but they cannot be idly tossed out because in the junk mail is most likely the deed for the house, a tax refund, a past-due insurance renewal notice, an invoice. But to us they are just papers, papers that make Mom miserable, make her crouch and eat garlic in the dark, make her fuss, make her sad—they become the reason for all unhappiness. The rest of the room is covered in what we like to call *mountains*—mountains of clothing, that is. No surface reveals itself; only the bed is available for use, and even that, while Mom is at work, is subject to mountains and papers brought in fresh from Dad. But right now it's just us three in the room with no space, only enough room for our bodies, savoring the last moments before Mom must leave again.

"Mommy," Junior begins, "you should divorce Daddy."

From the other side of her, my brows furl, my eyes widen; I try and telepathically send him a message of shock. How dare he? But I will say it too. With his audacity, he gives me the courage to dream things, to say things. If the tornado is to come, we must manifest it. But children are powerless. Outnumbered and in over their heads, sure, perhaps not the picture of family life they'd imagined or perhaps deeply harder than they could dream, and they are so damned tired. But here we are, with our opinions and our needs. I spoon as much of her body as I can hold in one arm, and so I feel her leave, though her body never moves.

I envision her eyes going blank, like an animal playing dead in the woods. She holds very still for a moment before returning and asks, "What time is it?"

A week later, I come home hungry and out of breath after playing with the neighbors to again find Mom sitting in the kitchen, nearly naked, wearing only a sheer nightgown and a pair of holey underwear on top of her head to protect her curlers. It's not her attire but her face that lets me know something is up. I start to catch my breath and lose my appetite. Her eyes droop. She hasn't slept. Something is keeping her up. She sees me standing there and looks at me, then away, then back at me, like what she has to say is unbelievable. She holds her face in her hands. Whatever she is feeling, I start to feel.

"What?" I ask, frightened. Back and forth her head slowly shakes. "What?" I ask again.

She finally speaks. "Nothing."

"How come you're not asleep?" I ask, concerned. She has to be at work in four hours, and from the glazed, puffy look to her eyes, I can tell she hasn't slept yet.

"Your Aunt Evelyn called."

I have some idea of what is coming, but I wait for more. She shakes her head. Despair is a common reaction to phone calls from my father's sisters. "She's coming."

Evelyn wasn't bad so much as she was rich and white, and seemingly judgmental. One of the very yuppies Dad always cursed. And perhaps even more than all of those things, her arrival meant we had to clean the house and Mom had to figure out how to make that happen in her sleep. Evelyn wanted to help, to check on us, make sure we were still alive inside our rat's nest. So every year, she got off her husband's yacht in Miami and flew to Oakland, where her eccentric brother, his black wife, and all of their millions of children (five) continued, to her amazement, year after year, to exist. How were we not dead yet? How had we not been killed by one of Dad's booby traps? More likely yet, how had we not been killed by a bullet on the murderous Oakland streets? And those public schools? So many things could have, and should have, killed us. That's what we believed about our aunt, and so even though she was nice enough—bought us things, bought things for the house—I remained skeptical. I watched for her judgments. I waited for her amazed reactions to my good grades in school, my full belly. But often, they never came.

I wonder how much time we have. "When is she coming?"

"Next week." Mom pretends to weep in her hands. "Just look at this . . ." She lifts her hands from her face and gestures to the mess around her. She describes the state of the house in shapes. It is in good shape or it is in bad shape. Before relatives visit, when we clean the best we can, we make things *passable*, as Mom says, meaning there are chairs to sit on, and more than just a narrow pathway through the front door to the kitchen. Bad shape is when we haven't had visitors for a while, when we forget our furniture is made of wood because we can't see it. Every surface is covered in papers, seeds, tools.

The house is in bad shape. I look around the house, and I see what I have grown accustomed to overlooking. I put myself in the shoes of my aunt who will arrive in a week. She will notice a chain saw near the front door, an industrial-size ladder resting on the couch. She'll see a coffee table covered in mail and plants. These are things I am used to living with; choosing not to see is the only way to not let it bother you. Horrified, I continue scanning the house as far as I can see.

Evelyn would have to step over boxes labeled in Dad's handwriting: *BILLS*, *TAXES*, *MAIL*. She would then enter the dining room, where she would see a repeat of the coffee table—more papers, surrounded by boxes stuffed, not with what their labels would have you believe, but full of more fun finds like pine cones, naked headless Barbies, photocopies of very important articles that Dad cut out from the *Oakland Tribune*, and old issues of *Outdoor Alabama* magazine.

The six chairs around the dining table are also covered. They are storage for phone books (all seven of them), and electronics Dad isn't ready to part with—a broken Walkman, dead batteries, a retired boom box, walkie-talkies with wires hanging out of them like guts.

Sufficiently horrified, I join Mom in her anxiety, knowing that when Aunt Evelyn walks into the kitchen, she'll find a room where from no perspective or angle could you see even a sliver of counter space or floor space save for the chair Mom now sits in. The surfaces are completely filled: a toaster, four or five half-full bags of bread, open jars of peanut butter with spoons inside (Dad loves peanut butter). More peanut butter behind the pile of plates (the first jar was hiding, so another and then another was purchased). A pot of rice from the day before. A skillet coated in congealed oil. Cans of soup. Packages of Jell-O and tapioca pudding that were on sale (they were for saving money, but no one ate them). Dirty mugs. Cardboard coffee cups stacked from the nearby coffee shop for reusing. Oily paper bags full of day-old pastries from the local coffee shop (they were left outside at closing time for the homeless, but Dad took them for us).

Aunt Evelyn would see our latest acquisition: a small TV for the kitchen, with a few fuzzy channels, that Dad presumably rescued from the street (he loves saving more than he loathes TV). It sits on top of a swivel office chair with a broken back. In the middle of the kitchen, near boxes and broken appliances, she'd see our one good chair. This is where Mom is sitting. Above her is the refrigerator, which we're proud of; water and ice comes from it. On top of the refrigerator is Dad's filing system for receipts. Every time you open or close the refrigerator, a shower of receipts falls on your head.

Mom sits there, beside the refrigerator, in the dark. Even though it is only afternoon, the house does not let much light in. Pink curlers poke up like antennae through the leg holes of the underwear she wears on her head. I can see the outline of her long breasts beneath her nightgown. They sit on top of her tummy; these are the biggest things on her five-foot frame, and what make her a mother—that stomach, stretched and round from carrying five babies, and breasts, kneaded into loaves from lovingly, generously nursing each one of those babies for a very long time, or until they pushed her away.

"This is my house," she says. "How can I live this way?"

She says this to no one, as if I am not standing there witnessing. My distress meter rises. Mom is not happy. I clench my fists, and my chest becomes tight as I internalize her state. I imagine her having this conversation with herself every day while I am away at school or out playing. She watches soap operas after working all night and sits there on that kitchen chair with her hands over her face asking herself how.

"We have a week," she says again, regaining some composure. She stands up and assesses the work. "We can get it at least passable by then." She looks at me, wanting me to acknowledge that she'd said *we* and not *I*. *We* would have to get the house into shape. *We* are on a team. Dad is not on this team. "We'll do one room at a time," she says, taking stock. "We'll start with the living room."

I like being on her team. I can see life come into her eyes. "Vivian will help," she says, and smiles at me. Now I am in the room. "We can do it." There she is. Now she sees me. "Maybe Claire will even come and help when she gets home." She mentally recruits.

The next day I walk home slowly from Julia and Josh's. I realize that it's finally summer, and all I have to look forward to is cleaning up the house. I have no plans for the next few months besides going to Alabama and bumming around with Junior until dark, riding bikes or rollerblading.

The last weeks of school before this moment had stretched out into impatient anticipation of summer, of freedom, however unimpressive my plans were. The days became longer, and much of the time I just found myself waiting for Dad to pick me up after school, sometimes waiting for hours. Those last few weeks before summer were lawless ones: I would find neighborhood kids to play with after-school who made the playground into their park in the afternoon. Sometimes my best friend Nellie would wait for her father too, so we'd entertain ourselves by playing on the monkey bars or making up dances to our favorite En Vogue songs. Some days Junior would pick me up, and we would take the long way home, stopping along the way to buy sodas and drink them with the tops open only a crack so we can feel the cans crushing in our hands and control the sweetness, make it last, guiding it into our mouths one drop at a time.

But now, finally, summer is here, and weighed down by the thought of my impending fate, I drag myself up the stairs toward the front door, wondering where Junior might be and how I might join him, get out of helping with the inevitable cleanup. As much as I am a patron for peace in our household, I also want to be free of my mother's worry, to take advantage of the lawless summer, to be free. I wish to be as strong-willed and uninhibited as him.

In the living room, I am surprised and delighted to find Claire. She and Mom are laughing. She is sixteen, beautiful, independent, my hero. She is home from the private boarding school she attends on scholarship in Danville, a wealthy town just thirty minutes north of Oakland but that is like another world. She's come to help, and likely carrying the same guilt Mom has gifted me. She is surveying the room while Mom sits and watches from the couch.

"Guess who's here to pitchfork!" Claire shouts when she sees me.

She calls cleaning for relatives *pitchforking*. It is a term she made up for the final moments before they arrive, when things get desperate and we stop thinking about logical places to put things and just start tossing entire boxes down the basement stairs, under beds, and into closets.

Claire stands with her hands on her hips. She kneels down in her long bohemian skirt, moving the curls that have flopped over her face.

"What in the hell is this?" Claire holds up an empty fish tank. Inside it is a sock, a tennis ball, and, as I look closer, what looks to be some sprinkler parts from Dad's job.

Mom is laughing so hard she starts to cry. Claire drops the fish tank with a thud and begins laughing too, cradling her forehead. The laughter is dread infused.

"And, I'm sorry," Claire says, scrunching her red lips, raising one bushy eyebrow, "but what the fuck is that doing in the living room?" She points to the chain saw near the front door. Mom laughs and laughs. She isn't wearing underwear on her head. She's taken her curlers out for Claire. When I laugh too, Mom stops abruptly.

"Okay," Mom says, stern, wiping her eyes where tears of laughter had just fallen. "Enough. Ain't nothing funny. I'm just laughing with you two old hussies to keep from crying. We had enough fun. It's time to get to work."

I'm sent to the store to buy large garbage bags, the heavy-duty black kind, and sponges for scrubbing. I walk the two blocks to the convenience store. I know most of the people who live in the houses I pass. Alexis, my friend from school, lives with her Filipina mom and mean, white stepdad. And

58

near them, a white, gray-haired lesbian with a little boy named Patrick who plays outside by himself. Sometimes Junior and I invite Patrick to play with us, and then we see his mother's face up in the front window of their house shaking her head no. Will walks past me and waves. He is a professor who teaches history at UC Berkeley. I can tell Dad thinks that's a worthy job to have because he mentions it all the time, unlike Julia and Josh's mom and dad, who he says are yuppies. Their dad is a lawyer and their mom doesn't work. Dad has made it clear those jobs are not as good as being a teacher.

"How are your parents?" another neighbor asks as he walks swiftly by me, smiling. "Tell your dad I love the new plant!" he yells from way up the street.

I nod with a smile to acknowledge him, being sure not to let him know that I am going to the store at this very moment to buy materials *specifically* for emptying Dad from the house, wiping him from every surface.

When I return, Dad is home. There is evidence of him, and my heart begins to race; he will not like what we're doing. A shovel lies on the ground outside his truck, which is parked on the sidewalk leading to our driveway. It does not fit in the driveway since there is another car there, a dead black Camaro from the seventies. It died without a proper burial, like many broken objects that lie scattered in and around the house. Dad's brown pickup truck is parked right next to it, leaving only a sliver of space for passersby. I step over the shovel and a hose that's also been unloaded from his truck and go inside to get to work.

"What took you so long?" Claire wants to know. No one

likes being asked to return home and clean, I imagine especially when this isn't your full-time home anymore. I say nothing, just hand over the bag of supplies. "What are you giving it to me for? You're helping too," she sneers.

The tension begins to rise in me. I still don't see him. Then I overhear Mom and Dad in the kitchen.

"They're *your* relatives," she accuses. "How do you expect me to live like this?"

"Stop yelling, would you?" Dad pleads.

"I'm not yelling!" she screams. "Are you going to help us, or are you going to get in the way? You tell me that. Because I would rather you get out of the way. Get out of *my* way."

"This *is* out of control. You're out of control, and you've teamed them up against me again."

"Yes," she says. "This is out of control! You got it. Now get the fuck out of my way."

"Watch your mouth!" he says. "You sound like trash."

"You want to know why I sound like trash? Because I live in trash!"

Claire and I stand in silence, listening. Dad storms through the living room, grabbing things as he heads for the door—the chain saw, the fish tank.

Mom appears next to us in the living room, and, together, we all watch as he leaves.

"Have fun with your mom—I mean, enjoy being wasteful and violent," he says. He stands at the door and looks at Mom. "How do you think this makes me feel?" They stare at each other for a moment, long enough for me to waver between whose side I'm on. When she doesn't flinch and doesn't answer, he leaves and slams the door behind him. We hear a crashing from behind the door, his chain saw or the fish tank thrown against the stairs outside.

She takes a deep breath. We take a deep breath. "I'm sorry you had to see that," Mom says, taking the box of garbage bags from Claire's hands, her face blank, words sterile. "We have a lot of work to do, girls."

THREE

A week later Aunt Evelyn arrives. Just hours before her plane touches down, the house is finally becoming passable. Dad paces nervously around the house, peering at what we're doing, making sure we don't throw anything away that's valuable. My job is to decide what is true junk and what is merely unidentifiable, and make a pile of unidentifiable "Dad stuff" for him to go through.

"What are you doing with that?" He comes running toward me. In my hand is a cracked plastic filing rack that I'm about to toss in my garbage bag.

"That's perfectly good," he says, taking it from my hands.

"But it's cracked," I say. "And we have a bunch of others that aren't cracked." I point to a pile that I've uncovered. He storms out of the room. I hear the front door slam. And five minutes later he returns, eyes on my garbage bag.

He waits until the very last moment to leave for the airport to pick up Evelyn. The house is in a state of disquiet, as if holding its breath while he creeps around angrily, ready to yell or curse or run off with a bag of garbage one of us has viciously filled. If we laugh, we're getting enjoyment from being wasteful and throwing out things that don't belong to us; we are just like our mother. If we're quiet, it is our duty; we are doing it because we have to, because he isn't very good at organizing. If we're quiet, he won't hear our resentment. The house goes on holding its breath as he does one last scan of everyone's work, scrutinizing our piles of junk before he leaves.

From the front window I watch as his truck pulls off and drives down the street.

"He's gone!" I yell.

"Pitchfork time!" Claire calls.

I run to the kitchen to join Mom and Claire as they stuff everything in sight into bags and begin tossing them down the basement stairs. Vivian has come home from summer school and is helping too. Junior isn't home; he always manages to be gone. I stuff several bags in our bedroom closet and other bags under Mom and Dad's bed.

The phone rings. It's Dad calling from a pay phone.

"He's stalling her!" Claire announces. "He's taking her to the botanical garden!"

We're relieved to have a little more time. Mom goes to the laundromat to wash sheets, towels, and a tablecloth. Claire sweeps and I shove the receipts on top of the refrigerator out of sight.

I have watch duty. From the window I see my aunt open the truck door. Her luggage is precariously loaded into the truck bed on top of a layer of gardening tools and the chain saw Dad took out of the house earlier that week in his fury.

"They're here!" I alert everyone to get into position, look normal, wipe the dirt and sweat from their faces.

I watch Evelyn look up and down the street, familiarizing herself with the neighborhood. Her red hair is exactly the same color as his. Her nose just as big. Claire says Evelyn married well. I think about Mom and I wonder if she married well.

I hear Claire and Mom scuffling in the back. Vivian has retreated to our bedroom. I wait in my place on the couch to greet Evelyn when she comes through the door. I am the greeter. I picture Mom and Claire hiding away in Mom and Dad's room, relieved it is over. Someone has to be the buffer between Dad and everyone, so I stay. Where is Junior? Where is Cornelius? They are boys and so not called upon by Mom for this kind of domestic activity. They will be called upon at the end when trash needs to be hauled away or large objects need destroying. Their boyness allows them to escape this part of the production. I imagine Cornelius free in his college dorm and Junior on a bike flying down some hill, and I am filled with resentment for my girlness, for my fierce loyalty, for my permanent position as family witness and peacemaker. I never want to help, but the alternative is abandoning Mom, which I don't have it in me to do.

When Mom uses good language she calls Evelyn *high and mighty*; when she is in a foul mood, she says Evelyn thinks she's *hot shit* because she married a surgeon. These are the times Mom likes to recall that she once had the chance to marry a doctor, but in the long run she was glad she didn't because he was black and *ugly*. She spits out the word *ugly*, meaning he was dark. "It's okay, though," she says. "Otherwise none of you would be here." I believe she means she's happy we're here physically, but also that we are here and light skinned. There is gratitude in her voice: *Thank goodness you are not black and ugly.* She is transparent in these moments, believing, without knowing she is believing, in the ugliness of black.

Evelyn looks like she's just stepped off a boat. She talks a lot about the yacht that she and her husband vacation on during summers off the Florida coast, and since I have never been on a yacht, I figure this is how boat women dress—her white capri pants and plaid button-down top. Her wedge heels are strapped up to her pale, freckled ankles.

She sings the word *hello* and comes toward me with wide-open arms, grinning. "Hello, my dear." She smells a bit like chlorine. When she lets go, she looks at my dad and asks him if she can use the bathroom.

Dad scratches his head where he still has a halo of red hair. My heart thumps. "We don't let our guests use the bathroom," he says, keeping a straight face. She looks at me for confirmation that he is joking, and laughs. "I'm serious," he says. "The café down the street is open, Melissa can walk you there."

"Oh Chris!" she says, putting her hands on her hips.

"We only invite guests who have superior, enlarged bladders." She laughs to be polite. "I thought we were related, but I guess not. My relatives all have enlarged bladders," he says. His joke doesn't land.

"Well if it's too much trouble . . ."

Dad stops his act. "Let me go ask Theolia if it's ready," he says, walking through the dining room he now barely recognizes. All of his things are missing from it. He doesn't know how to act, where to put his body, and he most definitely does not know what to say. And in his dismay at the state of his house, the absence of his things, he has ruined it all. The whole point is to pretend we haven't tried to make the house look this way, that there aren't bags of garbage hidden behind every closed door. He has to go and see *if it's ready*, as if we'd worked on this together.

He returns with the okay, but explains that the toilet is rigged, so if she has to number two she can go to the café if she wants to be comfortable. He explains that she'll need to fill the bucket in the tub with water and pour it down the bowl vigorously. This operation is to save water.

Evelyn opts to use our bathroom. When she comes out, we wait for her to have something to say or do because we have nothing to say or do. We don't even know where anything is. We barely recognize the surfaces she begins placing her things on: her purse, her sunglasses. Do something, Evelyn . . . say something, I think to myself. We have nothing planned besides having a passable house for her to enter.

Claire, Mom, and Vivian still won't come out. Junior still isn't home. I have Dad duty. I have to be here with him. I can't leave him alone to do something like offer to hang her sweater in the front closet where I know for a fact a garbage bag is stuffed. I watch in horror every time Dad opens his mouth.

Luckily, Dad's first instinct in uncomfortable situations is to leave them. "Evelyn, if you're up to it, I'd like to show you a job I've been working on not far from here. These rare ferns will blow your mind!"

"I'm pretty tired from the flight and the botanical garden actually—maybe tomorrow?"

"C'mon!" Dad says. "Don't be such a stick-in-the-mud! It's just one block for heaven's sake. Are you *that* lazy?"

I watch them from the couch, enjoying the space in the room, but feeling suffocated by their conversation.

"I take offense to that," Evelyn responds. "I just traveled three thousand miles to be with you and your family, and I'm tired. But dammit, if you want me to see this fern, let's go."

Dad backs toward the door and puts his hands up. "Okay, okay, okay," he says, giving up. "I'm the bad guy." He clears his throat. "I apologize." He opens the door, exits. "Would you like some Chinese food? I'll get some Chinese food while you rest."

Evelyn smiles. "That sounds fantastic, Chris."

After Dad leaves, Evelyn sits next to me on the couch. My heart flutters. I fidget. I don't know what to do with a guest either. After the cleaning part, there is a big question mark. What do people talk about with guests? I look at my hands when she looks at me.

"What are you interested in these days?" I shrug. "Oh, come on," she says. "You have to be interested in something."

"I like rollerblading. I got new Rollerblades."

"Great! I'll take you out tomorrow, you can show me around."

Evelyn leans closer to me. There's that chlorine smell. "Where is your mom?"

"In her room, I think." I try and say the right things. I try and cover for everyone.

"Hmm," she says, looking around.

We sit in silence for a while, then we make more small talk and I try my best to appear relaxed.

"How are your grades?" she asks as she gets up to touch a framed photo of her mother, my grandmother, on her wedding day. She's elegant and serious faced in a white gown, holding a bouquet of roses. "Just look at her," she says, not listening to my answer. "Is that your other grandmother?" Evelyn asks, moving on to another photo of Mom's mom in an oversize sweater in the same botanical garden Dad just took her to. In classic Dad fashion, and as a compliment to her, he had her pose next to the biggest, most admirable cactus in the desert garden.

I remember passing through the desert garden to our favorite place—the Japanese gardens, where Junior and I would entertain ourselves for hours, catching guppies and playing make-believe. On the way to the botanical garden—sanctuary to Dad and babysitter to us kids—Dad would quiz us. "What kind of tree is that?" He'd point to a redwood, a eucalyptus. "Good." He'd smile with pride when we answered correctly, and then he'd park his truck and release us into the closest thing to a forest he could find in the city, sharing his joy with us. On good days, trees, grassy lawns, and ponds become our playground; on other days, empty parking lots, lobbies of apartment buildings, and storefronts where he works become our caretakers.

"Yes," I answer. "That's Grandma Annie from Alabama." Evelyn looks around and continues to touch things and pretend to wait for my answers. I wonder where Mom and Claire are, where Dad is, where anyone is. In the lawless summer, Junior has begun to stay out later and later, riding bikes presumably with friends; he is nowhere to be seen and I quietly resent him and everyone else for it. Again it is my job to be here to absorb whatever happens and try to avert a disaster. I am the loyal daughter. I must be here. I must facilitate order and peace. Mom and Claire are in Mom and Dad's bedroom nearly blockaded in by mountains of pitchfork, catching their breath and transforming into social, polite people with lipstick and sponge baths. I feel like I'm holding my breath for what feels like an hour until Dad returns with bags full of Chinese food from around the corner.

We eat at the table for the first time in months. Fried tofu with greens for Mom, chicken chow mein for me, vegetable moo shu for Vivian, Szechuan chicken for Junior, and some other dishes we can all share. Vivian emerges when the smell of food drifts in. She greets Evelyn, makes herself a plate, and sits at the silent table. Evelyn attempts to fill the silence with questions, which Vivian responds to with one-word answers: Good. No. Yes.

Dad doesn't eat with us. He has things to do outside like always. Unloading the truck so that his tools won't get stolen, going out to turn off the sprinklers at a nearby job.

Before he leaves, he stands at the door for a moment. "I really did want to show you the ferns," he says, shaking his head. "I can't believe you're that lazy. Whatever. Leave some of the tofu dish for Theolia, will you?"

With the slam of the door, Evelyn, Vivian, and I are left alone. Our chewing fills the silent room. After minutes that seem like hours of some of the loudest, most uncomfortable chewing, Mom appears. She is dressed for Evelyn in a red blouse, jeans, and maroon lipstick. Her head is full of fluffy pressed curls, shiny with oil. Even over the smell of Chinese food, her perfume fills our noses. Claire follows. She wears a loose green knit sweater that slumps off one of her shoulders, jeans with holes in both knees, her hair an explosion of curls that she has to constantly move away from her face.

I am instantly grateful for their presence and furious with them for leaving me alone for so long on Dad duty. I relax into my seat and let them take over. Claire is good at talking to people; people like listening to her. I am too young, too shy, too awkward.

"Well, hello!" Evelyn shrieks. "Look at the two beauty queens!"

"Look who's talking, my beautiful aunt!" Claire responds.

"Were you two resting? Chris tells me how hard you all were working to clean the house. You must be exhausted!"

Mom shrinks. I can see the rage growing behind her eyes, a frozen Mona Lisa smile. Her body moves with a rigidity saved just for Dad's sisters.

The next day Evelyn, Junior, and I take a walk for some window-shopping and coffee. Evelyn walks ahead, waiting and looking back at us from every corner. Her long, freckled boat legs are faster than ours. She walks like she knows the place.

"Here," she says, pointing to a bookstore. We follow her in and then we all separate. I go to the kids' section and Junior goes to the comic books. She has a stack of books on the counter when we're ready to check out. She buys Junior and me one book each. I choose *Matilda*. Junior chooses an X-Men comic. On the spine of one of her books I read the words *Adult ADD*. I think of the times Cornelius has called Dad an "ADD-ass motherfucker" when they've fought. I know what it means. Kids have it when they can't sit still. Those kids grow up to be restless grown-ups. Maybe if he reads that book it will cure his messiness.

Later that day I notice the book is sitting out on the dining room table in plain sight. I don't move it. It stays there all day. I see everyone pass by it, reading its title, picking it up, putting it back down in its place. When Mom sees it, she picks it up too.

"What's the meaning of this?" Mom's voice is styled in its anger, almost British. "What is the meaning of this?" She sets the book back down and looks at me.

"It's for Daddy. Evelyn got it. She thinks he has ADD."

Her body moves toward me, in slow motion.

"Is that right?"

When I see the book again it is on the front porch. There is evidence of Dad in it—it's bursting with receipts and newspaper clippings, an envelope of seeds. Dad is a poet in the way he believes in life, the growing of things, of children. But his poetry is the kind people don't understand, maybe he doesn't either, the way it grows out of control, the desire for life so great it escapes even him; he cannot control this life. He loves children, which are another kind of life. I have observed the way he admires babies. He holds them awkwardly, kind of like the way he dances, as if his joints do not easily bend, moving choppily to a rhythm

71

only he can hear. Instead of the normal way of holding a baby—bringing it to your chest, rubbing its back, smelling its skin—instead of the cooing and pleasantries most people make in the presence of babies, he stares into the child's eyes lovingly, with reverence, while holding its head in his sandpaper palm. I have seen him do this with my baby cousins in Alabama. I have felt the discomfort of the people around him, wondering what this white man is trying to transmit into the skull of this black child. It is usually a black child he holds up with this kind of reverence. He thinks the brains of children are beautiful. I wonder how many times he stared into my eyes and held my skull, speaking to me in a language I may have understood then. I wonder how many times he stared into all of our baby eyes, holding our skulls in his palm, planting seeds, growing life, or so he thought.

Dad doesn't look at me anymore. His eyes dart at the pace of a hummingbird looking obsessively for nectar, busy, with a hyperactive focus that has nothing to do with me. I cannot relate, and this makes me nervous. I am nervous about having a father like him, nervous about the way I feel I need to look after him, nervous like a parent with outstretched arms, ready to rescue a newly walking toddler on the verge of falling or eating something poisonous from the ground. I am nervous that he made me.

In the distance, though, I can feel him admiring me. I know he has looked at me because he has commented on the broadness of my forehead, a feature I despise; he says it means I'm smart. I wonder what he sees when he looks at me; I wonder if he's satisfied with the way my brain has grown.

Before Evelyn leaves she takes Junior and me to the county fair. It's just us three since we are the youngest. We are full of energy, a sense of desire awakened by the act of being taken somewhere with the sole intention of having fun. Junior is practically bouncing with excitement. I imagine him as a rabbit, hopping from ride to ride in giant leaps, stopping in front of each one and breathlessly asking, "Can I go on this one?" It makes me laugh and it is infectious. It has come over me too—desire. I can want things and ask for things. I see fists full of giant pink cotton candy and cones of ice cream. I see kids throwing balls at tanks of water, trying to hit a target to make the man sitting on the board fall in. I see huge stuffed animals being won. It is dizzying. Finally, I can't control it. I scream out, pointing, bouncing, "I want cotton candy! Can I have that? I want that!" I want everything.

Evelyn stops, grabs my hand hard because I'm closest to her; Junior is already ahead of us and uncontrollable. "Stop it!" she yells, exasperated. "Stop nagging me!" And then she makes an unintelligible sound and shakes her head as if to shake off my request. I hear: *Stop wanting*. I am fitfully silent for the rest of the trip. I will want nothing and I will punish her with how good I am at wanting nothing. When Junior comes over, he raises an eyebrow at me, knowing I'm unhappy. He quickly follows suit, both of us reverting to silence. We sit in the back of her rental car quietly, only glancing at each other occasionally. He has taken my side and protects me with his silent solidarity. Adults are a problem, a hindrance to our freedom, the expression of our desire, and they can't protect us. We must offer each other these things.

When Evelyn leaves, I am glad. It means everyone can relax again, but it also means the papers will come back. First a receipt, then a sprinkler part, then a school bag, a book, someone's marked-up homework, mail, dirty socks. It all returns with a vengeance, as though angry for having had to hide, as if the mess itself is alive. It regains control of the house and of us. The front door returns to its permanently closed position.

SUMMER CONTINUES, BORING, nothing, a string of hours marking days passing until hopefully something, anything, happens. And finally it is upon us: our annual trip to Alabama. It is the only place Mom and Dad or any of us ever goes, so it qualifies as a momentous occasion. This year Claire and Cornelius are staying in Oakland, busy with school and work, but the rest of us start to prepare. Mom tears the house even further apart to find things to take in her and Dad's oversize suitcase. As if she is moving there, as if bringing gifts for her relatives in another country, she stuffs the luggage with far too many objects—lotions, perfumes, good olive oil—almost inevitably having to remove items from it at the airport because it's over the weight limit. But Alabama may as well be a foreign country, and so it is custom to overpack with gifts and treats from the promised land.

On the day we leave, I watch as my parents run around—Dad finishing up jobs and making last-minute calls in Spanish to his employees to remind them to water certain plants at certain sites and move his truck for him on street-sweeping days. Mom, trying to enjoy her first days of vacation at home, still wears the stress of work, frantically packing the suitcases and periodically asking us kids, but really asking herself, "Are you ready?"

Cornelius arrives in his green Hornet to drive all that can fit to the airport. And the rest arrive in a yellow taxi. When the taxi is outside, Dad realizes he's lost his keys, so Mom has to search for hers at the bottom of their overstuffed bags. Just when we think we are ready, Dad realizes he's also lost his ID, but Mom anticipated this and flashes it to him. He nods, locks the front door, and finally we are off.

Alabama is our other home. We walk around the Montgomery airport squinting our eyes, trying to surmise which of the people passing by us is our relative. This is the land of my mother—my motherland. Everyone is black and looks vaguely like someone I've seen before and therefore liable to be my cousin no matter how many times removed. We stick out because we are with a white man who doesn't act like the white people around here—in fact, there are no other whites in sight—and he is with her, proudly, his chest puffed up like an orange bird next to his wife, his harem of brown kids with explosive heads full of all possibilities of curls, frizz, and naps behind him. We are looking for our real relative, Uncle Woody—the Black Wolf as he's known affectionately—who will drive us out of this small town and deep, deep, deeper into the country just outside Selma where our mother is from.

Outside, a humid warmth blasts me and wraps around my body. It's nothing like the heat of Oakland, whose dry summer air moves with the breeze of the bay, whose fog sometimes never clears. This heat hangs, is wet and land-locked. I accept this land as home because it is Mom's. She is awake here—alive, light, funny—a person I only get to meet in Alabama. Her hair is freshly braided in a springy bob, which she playfully shakes out of her face, only to have it return seconds later. Her teeth are always showing, as if in pose, awaiting a camera. She has lots of cash, a white hus-band, and a throng of mixed children. For two weeks out of every year, she gets to be rich, exotic. Even the way she touches me here radiates a certain air of regality, of hav-ing made it. *We made it*, she says silently in her winks and touches. *I made it. I got out.* Her attention is intoxicating.

Even though the air is still, there is a hum that excites me, that lets me know something is happening in it. This is the country. Country as in dirt roads and slow-moving people, lazy cow pastures, horse stables, everyone knowing everyone. Plantation-style homes. Old cotton fields now full of lush, green weeds. Mom points it all out as we drive. "There," she says, "is where Mr. So-and-So lived, and Mr. So-and-So over there. And right there is where we picked cotton." Her finger elegantly points to some green pasture, and I try and see her in it, not as my mom, but as a girl who lives in a shack up the road, missing the first weeks of school to pick the cotton at its highest to earn a few extra cents. Her parents got out too, but only up the road, just outside of the county where my grandfather's father and grandmother's mother had been slaves. The house where my grandparents live is less than ten miles from the plantation. It takes so long to leave. When Mom took a Greyhound bus to San Francisco and married soon after, it was the equivalent of sending your child to America. San Francisco was a different country for a Southern girl who had never been far from the literal plantation. It was a different kind of America, at least on the surface.

I drink in this mother I meet anew every summer. I watch her closely. Who is she? Even the way she speaks here is different; it's more natural and lyrical, less fake British than she sounds at home. There is something musical in the way my family speaks, something special about the small talk that my proper, literal city ears must work hard to decipher. Everything is a question: *Ain't it?* The ends of most words are chopped off and all the words roll into one languorous stream of language: *Go-on-n-fetch-me-one-o-dem-thangs-from-ovah-yondah*. There are magical words like *yonder*, meaning there—over yonder. I am slow to respond because my brain must translate, even after coming here every summer for my entire life. Words like *girl* and *baby* are stretched out into song. My name is Baby or one of my sister's names, or I am just "one of Tho's chilluns." No one is called by their real name. Mom is simply Tho because no one can pronounce Theolia anyway, always Tho or Thee, or sometimes Theelo. Aunt Bernadette is Bobbie Lou, Aunt

Annie Pearl is Boo Jack, and so on. There are some cousins whose real names I have never known—Butter Roll and Lil Woody must be on their birth certificates.

Alabama is the only place that makes Mom happy. I call this place Alabama in the abstract—imagining this big, rectangular state to be this one experience I have each summer in a house on a dirt road in Perry County. Mom calls this place home. The three-day Greyhound buses we took—and now the planes—transport us, not to some abstract place, but home. It is the place where I get to see my mother.

When we spot my Uncle Woody at the airport, Mom looks like a child resisting the urge to jump up and down from the joy of having spotted her younger brother in the crowd. We make our way to the parking lot to his truck. Mom and Dad sit in the front, and I'm squeezed in the middle of the long seat next to my uncle. I peek back to the truck bed, where Vivian and Junior are piled in like cargo, wildly laughing, their hair blowing in the hot wind as we approach the highway. Junior gives me the middle finger with both hands and waves them around, makes a silly face. He knows I can't do it back because I'm with Mom and Dad. Alabama is lawless, so it seems; we don't wear seat belts and it's all right if all the kids sit in the bed of the truck. Mom and Uncle Woody point out green land all the way home and talk about the people who used to live here or there, where now there are only fields of grass, a hotel, or a car lot. To them, everything has changed, but this is just how I remember it: a two-lane highway, a long drive to Grandma's, everywhere green. Green kudzu and Spanish moss draping the green poplar trees, neon-green meadows, colonial homes with swing sets and perfectly mowed green grass, a green horizon consisting of the peaks of pine forest as far as the eye can see. Houses are miles apart from each other; trailer homes are scattered in the wooded distance. There is a buzz in the air—even it is green and electric.

While Mom loosens as we get closer to the place she calls home, Dad tightens. He hates sitting still. He hates small talk. But mostly, he is reminded, as he is each summer, of his absolute whiteness. He cannot loosen his tongue. It is impossible. His words remain sharp at the edges while everyone around him code-switches fluidly. He feels the blood in the soil but can only relate to it through his knowledge of a not-so-distant history he's learned through books. He cannot relax his body, is writhing in his seat, so he cuts in when he can't take it anymore. "Instead of talking about dead people, let's talk about something with real *meaning*." The way he says *meaning* embarrasses me. I glance at my uncle who says nothing, but raises one eyebrow. Mom glares at Dad and punches his leg.

"Chris, don't you start," she warns. "You hear me?"

Dad holds a different abstract vision of Alabama. He imagines slavery, extreme poverty, and Jim Crow. It angers him, and he flaunts his white privilege around Alabama in the way he demands that people talk about it: *Tell me what happened to you*, he wants to know with good intention. *Tell me how you struggled. Ease me of my burden and let me admire you; I want to respect you.* He imagines the civil rights movement, fed up and impassioned black people marching across the Edmund Pettus Bridge. He'd like to imagine Mom there, demanding justice, but she wasn't there. She was picking cotton in some field, without transportation, without the privilege of books, only the innate political consciousness that comes with being born black and poor and country. What she wanted more was to buy her parents a toilet. Dad wants her to talk about it. *Tell us*, he demands impatiently. *Tell the children.* He wants to admire her. So much of himself is dependent on his admiration for her.

Dad pulls out a crumpled-up newspaper article from his bag. "Listen to this," he says. "This has *meaning*." He begins to talk about the civil rights movement and a museum in Selma, where Mom is from.

"We'll look at it later, Chris," Mom says. She is engaged in light conversation with Woody, whom she hasn't seen in a year.

"But, you lived this! And here we are . . . The people you're talking about are not here, let's talk about something relevant!" The way he says *relevant* makes me put my head back on the seat and sigh. My uncle chuckles and passes me a bag of something.

"Here, Claire," he says.

"I'm not Claire."

"Vivian," he says.

"My name's not Vivian."

"What your name is, girl?"

"Melissa," I say, looking up at him. He shoves my head playfully. My parents are still arguing. I look in the bag, and it's full of a substance too puffy to be potato chips. I take one out of the bag and lick it. It smells funny. Tastes like grease and barbeque.

"What, you ain't never ate a pork rind?"

"What's a pork rind?"

He laughs at me. "It's good," he assures. "What your mama be feeding you in *Ca-li-for-nia?*" He takes great, mocking effort to enunciate this word.

We get to stay in Alabama for two weeks every summer for the family reunion. At night, an unreal buzzing of god only knows what—crickets, frogs, snakes, ghosts—comes from the ground outside and makes me grateful to be in my grandmother's house, safe in bed. There are no other houses around for miles. It is hard to imagine my mom living here as a kid, in a shack down the road, with thirteen brothers and sisters, in a structure, not quite a house, with no walls and no toilet. I try and imagine this pleasant smell of summer I look forward to replaced by the smell of a season's worth of hot shit rising from where the land starts to slope. When Mom moved to California, the first thing she did was save up enough money working as a maid in San Francisco to build a bathroom in the new house and install a septic tank.

In the summer, when the house is full of visiting relatives, the water gets low and we must take short showers; we mustn't wash our hair. Water is a precious commodity that must not be taken for granted. We visit the ceaseless natural spring down the road and fill up dozens of recycled bottles with water for backup sponge baths, toilet flushes, and drinking. This water is delicious, magical to me. Year after year, it pours endlessly from a rusty metal pipe in a seemingly ancient moss-covered stone receptacle surrounded by ferns, lizards, and dragonflies. I put my mouth right beneath the spout, close my eyes, and gulp as much of it as I can.

When Uncle Woody's pickup pulls into the red dirt yard of Grandma's house, the screen door screeches open and out waddles Grandma with open arms. We unload our suitcases onto the brick-colored dirt. My legs immediately itch, and I slap at red ants, wave away mosquitoes. Grandma pulls me into her chest, and I drink in her earthy buttermilk smell.

"Baby," she coos, and squeezes me, laughs in a muffled hum. All old women must hum like this when they squeeze their grandchildren, I think. Vivian and Junior line up for their squeezes, and we march in to greet our cousins and any aunts who have already arrived from North Carolina, Tennessee, Florida—places I imagine are like mountainous, green suburbs where the women bake peach cobblers and biscuits and leave a trail of perfume behind them wherever they go.

Cousins Shawn and Sheneka, the same age as Junior and me, and therefore our companions each summer, emerge from their bedrooms shy at first, their sturdy, mosquito-scarred limbs waddling cautiously toward us; we haven't seen each other in a year. Aunt Bernadette walks out from the living room, which she's undoubtedly already dusted and vacuumed twice that day. "Give Auntie some sugar!" She comes in for a hug and whispers in my ear, "You should've been my baby." She says it every year, reminding me, with a loving look of ownership in her eyes, that my mother once attempted to give me to her, in a casual Southern family adoption—*here, sister, have one of my babies, I already have four*—but when Dad found out he wouldn't allow it. He had to remind Mom that I was *his* child. Aunt Bernadette doesn't have children yet and her husband is white, so I could have passed for hers. Every summer she looks longingly at me and whispers sweetness in my ear, reminiscing about when my mother brought me there as an infant with the intention of giving me to her, but changed her mind at the last minute. It is a story told with humor, how I was brought in secret one summer. No one in Selma knew I'd been born. In those early days Dad never came to Alabama; he had to stay home and work at his demanding city job, so Mom would ride the Greyhound bus alone with us through Texas—it seemed we spent the entire ride trying to get through monstrous Texas; the other states were a breeze. Mom hid down the road with the other children while Uncle Woody held me, wrapped up in a blanket, and took me into my grandmother's house. He announced that he'd found a baby in a ditch; someone had presumably left me there to be taken.

This theater was performed although the transaction between Mom and Aunt Bernadette had already been agreed upon. My mother's sense of humor is a dark one. All who were home participated in washing the baby from the ditch, powdering her, wondering what to do with her, wondering who'd put her there. Then someone said, "This looks like one of Tho's chillun," and that was the end.

My mother entered the scene, laughing, proud that her joke had been successful. Maybe she wanted to see what it felt like first, to try on the feeling of not being my mother. When Mom tells me this story, I do not laugh; I don't find it funny. She has no memory of the not wanting, but my cells remember and I see in her both my mother—my infinite mother—and a woman—overwhelmed, pregnant, thirty-eight years old, sleep-deprived—who briefly allowed herself to imagine the relief of giving away her fifth baby.

Aunt Bernadette, my almost mother, pushes me aside to invite Junior in. "Handsome," she says, then pushes him away to hug Vivian. "Tall." Her lips leave smudges of burgundy lipstick on our mouths and cheeks. She looks like a younger version of my mother. Her red-brown skin like the dirt outside, dotted with freckles and pretty moles like a black Cindy Crawford. Her short, pressed hair doesn't move, but she throws her head to one side and another as if it does, moving an imaginary long mane from her face like a movie star. I try to picture my life with her; I can't see it. Life without my siblings is one I cannot imagine.

The days go on and the excitement of arrival wears off. It is too hot to be outside. I watch more cable TV than I have in all my life. I'm in heaven until Dad finds us and tells us we're rotting our brains and asks us if we want to be lard asses. He makes us—me and Junior, Shawn and Sheneka—go on a hike with him. We follow him far behind the house where the land erodes into a sudden decline like entering the deep end of a pool. The decline leads us to a shaded forest where slick lizards and frogs live and a peaceful creek flows.

Junior has beaten all of us, and I can hear him calling from up ahead. "Creek!" he screams, his voice echoing through the magical forest we think we've discovered. The forest is so deep, so hidden by shady layers of pine it may as well be underground. "I found a creek!"

We move more quickly and catch up to him. Junior looks at the creek the way I've seen him look at other things he wants to get into—driver's seats of fast cars, gushing waterslides, locked cash registers. He wants to know how things work; he is quicker than most, wants to skip the steps of learning, go full speed ahead to doing the thing, whatever it is. He looks into the creek, but his body is already somewhere else; we are only now catching up.

I pick up a rock and throw it in. "Frog!" I point to the jumping animal I seem to have disturbed. We are never alone in the woods. Dad tells us we can take our shoes off and put our feet in. He is ignorant of the snakes and leeches we have been warned of our entire childhoods, but his innocence is endearing so we follow his lead. Shawn and Sheneka look at each other with raised eyebrows. Junior has already taken his off.

Even though it's July, everything is the color of spring down there. Pine branches shoot out fresh, untouched needles, and soft blankets of moss cling to the trunks of the fallen branches. Dad speaks to us in Latin, telling us the scientific names for every fern, helping himself to the ones he finds most interesting.

"Wow!" He stops to examine a large one. "It's definitely the Dryopteris genus, but I've never seen one this big!" He unearths it at the roots, gently detaching the plant's white tendrils from the sandy red dirt. In black rubber boots, his pants rolled up above his knees showing his skin as bright and pale as the moon, his hands full of soft stolen ferns he intends to bring back to California, their roots dripping dirt as he directs our attention to cow patties, giant mushrooms, and the droppings of potentially wild animals, he looks like a wild man, a happy man.

Shawn and Sheneka have fallen behind. Their chubby legs are unaccustomed to walking for fun, especially in the summer. They anxiously stumble over fallen tree branches and hardened cow patties. Even though they are from this land, they do not trust it. We are not of the generation that had to be intimate with the fields; Mom, all of our aunts and uncles, our grandparents, and the generations before them had to know all of its animals, ghosts, fruits, and critters. They now enjoy the AC inside, while Dad makes us discover this land as if it has never been seen before.

"Did you know this was here, behind your house?" Dad asks Shawn and Sheneka when they catch up, with a slight inflection of disbelief, a little reproach. They shake their heads. Who knew there was this magic world hiding behind a place we thought we'd seen and known, inside and out, year after year? It had always existed, but we'd been blind to it. It was always available to us, if we could only see it. If only someone would show us. What more was out there? In the woods or in the street, it didn't matter. What other places existed? I wonder, What is beyond our house in Oakland?

Alabama is mythical. Summer is not inhabitable by humans, but here we are. It lends itself better, I think, to fantasy or magical realism, to stories where little girls are the observers or the initiators of very strange events. What is real and what is imagined?

After a powerful crack of thunder, the power is out. Outside in the night, it rains relentlessly, and all we can do is wait in the dark. Veins of lightning shoot out over the sky and then fall like fireworks, and for a moment you can see the fields beyond, the tops of trees beneath the electric sky, and then nothingness, just the steady, merciless sound of torrent against the tin roof and earth. The unknown of the darkness inside and out terrifies me. Even the adults are scared. The next bark of thunder has me ducking, afraid, looking for some place to hide where I won't be struck.

In the corner of the living room between the brown floral couch and the side table with stacks of *Jet* magazines, I crouch down and hug my knees. Aunt Bernadette sits across from me on the love seat. All I can see is the glimmer of her polished toenails. We sit in the dark, our bodies still, sweat beads starting to form along our spines from no air conditioning.

"Throw me one of them magazines," she says. "Oh wee, it's hot."

I toss her the one with Janet Jackson on the cover, and she fans herself with such force I can feel the air from across the room. I am grateful for it, and grateful to have her in the room with me.

Laughter rumbles from the back of the house followed by feet pounding down the hallway. This is the particular sound of a child who cannot be contained. Junior, shirtless, wearing only swimming trunks, makes a run for it toward the front door. His laughter becomes high-pitched when the rain touches his face. I watch from the window as he grins, jumping up and down in a pond-size puddle just beyond the front porch. Why isn't he afraid? He brings an object up toward the sky and then rubs it under his armpits—a bar of soap. He laughs up at the sky and takes a shower right there in front of the house, in the darkness. Even though he looks crazy, I want to join him. But I'm frozen by the thought of what all the grown-ups have said about getting struck by lightning and the leeches, how they find your feet in the water and suck your blood.

A rush of Aunt Bernadette sweeps past me, and she's at the front door calling to him faster than I can turn around. "That boy don't have no kind of sense," she mutters. "Junior!" she calls outside over the rain. He ignores her and continues to jump and rinse the soap from his body. "Boy, get back in this house before you get struck by lightning!"

When he doesn't answer or even look at her, she calls toward the back of the house. "Theolia!" she yells to Mom. "You better get that boy!"

The next thing I know, Mom is dragging him back into the house by his arm.

"Man," he huffs. He leaves puddles of water behind him as Mom pulls him through the candlelit hall.

"Go put on some clothes," Mom demands. She warns us not to show our true colors, warns us regularly—before we go to the neighbors', before we go to school, before we go to Grandma's. What color is that? Sometimes it is the color of desire—don't show hunger, don't show need or want of any kind to outsiders. But often it is something else—the color of the city, the color of the cement, the color of the curse words that often slip from our mouths, the blackness of our bodies that mixes with the white to make us what the little Southern kids call *bright*. "Why are you so bright?" they ask in earnest, and I look at them bewildered, wondering with my literal city ears what brightness they see in me. Bright, but still very much not white. Is that the color Mom means? The not-white? Or is it another color?

She would prefer we act like we don't come from the city, like our feet were born dusty, like we came from roads, not streets. She would prefer we act full, satisfied. Junior doesn't care; he always shows his truest colors. He wants things, is hungry, curious—a wild city creature. "I'll get you when you least expect it," Mom says as her final warning after the shower spectacle. She makes an effort to beat the boys when she's not angry anymore; she makes an effort to beat them with intention, not emotion, as if doing so will make the warnings penetrate more completely, encourage them to hide their truest colors, protect them from these colors. If not her, then who? She does not beat me because I am becoming a woman; it is not necessary. I have already learned to hide, to make myself small. My body, crouching, blends into the furniture, and I watch in the dark and wait. I know soon she will attempt to beat the wild out of him; she will do it in the name of protection.

In the morning it's like it never rained. The sandy red dirt drank up all the rain of the night before, and Junior's shower is a memory that makes me smile as I swing under the peach tree. It's still hot, but the shade helps—better than being under the freezing air conditioner. As I pump my legs, I watch Mom walk around the property in her made-in-China African dress. She sees me and waves, bends over to inspect a daisy. She plucks a skinny branch off a pink blooming crepe myrtle tree and calls Junior's name. He appears moments later, but when he sees what's in her hand, he takes off running down the road where we aren't supposed to go. Mom runs after him in the dust he kicks up, waving the branch over her head, yelling about how he's not going to make no fool out of her. For a while I can't see them; the road and the kudzu have swallowed them, it seems. But it spits them back up: Mom first, her branch gone, her nostrils flaring as if emitting fire; Junior follows, a safe distance away, walking with a bit of a limp. He picks up rocks along the road and throws them, making little clouds of red dust in his path. His face is bright red.

Dad walks into the scene too late. "What the fuck, Theolia?" he says when he sees Junior's red face. "What he did was harmless."

She ignores him and walks into the house. The two Chrises look at each other. Chris Sr. looks at his son with apology. Chris Jr.—Junior—looks away and walks toward the back of the house where Aunt Bernadette's dog lives. He is too defeated to be seen by anything other than an animal. They can't protect us.

The next day Junior slaps Mom in the face with a fly swatter and gets his mouth washed out with soap. Over his tears, while it happens, he gurgles out cuss words. "Fuck you," he screams. "I fucking hate you." He sounds like he's underwater. This time Dad does it and Mom thinks it's too much.

90

"Chris!" Mom hovers over them. "Enough!" I watch and I learn that Junior's transgressions mean something different. His body, his mouth, are subjected to punishments from which I am spared. His punishment is both for who he is and who they are afraid he'll become. His boy body, his boy mouth, pays the consequences for the burgeoning man inside, the man they can already see forming. They fear for that man. They punish what they think is his future body, his future mouth, whose power and recklessness are feared, deplored. They must be washed and beaten out.

This is when we first begin to part, the first time the edges of our selves leave each other and seek belonging outside. He becomes a man and I become a woman. This process is slow but intentional. It involves many people and many messages; it begins while we are still in our child bodies. Junior has always been bad. Bad is a self-fulfilling prophecy that, heard enough times, is believed: *I am bad*. The constant question, *Why are you so bad?* That time he stole. All the times he stole. He is always stealing, always wanting more. The answer he receives is always no—no matter how practical and from the heart the thing is that he desires—because he will surely ruin it, for he is bad and he must be punished for his badness. This is where we diverge. I become a black woman in the way I have been taught: silent, undeserving, inadequate in every way. And he becomes a black man: unpredictable, scary. Bad.

FOUR

We return to Oakland mosquito bitten and bronzed. Fall arrives with heat waves, what we call earthquake weather. An eerily quiet heat moves over the city, hushing the activity of the summer and marking the beginning of a new school year, a new season. Junior will begin at his new school in the hills, and I will continue at the elementary school he graduated from a few years earlier. I'll begin third grade and he'll begin seventh; we are seven going on eight, and eleven going on twelve, respectively. Vivian has begun high school at the neighborhood school. Cornelius is living at UC Berkeley in the dorms. Claire is back in the dorms of her boarding school. It is all glamour to me; I look forward to the day when I can have that kind of freedom, but I am left at home, the smallest one, the furthest behind, as all of my siblings carry on with growing up and into their independent lives. Sixteen, I think, is when I'll have a taste of freedom; it is the age my imagination allows me to visualize. In this vision I am big, unafraid, and free. I watch Junior closely since we are nearest in age, his life an example of my very near future. He is closest to the freedom

I imagine. I watch him as if he is my mirror. I watch as he returns from his new school; I look for the little ways he changes.

"Look," Junior says. I am passing by the room we share, on my way from the bathroom to the kitchen. He motions for me to enter, and I know his look is one of trouble; I know the thing he wants to show me is illicit. I have seen this look evolve over the years. It is a twinkle in his eyes, a glimmer in his smile, a look of absolute pride: *Look what I can do*. I enter the room. He closes the door behind me and shows me boxes he's got stashed under his bed. Gel pens from the stationery store. Entire boxes of all the flavors of bubblegum from the convenience store: grape, strawberry, classic bubblegum. My eyes are curious. I look at him. "Where did you get all this?" But I already know the answer. He smiles, not needing to speak. I run my hands over the pens and packs of gum. I feel wealth. It is cool to the touch and smooth. I feel joy. I want to possess it.

"Can I have one?"

"Any one you want." He waves his hand over the boxes, presenting his booty to me. I am an accomplice. An accomplice to this wealth, this joy, I tell myself. It matches my vision of a future in which we have things, in which we are big. It is mine by default. Junior tells me he intends to sell these hot items to the rich kids at his new school. The immorality of this doesn't enter my mind. It is genius. We will be rich. We. I include myself. I invite myself to share in this business as his accomplice. We will come up together. Sooner than I can offer him a future he can touch, he can offer me one, built from the profits of stolen candy. We will be rich. I am certain of it. Soon the boxes of candy and pens will turn into cash.

I think back to little Junior just a few years back—what did he want? I remember meals around the table on evenings when Mom would be awake enough to cook, and there would be enough space cleared around the dining table so we could eat and look at one another. We loved to eat. There was a sense of normalcy when we ate around a table together. It was a ritual we craved and that, when we had it, gave us such joy. Junior, Vivian, and I liked to pretend to be actors in TV commercials advertising food. We'd take turns chewing passionately. "Watch," Junior would say when it was his turn, and he would perform his own commercial for an imaginary brand of canned food he called Generous Portions. He smacked his lips and made sounds of pleasure while he took a bite for our pretend camera. "I'm gonna be rich," he'd say when he was finished. That was one of the first things I remember him wanting.

I unwrap a piece of strawberry bubblegum and pop the pink cube into my mouth. I close my eyes and savor the first burst of saccharine flavor, knowing it will end soon. It is so good. I open my eyes to Junior's pleased face.

"You like it?"

"Of course I like it. Let me take some," I say, eyeing the flavors I intend to take for myself. Junior doesn't object. "So, did you take these entire trays from the corner store?" I ask, shaking my head, preemptively scolding him because I already know the answer.

"You should see the cars those kids get dropped off in at school. They can afford it."

I roll my eyes and move on to another subject. "Do you take the bus home by yourself after school? Or do you make Daddy pick you up down the street?"

We both laugh because for years we've asked Dad to drop us off or pick us up a few blocks from school so we wouldn't be seen in his dirty work truck with piles of tools and tarpaulins flapping off the sides, us emerging from the front seat like the contents of a clown car. How many children can fit in a truck cabin? Leave it to Dad to find out.

"I've been taking the bus." He pauses for a moment, probably thinking about the last time he was robbed and bullied. "But it's okay," he finally says. "I have a friend who rides with me."

"That's good," I say.

"Yeah, he lives in West Oakland. He's new too. His mom made him go because he was fuckin' up at his last school."

"Sounds familiar."

"I go over there sometimes."

"To West Oakland?"

"Yeah, he has a bunch of friends over there. It's cool."

"Okay," I say. "Just be careful."

It is those lawless after hours, the hours in between school and darkness, the hours when Mom is asleep and Dad is working, that cause alarm. I feel something in me becoming protective of him in a new part of town with a new boy, but I push it away.

That fall, Mom and Dad are preoccupied. They don't know Junior is stealing and hanging out in West Oakland after school. All they know is that Junior's teacher said his grades were good, and so they relax, believing they have made the right choice for him. We are a family of seven. Some of us are still living at home, one in college, one away at boarding school, one of the children at home prone to trouble—but now they can relax a little knowing Junior is at least doing better in school and he's not being bullied. There is hope yet, and so when they announce Mom is pregnant, they do it with a sense of readiness, of confidence and pride for our growing family, however feigned, however uneasy they may actually be to make us eight.

"You will have a little sister," Mom says as she sets the dinner table for Junior, Vivian, and me one spring night before getting ready for work. Dad is pleased, messing with something on the counter, close by and pretending to be busy as Mom makes the announcement.

"When?" I ask.

"Soon," she says, smiling. "I have only a few more months. So, looks like when we go to Alabama next, your sister will be joining us." She is gleeful, touching her belly as she speaks.

I am shocked. What baby, I think. I don't even see a baby. She is easily hidden beneath baggy clothes and Mom's already-round belly. I'd always imagined myself as the last child in the family. In my mind that was firm. Junior and I, we were the last babies, a complete duo. I feel betrayed for not being notified sooner.

For almost eight years I've reigned as queen baby, as right-hand man, and now I would be dethroned, demoted to someone less important, someone big enough to take care of myself. This new order makes me align with Junior all the more. I follow him wherever he'll allow, always the witness to his life. In return he offers fierce protection. We are each other's eyes. I know who will take care of me: he will. This is understood.

She is born in early summer just a month before we head to Alabama. Mom's vacation commences as soon as she delivers: a long maternity leave followed by a vacation back home. All of us—Vivian, Junior, Cornelius, Claire, and I—wait outside the hospital room while she pushes out our sister with Dad by her side. When the baby arrives, we all gather around Mom to behold the tiny red-faced, bright-eyed girl-child. She is named Angelica. We become wrapped up in this new being. In the first days of her life, Junior and I walk to the hospital every day to visit Mom and baby Angelica. We all sit on the hospital bed together, passing her to and fro between us, captivated by the sounds and faces she makes, her little smiles. We kiss her nose, her eyelids, her miniature fingers, and stroke her soft head, her brand-new hair more like little feathers than curls.

I observe Mom. She's happy sitting with us—her smallest children—enjoying with unabashed glee the cleanliness of the hospital, however sterile, and the sense of being served, however temporary; she will stay as long as they'll let her, holding the little bundle of person while the nurses wait on her. It is as if this might be her natural state.

In the way she holds Angelica, I understand how deeply she loves all her babies. Like seeing her relaxed and smiling in Alabama, I witness a new mother in this hospital room, awakened in new motherhood. I receive some extension of the love I see being given to my sister, if only in the joy I derive from being able to witness my mother happy.

When the nurse comes in to bring Mom a tray of gray food and apple juice, Mom offers it to Junior and me, and we share it ravenously, as if underfed. I shovel mounds of gray matter—sliced meat slathered in salty gravy beneath a mashed-potato substance—into my mouth and stare at Mom staring at her new daughter. She is such a tiny thing. Some part of me wonders how she will be cared for. Who could be trusted to do it? When Dad is working and Mom goes back to being asleep, who will do it? A tiny sense of burden creeps into this happy moment, a sense of responsibility too mature for my seven years: we will have to do it—me, Junior, Vivian, and the others.

Our home is abuzz with Angelica, this new member of our family. Even Cornelius and Claire come over more frequently. Soon we begin packing bags for Alabama. This time it'll be just me, Junior, and Angelica going. Vivian is staying back to make up a class in summer school—she is struggling in math and science—so Cornelius promises to stay at home and keep an eye on the house and fifteen-year-old Vivian while we're gone for two weeks.

UNLIKE IN OTHER years, we rent a car when we arrive in Alabama, perhaps because this year we have a tiny baby with us and must strap her up in a special car seat. We cannot allow her to ride in the beds of trucks or on long truck seats on a lap. Not yet. It is our job to protect her. Junior begs Dad to give him a driving lesson in the rental car, and

Dad refuses as he concentrates on finding what he thinks is a good talk-radio show instead of focusing on the road, swerving a little as he turns the radio dial.

"Can we please listen to music now?" Junior pleads.

Dad starts tuning again and settles on a classical music station. He turns the volume up so loud he has to yell. "Do you know who this is?" he quizzes us. We do not. Junior and I sit in the back on either side of Angelica's car seat and glance at each other periodically, rolling our eyes.

"Mozart!" Dad yells, educating us when we don't respond. "Your brother Cornelius has the same middle name," he announces proudly. "Did you know that Amadeus was Mozart's middle name too?" He responds to our shaking heads, which he sees in the rearview mirror, "That's right. I thought he'd play the violin like Mozart. Maybe if there was a football involved." He pauses for a moment. "This is a beautiful part!" He turns the volume up even louder. Junior and I cover our ears. "Can you recognize the different instruments in this section?" he shouts. We can't. "Mm," Dad remarks, clearly pleased with his music selection. He is in his happy place: in perceived control, driving, wife and kids in his care and under his influence, on a family vacation.

"Nice music." Mom looks back at us and nods her head, smiling an enticing smile like she's just seen something tasty. Angelica has miraculously slept through the whole music lesson.

"Can we listen to *good* music now?" Junior asks.

"Now, hold on," Dad says. "This is good music! Do you hear this? Wow!" He eventually tapers off, no longer talking to us but to himself, making sounds of appreciation as we drive into greener and more spacious land. It feels like we're foreigners in an alien land, blasting strange music in our spacemobile. Everything about us is wrong: interracial marriage, mixed kids, together and loving one another in this place, which we know is very much still segregated, remnants of slavery intact and all around us.

Junior and I would like nothing more than to find the local rap station and see if the popular songs we love have made it all the way to Alabama, to feel a little less foreign amid this classical music, in this car, in this town. "I'm not putting on any shoot-'em-up music if that's what you mean." Dad hates rap music, calls it *violent hate music*. Sometimes he jokes around, dancing to an unknown beat and imitating rap music, singing, "Beat 'em up, shoot 'em up. Boom boom hip hop, shoot 'em up, kill motherfucker, bitch," and other offensive, off-base imitations of music we both love. He blames it for drawing Junior to a bad crowd.

I look at Mom's profile as she looks out the window, the scenery passing by her in flashes of green trees and blue sky, framed against the outline of her soft brown skin, her long black braids curling at the ends. I copy her, surrendering to the music and to Dad's banter, and stare off into the distance until I fall asleep.

I wake to my car door opening and the slap of Southern heat on my face, my arms, then my legs; it wraps my entire body in a familiar welcome. I instantly wake up and start greeting my cousins, my grandma and grandpa, my aunts and uncles.

It is nonstop reunion prep the moment we arrive. The

reunion will take place in two days and the inaugural fish-fry party in just one. Grass must be mowed, trees must be trimmed, new flowers must be planted, picnic tables and coolers must be washed, ribs and chicken must be marinated, the smoker and the deep fryer must be unearthed, the vegetables must be prepared, and the children, in order not to be in the way, must either offer to help or disappear. I opt to disappear, to avoid helping and to avoid Dad. Dad in Alabama is like a puppy off its leash—mischievous and wound up. His inability to sit still makes me nervous. He hears gossip and he wants to act, cannot understand even after all these years, that people enjoy simply talking—casually talking about the weather, about politics, about other people. I walk through the living room of the trailer where my aunt lives. Mom and my aunts are sitting on all the couches and chairs with buckets between their legs for the scraps of the black-eyed peas they shell and the corn they husk. They engage in light gossip about distant relatives who they are expecting to come, but only to pack stacks and stacks of to-go plates and leave. I hear Dad proceed to lecture the ladies that they mustn't just talk about it, that they need to *say* something if it bothers them that much, or better yet *do* something. "Oh no," I groan to myself, and walk right out of the room and into the yard, where I feel instantly less burdened. I don't want to shell peas, and I don't want Dad duty. I choose the heat.

I eventually make my way back into the house, where I find Aunt Betty gossiping in the kitchen with some other aunts. They're about to prepare peach cobbler. One of my aunts has Angelica on her knee, and Aunt Betty begins clearing the table. "Baby, get your auntie some more flour, will you?" Immediately I get sucked in to working, but I don't mind. I sit in a chair next to my aunt and my baby sister. I listen to their melodious voices and wait for Betty to ask me to do things. She stops asking, and now simply commands: "Crisco." And a few seconds later points to a cabinet: "All the cans of peaches." "A pot from up yonder," she says, pointing below the dish rack. "Butter—all of it," she adds, pointing to the refrigerator. I don't mind being bossed around in this room. I enjoy their soft talk and the hum of the air conditioner and the quiet of the house, the calm before the storm of people that will arrive in a few hours. For my help I am rewarded with a stroke on my head and a compliment; I am told I am "a sweet baby, the sweetest girl from California there ever was."

Aunt Betty makes it clear she thinks of California as a foreign place full of bad people, and that I'm an exception to the immoral people who live there. I'm just happy to have the positive attention, and soak it up. My relatives don't know much about Oakland. They don't know we have a big sparkling lake in the middle of the city and hills that looks like Christmas lights at night as far as the eye can see and a massive bridge that takes us to San Francisco, where they have real-life *Full House* Victorian homes. They don't know we have the twenty-four-hour doughnut shop Happy Donuts, where Dad lets me have whatever I want on the nights I go with him to drop off Mom, or the Berkeley Marina where we fly kites, or the UC Berkeley campus where Junior and I used to feed squirrels nuts right from our palms after Quaker meeting, or Piedmont Avenue with its toy shops and bookstores, and parks in every direction. They don't know about my best friend Nellie, whose mom takes us to interesting places like Adventure Playground on the Berkeley Marina, where we run wild building things and imagining other lives. They don't know Oakland is not a bad place.

It is almost showtime. Slowly the closer relatives start to arrive. Cars begin to line up in the front yard. I bounce from room to room, helping, observing, playing, and then sitting on the porch with Grandpa, where he swats flies like it is his full-time job and occasionally yells out corrective feedback when he sees someone in his line of vision doing a task that could be done better. From the porch, I watch Junior and our cousin Shawn in their swimming shorts hosing down big coolers, taking breaks to spray each other and squeal. I see Dad emerge from the trailer. He observes Junior for a moment, a nod and a pleased smile come over his face, his hands on hips. It is a familiar look he wears when he confirms his child is safe. He walks up the few steps to the front porch, pats Grandpa on the shoulder, and pokes his head inside the house to see that Angelica is in someone's arms. From just inside the screen door, he salutes the person who cares for her. "Everything okay?" he says, enunciating hard as if English isn't spoken here. He nods and moves toward the rental car, announcing he's heading to town to run an errand. I take a deep breath.

Once all the guests have arrived, all the food has been placed on the tables, and everyone has a plate and a sense of calm—the moment before a meal—my oldest aunt gets up to offer a prayer of gratitude for our togetherness and for our food. She then invites our oldest living relative to lead us in song before we begin lunch. We are a family of singers. Uncle Red is my great uncle, Grandpa's older brother, and he humbly accepts. "All right now," he says, and stands laboriously and begins a song I have never heard. As everyone joins in, I watch the adults happily sway and hum and sing along harmoniously, like they've practiced, like they're all suddenly a choir.

Once we've finished singing, the quiet buzz of people focused on the activity of eating begins, followed by the buildup of conversation, soft at first so as not to be disrespectful of the transition from song, and then more confident and boisterous. Before my uncle presses play on his soul and R&B mix, Dad gets up from his seat and starts banging on a tin can with a fork. He has an announcement to make, he says, and needs everyone's attention. I begin the process of shrinking. I elbow Junior, who is sitting next to me on our picnic bench, for support. What will our father say? There are too many people for me to talk back, too many people for me to run away, so I just listen. He announces that he has an image to go along with what he has to say. Next he passes around a stack of papers. When mine arrives, I study it and shrink in shame. It is a color copy of a satirical painting: a family of pigs sitting around a dinner table covered in food. He must have gone to the library in Selma, found the picture in a book, and photocopied it.

My perception is not working properly, my senses are scattered; I am trying to listen—for ammunition for future arguments, and for evidence that my father is actively trying to oppress me with a growing list of transgressions: unsightly vehicles; a messy house I can't invite friends into; classical music and opera; broken, water-saving appliances; knee-deep dirty shower water; a toilet I have to flush with a bucket of water; and now this, at *my* family reunion. Mine. This is *my* Alabama, *my* family, *my* place. I feel protective of this space and thus resentful of how he has taken it from me without even knowing he has. It is the not knowing that hurts me most. I am unsure if it is his whiteness, his otherness, his restlessness, or his manic need to problem solve other people's lives that makes me feel protective over this land and these people—my family—but I do. I scowl at him. Half listening and half trying to monitor my body, hold back tears, tighten my fists, glare with precision, I can only hear bits and pieces. "This is meant to be amusing," he says. "Obviously none of us are literal pigs, but some of us can act like them." He continues, "And so just think about this picture as you go in for second or fourth to-go plates. Before you act in greed." He clears his throat, aware he is on the spot and not receiving the reaction he'd like—laughter, a thumbs-up from someone. "Before you act like a pig, just consider the work and money that went into this meal and think twice. That's all." He clears his throat again and closes abruptly, and then makes himself a plate and sits down next to my mother, who glares at him.

Despite my embarrassment, Dad is proud of himself. As a principle and personal value, he wants to help people and he imagines that is what he's done. He has done what's right, he thinks, done what others weren't brave enough to do, spoken up for the weary. If no one else is grateful it's because they are blinded by their ignorant, gossiping ways. He stands taller, feels the opposite of shame when he approaches people in conversation, unaware that he may have offended. I am left to hold my own shame and embarrassment and balance it with his pride, his sense of justice and my love for him, my desire also to protect him. I eat up all of these feelings, and top them off with seconds of macaroni and cheese and peach cobbler.

Gradually, the group shakes off his announcement. I hear my aunt say, "Go on and eat just as much as you want. We got enough food, you hear?" Slowly, the talking and laughing eases back in and the comments are forgotten, the pig pictures start to fall to the ground. From behind my plate I watch as he is forgiven by all. I expect a coup, but everyone smiles and moves on. He's the eccentric white in-law from California who doesn't understand black Southern ways. I, too, let it go, eventually letting my body relax but continuing to be hypervigilant, avoiding rooms from which I can hear his voice. I can't relax when he's near. The day goes on as if Dad's interruption never happened. The crowd dies down and guests head back to Mobile, Montgomery, Marion, Tuscaloosa, Birmingham, and Atlanta. Those who have traveled farther stay a while—North Carolina, Tennessee, and California.

That night Junior does what he's been waiting for all along. When Dad heads to bed early, tired out from overeating and the hot sun, Junior finds the keys to the rental car. "Look," he says, walking into the living room where I'm watching TV with our cousins. He shows us car keys in one hand and a cigar in the other. He must have swiped the cigar from one of the men outside. The adults are putting away food in the trailer, watching the video from the day's events that our uncle recorded on his camcorder, or outside drinking moonshine and whiskey around the smoker. Mom and Dad are asleep with Angelica.

He motions for Shawn to come with him, and they giddily walk out the door. I am not invited to join this time. I watch longingly as the screen door creaks shut after them, wishing simultaneously for an invitation and for their safety. Junior doesn't know how to drive, but I have a feeling Shawn does. You can do things in the country you can't do in the city. Sheneka and I play UNO in the living room and watch TV until we are too tired to blink. Junior still isn't home by the time I get ready for bed. Sheneka retires to the bedroom she shares with Shawn, and I lie out on the small couch in the living room, where Junior and I have been relegated to sleep. I save the big couch for him and leave a blanket out. In separate rooms Sheneka and I both wait for our brothers.

I wake to the sound of the groaning air conditioner and to the smell of biscuits. It takes a moment to register just how freezing I am, the air conditioner ferociously blasting and the sheet that was my cover at my feet. Once awake and aware, I immediately look for Junior. Relieved, I see him across the living room, balled up in a fetal position, his face in a soft scowl of sleep, and I walk over to cover him with his sheet, which has slid to the floor. He's home; I can relax. I then move the dial of the air conditioner to its off position, return to the couch, and hold myself in my arms. Soon it will be sweltering, but I enjoy this moment of quiet air and listen to the sounds of the motor slowing, feel my skin soften, start to hear the sounds of the house and of life around us.

I hear Mom's voice first and the sounds of utensils on pans, the sizzling of grease, Angelica whining. I follow the smell of biscuits through the hallway and into the kitchen where Mom, Angelica, and Aunt Betty are. There is always urgent talk. All gossip sounds urgent—exaggerated whispers and raised eyebrows, hushes and averted eyes when other people enter the room, a look that says, *We'll finish this later*. I walk in on what I think is this kind of talk. Over Angelica's baby sounds, I hear Mom repeat, "My children, my children are okay, I'm so grateful." This must be one of her sermons—perhaps she's comparing herself to someone who's had it worse. I slide into an empty chair around the table as invisibly as I can, but I am noticed. The talking stops, and my Aunt Betty begins wiping the table off around me. "You hungry, baby?" I nod my head silently, and she places a plate in front of me—a heaping pile of grits, salmon cakes, and a biscuit. A roomful of adults is somehow silencing; I feel very small. I eat quietly, but there's something more that I try and decipher in the energy. Mom is bouncing Angelica on her knee, quietly looking down. Junior emerges from the living room and takes the seat next to me, still rubbing the sleep from his eyes. I wonder if Dad has noticed his car went missing last night.

Betty pipes in. "Lord have mercy, girl." Mom is the girl she refers to. "Girl," she says again, this time drawing it out. She shakes her head while she fixes Junior's plate.

Grandpa enters the room next, the sound of his cane making an entrance before him. He sits down slowly and heavily.

"What's going on in here?" he asks, likely responding to the quiet.

I watch and wait. Junior and I shovel grits into our mouths and observe the people in the room with wide eyes as if they're a movie. Mom lifts her head from where it'd been resting in her palm. She shakes her head and stares, not making eye contact with anyone. "I just don't know how much more I can take."

"Girl, isn't that the truth?" Betty adds from the stove, fixing a plate now for Grandpa.

Mom lets out a heavy breath, one that seems to have been reserved for this moment, and starts to speak. She distractedly bounces Angelica, who has begun to fuss. "The house," she starts. "The house is gone." Junior and I stop eating. "It's gone," she says.

"What do you mean *gone*? What about Cornelius and Vivian?" I break my own silence.

"Melissa, the house burned down. Vivian and Cornelius are okay. They're staying with the neighbors up the street until . . ." She fades, her eyes becoming wet. "Until I don't know . . . I just don't know. We have to go home as soon as we can."

"Huh?" Junior says, swallowing his food. "For real?"

"What's this I hear about a fire?" Grandpa says after he's gnawed his first bite and washed it down with a swig of coffee. Angelica begins to wail, realizing she's being ignored. "Give me that baby," Grandpa demands. She is passed around the table like a side dish and begins to laugh. He bounces her now on his knee. Once she's calm again he inquires, "Now, what is this about a fire? Is Oakland short on firemen? How in the hell did the goddamn house burn down?"

Again we look to Mom to tell us, but before she can open her mouth Dad comes stomping into the kitchen from the bedroom, where he's been on the phone.

"Theolia, I need you." He motions for her to come into the other room with him. "Insurance," he says.

Junior and I look at each other and eat uneasily. We need more information. What does all this mean? Aunt Betty serves anyone who enters the kitchen—Grandma, our cousins, our aunts and uncles. One by one she piles grits onto Styrofoam plates and tells them what has happened to our home, whispering things like *pity* and *shame* under her breath with a stoic look on her face. We quietly finish our breakfast at the kitchen table, where a dark cloud seems to have come over our family.

Cornelius and Vivian call throughout the day. The fire happened mysteriously in the middle of the night in Cornelius's old room at the back of the house. He fell asleep on the couch that night, so the smoke took a while to reach his nose on the living room couch. When it did, he jumped up without thinking and ran to the room where Vivian was sleeping—the room I share with Vivian and Junior. He banged on the locked door as the smoke grew thicker and the flames licked at him. He kicked the door down. Vivian had already begun suffocating from the smoke. He picked her up out of bed and ran toward the front door, toward air. Outside,

Vivian coughed and coughed, wearing only a T-shirt. The fire department came and put the fire out, but it had already destroyed everything. When the fire was finished, all that was left of the house was the structure itself, the facade and the charred wood columns that held it up from the inside. From the front it still looked like a house, except for the windows blackened by smoke. This is the story we are told.

I ask Vivian to tell me this story over and over again. Cornelius is a hero in my mind. "But how did it start?" I ask. The answer is not clear. "Weren't you embarrassed to be in front of the neighbors and the fireman in only a T-shirt and underwear? Cornelius saved you . . ." I recount the details until it becomes real.

On our minds is only fire. I carry on as normally as I can, trying to scoot into rooms and overhear anything that will be meaningful to our lives. Where will we live now? I try and connect the dots. Ironically, a year earlier there was a massive fire in the Oakland hills that just missed us. I was so scared the house would burn down. The news was on all day and night with updates for which neighborhoods needed to evacuate and which ones were still safe. Images played of long lines of cars stuck in traffic, families trying to get away from the fire, having left everything behind in flames. Our house was so close. Ashes rained from the sky, and Junior and I caught them in jars as if it were a game. Later that evening, as the sky became darker with both night and smoke, I packed a bag—a giant black trash bag of the belongings I'd take when it was our turn to evacuate. "We shouldn't sleep here tonight," I said when I entered the living room where my family watched the news, but they laughed, knowing, I guess, that it would not come to that. But a year later, fire retuned for us, thankfully taking no one—just the house.

I want to evacuate now. I want to pack a garbage bag full of my things, but then I remember I have nothing. What I have with me now is all I have. We preemptively evacuated when we came to this reunion, and left Cornelius and Vivian there at the helm of fire and disaster. I want to go home. But then I remember: I no longer have a home.

The next day I still don't have answers. When I ask Mom and Dad where we'll live, they say they're doing their best. Their best feels like an unknown forest of danger and disaster—chaos. From the conversations I overhear and the looks I observe on Mom's and Dad's faces, they are more afraid than they've ever been. If Dad knows about Junior's joyride at all, it is now forgotten and trumped by our impending homelessness.

Outside in the early evening, I seek peace on the swing under the peach tree out front. I watch Aunt Bernadette and Uncle Larry pull into the yard, returning from an errand with their ill-mannered show dog—a wrinkled shar-pei so ugly it's defaulted to cute. When Bernadette hears about the fire, she puts her arm around Mom and covers her mouth in shock. She motions for Mom to walk down the road with her while she lets her dog relieve himself. They stop, and Bernadette takes Mom's hand and squeezes it. They linger together for a moment in the approaching darkness before turning back, their nearly identical profiles more pronounced in the fading light of dusk.

During dinner, Mom makes an announcement while Junior and I eat. Finally, news. Perhaps there's a plan now. Perhaps the insurance details have been sorted out and we can have our home rebuilt. I listen attentively. "Your father and I think it would be best if Junior spends the rest of the summer with Aunt Bernadette and Uncle Larry in North Carolina," Mom says.

So Dad must have discovered evidence of Junior's joyride after all. Even the fire isn't big enough to distract from the priority of keeping him safe. This is when Junior leaves me. He is older and growing apart from me as he becomes a man. But this separation, this North Carolina decision feels different. We both know why. He is bad. He is a troublemaker, and Mom and Dad no longer have even a home in which to contain his wild spirit. It is presumably out of love—that he be watched; this is another message, another kind of punishment. Mom knows the danger of his body and tries desperately to protect it. His young black boy body on the streets of Oakland, free to run wild, free to meet with the wrong kind of friend, free to collide with police, without a home and without structure to contain him. It scares her to her core, more than it did with Cornelius because he had a quieter manner, wasn't so consistently bad. It scares them possibly more than the fire itself. Two children made it out of the flames, better not try their luck and risk a third.

Junior stops eating and suddenly has little boy eyes. No matter how old he gets, how offensive his body odor becomes, how freckled his skin, his eyes do not change. They remain the endlessly round hazelnut saucers of his little boy face. "Huh?" is all he can say, his eyebrows contorting with horror. For him, as for me, this news must be at once exciting and horrible—the rest of the summer in the North Carolina country, a replica of Alabama in my mind, but without cousins. It means newness, but it also means a level of boredom beyond imagination.

Aunt Bernadette steps away from the stove toward Junior and squeezes his shoulder. "You're my baby, Junior." He looks uneasy about this declaration. Bernadette is our beloved aunt, but she is not our mother. "You're going to love North Carolina!" she continues. "I'm going to buy you everything you want." This is a common bribe.

Junior looks at Mom for some sort of recognition. Is she hearing this? Did this agreement really take place? Is he really being sent away? Mom nods. "I think it'll be good for you," she says. "The country is a better place for a boy your age."

"When do I get to come back?"

Mom lowers her head and says, "I don't know yet. We have to figure everything out. We don't even have a place to live. With Bernadette, you'll be safe. I just don't know how long it'll take to get this sorted out." Junior will start the eighth grade in the fall and next is high school. "Say yes," Mom says next, even though she hasn't asked him what he wants or given him any option. Junior doesn't protest but he doesn't concede either; his eyes remain locked in an alarmed state. He is twelve now, but by the end of the summer he will be thirteen, a teenager. "Your auntie will take good care of you," Mom continues. "Lord knows I need help." She woefully shakes her head then looks up, presumably at God.

Junior looks back and forth from Mom to Bernadette,

these two Southern ladies negotiating where his body should be, making a case for why it is not safe in the city, especially in the summer when school cannot protect him and his parents' house cannot protect him, not anymore. *Danger*, they say, giving warnings. It is too dangerous for a boy like you. And it is. *A boy like you.*

Bernadette then switches from her fear voice to a loving voice. Her face turns from severe to tender; she finally gets a child. She comes for him, cups his face in her hands, and kisses him for too long, leaving a smear of maroon lipstick across his cheek. "Your auntie loves you," she says, referring to herself in third person. He reels when he is released, and no one but me can detect his apprehension. We make eyes from across the table.

Aunt Bernadette continues to pet him and stare into his eyes. "We're going to have so much fun." She is fantasizing about him being hers, making him meals, showing him off to her friends, taking him shopping. I don't know if I'm jealous of him or afraid for him. If he is a master of anything, it is garnering the attention of every adult in the room. It is silencing for any other child, for me. Because he is bad and must always be punished, and because he is also funny and always entertaining, he is the center of our attention, and now I watch as my aunt fawns over him. He is my brother, my protector, my confidant, the boy version of myself. Whatever jealousy I have is usurped by a sense of sadness: What will I do without him? Who will I be without him? I suddenly feel exposed.

"Are you excited to come with your auntie, baby?" Junior is getting too old to be called *baby*.

"Do it for me," Mom pleads. "Do it for your mama."

Finally he nods in agreement like the good boy she remembers and wants so badly for him to be again.

"Yes," he says politely.

My head turns back and forth between them. I listen, but keep all my thoughts to myself. I fast-forward to the airport, to the ride home across the Bay Bridge, to seeing the house for the first time. I let myself become consumed with the fire, with the pure potential of my new life and what will become of us, and I push down the thought that has begun to creep up—that I will miss him.

"Are you scared?" I ask him later when we're on our couches in the dark. In the morning we will leave and he will stay.

"Of what?"

"To leave," I say, but I mean so many other things: Are you afraid we'll be homeless? Are you afraid Mom and Dad won't be able to take care of us anymore? Are you afraid of life in North Carolina? Are you afraid of Aunt Bernadette's crazy dog? Do you feel powerless? Are you fed up with being a child and having no control? Do you feel small? Are you afraid to grow up? Are you afraid?

"No," he says, "and you shouldn't be either. Everything's going to be okay."

"Mom and Dad don't even know where I'm gonna sleep. They said some Quakers offered to host us. I wish I was going with you."

"You'd rather kick dirt in North Carolina?" We both laugh at the thought. "Man," he says. "It's gonna be so fucking boring."

"I wonder which Quaker we'll stay with." I start daydreaming about it, and he probably does the same about his new life. I break our momentary silence. "Can I tell you something?"

"Uh-huh."

"In a way I'm happy."

"What? Why?"

"Because all Daddy's crap burned up. The house is finally clean." I smile to myself in the dark.

WE RETURN TO chaos in Oakland, without Junior. Junior won't see the house, now just a facade of what it used to be. I look up through the brokenness of it and see the sky above. What used to be the terrible green carpet is now a flaky black sheen of ash, what we walked on now chewed up and spit out by fire. Junior won't see our old bedroom—completely destroyed, nothing left to salvage. My feet squish beneath me, being gently suctioned by wet black ground as I explore. I imagine the house being devoured by powerful flames and men fighting the fire with a giant hose of water.

I stand in the sludge and face the wall-less end of the house and stare at what's left of the garden. Junior won't see the backside of the house, now a blackened cavity that bleeds into a backyard whose wet earth stopped the flames. He is the one who can read me. No one else can interpret the look of sick pleasure on my face: All of it is gone. All the stuff. All the trash. No one died. This is my second chance. The only thing that was sacrificed was a houseful of trash. I want nothing to do with that house and all its things, all its silence and darkness. Mom and Dad see what I can't—life, memories, photographs, documents, pride, their first and only home together, family, the future—and they exist in a state of uncertainty and stress, unable to give straight answers or speak without shaking their heads. While I see possibility, Mom and Dad see the life they proudly started now a pile of wet black sludge. They understand they no longer have a home to contain their family, and this understanding makes them walk around with permanent furrowed brows, considering every option, trying to make the best decision for the family. I am eight and not involved in these discussions. They have asked for my patience.

"We're gonna be okay, you hear me?" Mom finds me in what used to be her room, picking out recognizable objects from the rubble. Dad is outside with someone from the insurance company. I am eased, not by what my mother has just promised me, but by the possibility I see around me. Of course we'll be okay, I think. We'll be better.

"I know, Mommy." We walk toward the back of the house, what used to be a wall and a door leading to the backyard, now just a giant opening, as if the Big Bad Wolf blew and blew until he blew the whole house down. We stare out into the backyard together, taking in the destruction. I want nothing to do, ever again, with the isolation of it, the darkness of it, the lonely silence, but I say nothing. I imagine a new world where Mom is as I know her in Alabama; she is awake and her face is always in light. I imagine a world with space for us.

Next, we separate. "The Quakers have been generous enough to put all of us up until we can figure out what to do next," Mom says. She calls them all "The Quakers" even though she is one of them; she also belongs to the Berkeley Friends Meeting. Many families have offered to put us up in groups, and so we separate and hop around between the kind homes of Quakers. Cornelius and Claire join Vivian with a family in Oakland hills. Mom, Dad, and the baby stay with a different family in Berkeley. I have presented Mom and Dad with an alternative for me: "I can stay with Nellie," I offer. They discuss it with her parents and it is done. I don't see my family for three weeks.

Dad drops me off at Nellie's house in East Oakland close to Lake Merritt. Dad talks to Nellie's mom for a while on the stoop, and all I can hear is Ellen's voice saying, "It's nothing at all. She is welcome here." I am welcome. I enter their duplex with a sense of adventure and my pink suitcase filled with only the things I took with me to Alabama. Even though I have been here many times, I experience it with a newfound curiosity. I am never going back home. I have no home. This is my new life; this is my new home. As an explorer in a new land, I walk through the dusty corridor, Ellen's sparse bedroom that follows, the bunk bed in the next room that Nellie and her little sister share, a bay window big enough to play in scattered with toys, Nellie's dad's bedroom erupting with drums and unfinished sculptures, a deck displaying Ellen's ashtray full of hand-rolled cigarette butts, the kitchen where an old TV is held up on crates and the kitchen sink bears stains older than me.

I look at it all like a freed prisoner in a new life. It is *my* dusty corridor, *my* sparse bedroom, *my* bay window, *my* cigarette butts, *my* sculptures. Ellen gives us her room, and for three blissful weeks, Nellie and I share Ellen's queen-size bed and indulge in stories at bedtime, eat homemade meals of pasta with soy sauce and veggie hot dogs, and listen to the banging of Nellie's dad's drums night and day. I feel spoiled and expansive in my new life here in this dilapidated Victorian with its single palm tree and dried-up grass on the lake side of East Oakland, a mostly Asian, Pacific Islander, black, and Mexican neighborhood, where Nellie's is the only white family around.

My fun is interrupted with word from Mom and Dad that the Red Cross has granted us vouchers for food and two hotel rooms in Downtown Oakland. We can now move temporarily into the Best Western and eat a few of our meals at Denny's. I can invite Nellie to the hotel, my new home, where we can swim in the pool all day and eat tuna straight from the can like little stray cats, because that's all there is, and I don't know how to make tuna properly. Mom is still on maternity leave, so she can accompany Dad all around Oakland, baby Angelica in tow, responding to ads in the paper for house rentals. They have a sense of relief now that the insurance has processed and approved the rebuilding of our house. Their attention is divided between finding a house to rent and hiring a contractor to build us a new house. Vivian and I, and sometimes Nellie, entertain ourselves between the two hotel rooms and cable TV; the pool is our babysitter most days, with Vivian loosely watching, painting her toenails on lounge chairs or straightening her hair inside, preparing for school to start by experimenting with hairstyles. Claire and Cornelius both have jobs, sometimes stay with friends, and come around only sporadically.

My summer has become an adventure, what I feel could be a new beginning, a turning point for my family. All that's missing is Junior. I wonder how he is in North Carolina, wonder how long Mom and Dad will make him stay away. I wonder how he'd do here with all this uncertainty and with no one watching. I wonder if he misses us. My recurring wish for him is that he do better. Do better, I repeat silently, like a prayer, as constant as my breath.

Eventually we move out of the hotel and into a house in a hilly part of East Oakland right beneath the bright and stunning Mormon temple that I only know for having the most impressive nativity scene in all of Oakland during the holidays. The neighborhood is mostly white, with a few Asian and black families scattered throughout. The house we will call home rests at the top of a hill one block away from the temple in a quiet residential neighborhood of single-family midcentury houses beneath what I think of as a real-life castle. I savor every moment of my first encounter with our rental, my small castle in my new life. The steps leading up to the house are painted red. There is a short pathway to the front porch surrounded by shapely spruce bushes on either side. The front door opens to a spacious living room, a dining room, and a sliding door opening to a side yard. Three bedrooms and one bathroom surround these rooms. The room that is to be mine is next to Junior's future room, and opens to a big red deck overlooking a garden with plum, fig, and citrus trees. I can't wait for Junior to see this new life. Whereas we used to share one bedroom between the three of us, in this house there is a room for each of us who still lives at home: Vivian, Junior, and I. Angelica shares with Mom and Dad while she is still little. Cornelius has found an apartment off campus and a job. Claire began and then dropped out of college on the East Coast, and then returned to live and study in San Francisco with her boyfriend; she works at a coffee shop and seldom comes around.

We begin to settle in, and I start to prepare for the school year in my new neighborhood by staying outside as long as possible and having Nellie visit me at my new, wonderfully empty home. Because we have nothing, this house doesn't fill up with junk; only a few pieces of furniture given to us by the Quakers decorate the house.

One of the first letters we receive is from Junior, stamped from Jacksonville, North Carolina. Dad posts it up on the refrigerator, and every time I open it I see his handwriting and his closing: *I miss everyone. I'm ready to come home.* But still he isn't invited to return just yet. Mom and Dad announce that they think it's best Junior finish out middle school in North Carolina so he can come home refreshed and have a new outlook for high school. They hope that perhaps the Southern way of life will help him, make him more respectful of authority, teach him better manners, make him more grateful for his opportunities in the city, buy Mom and Dad time to figure out what to do with him. But it does none of those things. The reports from Aunt Bernadette aren't good. He refuses to call adults *sir* and *ma'am*, and this causes problems at school. He's bored and doesn't fit in at school, so he looks to the street for entertainment and finds it. I can hear Mom and Dad on the phone urging him to adjust to Southern life, saying that he'll be able to come back as soon as the school year is over, that things are still only just settling here after the fire, begging him to have patience. Do better, do better, I think, repeating my silent mantra. I am ready for my brother to come home.

At night in my new bed, bought on voucher from the Red Cross, staring into the black ceiling, I imagine a life in which I make new friends and invite them into my house. I close my eyes and practice saying, "Come in, come in." In this life I am not afraid to speak. I am admired, I have nice things, but most importantly, I can let people inside.

Reality is a disappointment. The real me is silent, terrified of raising my hand in school even though I know the answers, never volunteering to read even though I read well. Yet somehow, swimming in oversize and out-of-fashion hand-me-downs, and without speaking much, I am still liked by the other kids. As if outside myself, watching life happen from above, this outcome is a surprise to me. My new school is close enough that I can walk there and back. At the end of the school day, I take the long way home. My school is all the way at the bottom of our street, where the neighborhood is starkly divided, as all of Oakland is. It doesn't take long to reach the bottom. I know by now that nice and good are myths. There is no good, no nice. And if there is, it is impermanent. There is proof all around me: a homeless summer and a burned-down house full of trash that was masquerading as good, as nice; a brother whose *bad* follows him wherever he goes, no matter how nice—there is no protection from black boyness. *Good* and *nice* are only illusory feelings, but, at least for a moment, I enjoy wrapping myself up in the illusion.

There is an invisible line across MacArthur Boulevard where my school is, which spans the whole of Oakland, with the invisible words *good* and *bad* written along either side. Once you cross the threshold, the quaint hillside neighborhood we believe keeps us safe and makes us good—with its immaculate gardens, two-car garages, and barless windows—you start to see the signs of reality, of permanent homelessness, drugs, sex work, and kids who have chosen the street over school, because school, too—its protection, its goodness—is another illusion.

I walk this line, aware of both reality and fantasy. On my walk home, on the gradual incline into imagined good, I let myself become the homes I pass, the gardens, the large windows exposing clean, warm houses, the fancy cars, until I can see the castle all the way at the top. Despite what's real, I let all this become mine. I no longer have to imagine. A miraculous fire came and burned away my old life and replaced it with this one. All that's missing is Junior.

PART TWO
PROTECTION

Oakland, CA
1993–1999

FIVE

I turn ten, and for the very first time in my life I invite friends from school over to see my life, let them into my home. I am so proud of its emptiness. We do things I think other kids my age might do at parties: we paint on T-shirts, play tag and run around the quiet hills, eat delivery pizza and birthday cake. For one year I am normal. I attend sleepovers at other people's houses—other than Nellie's— and take copious internal notes, give myself reminders to relax and enjoy the feeling of having friends. I pretend I know the games they play, to have seen the movies they have seen, to feel ease when they come near to hug me or lean on me or just be close. This is what people do, I remind myself. For one year we celebrate Christmas in the proper way, as is done in movies. For the first time I receive presents. I get a Kenya doll with a kente-cloth dress and the black American Girl doll that used to be a slave, and I am elated. I think some spell has come over Mom and Dad—this intoxicating newness, this hope—and it has infected our household. Maybe for the new baby; she has no memory of darkness or trash or silence or isolation. Maybe it is the relief Junior is safe in some place that isn't here.

When Junior returns from North Carolina he is older (nearly fourteen), darker, and more internal. He is teetering on the line between childhood and adolescence when tenderness is harder to detect; he is beginning to change on the outside and harden according to what is considered cool, what is considered tough. He is still my soft brother, but he wears a cool disguise. Most notably he smiles less and moves with a new stiffness. There's a slight limp in his gait; a head nod replaces the emphatic wave he used to give other boys his age.

He returns to find me ten and hopeful about the future. There are few things more exciting than the idea of a clean home I can invite friends into, invite my brother into and show him. Look: We have a backyard. We have a garden. We have wooden floors. We have light. We have a view. In the hills, there is a sense of possibility. I want to share this with Junior when he comes home: Look. Look at your room. We don't have to share anymore. Look at the space. But he is less trusting of it, less impressed by it, and behind his mask, I feel he knows something I don't about the future, about the world. I look for clues in his face.

There are just a few precious days of summer remaining before I start fifth grade and he starts ninth. Vivian spends her days brooding in her room with the door closed, listening to Toni Braxton, and painstakingly plucking every stray brow from her face and twisting a curling iron around and around the bangs that drape her face. In her middle years of high school, she, too, has become more internal. With our own rooms, we now have the luxury to discover our own preferences. She has discovered certain books, like *The Autobiography of Malcolm X*, and as a result of her awakening, she has begun to fight more with Dad, become very angry at whiteness, which he, of course, embodies.

While she spends her summer indoors, in between vicious arguments with Dad and bussing to summer school to make up more classes, Junior and I honor our last days by struggling up the great hills that surround our new home and savoring the joy of racing down again and again on our bikes, until there is some reason to go inside, like hunger or darkness. In these moments, I see his joy return. We make a playground out of the Mormon temple, running around its perimeter, admiring its massive gardens, its golden, sparkling point at the top. Our personal Eiffel Tower. I pretend we are royalty, pretend we belong.

We will both be going to the neighborhood schools. I am already familiar with mine, but he will be the new boy at his, yet another adjustment from life in North Carolina to a brand-new life in Oakland. Mom and Dad send Junior to a school on the highest hill in Oakland—blindly attributing goodness to the hills, to whiteness, because of its distance from "the street," and because last time he went to a school in the hills his grades improved. It happens to be our neighborhood school, King Estates. They are proud of their new zip code and imagine the schools will reflect our small pocket of Oakland. They imagine a school full of well-adjusted, privileged, "good" kids. And what a name for a school—a place for kings. Here in these hills we will be safe. Finally, with a house, a plan, and a new beginning, Junior can be safe. He can be good.

The school year begins without much production. We don't buy new clothes; we wear the same clothes we've always worn, that we are now starting to outgrow. Mom returns to work after a long maternity leave. The ritual of getting her out the door and off to work, and waiting patiently for Mom and Dad to leave, continues, but now it is done with more closed doors and with a toddler waddling around the house making everyone a little bit happier.

In the back of the house, in my room, I wait for the sounds of their exit over the thumps of Tupac coming from behind Junior's bedroom door. Angelica will go to San Francisco with them. I remember being small and experiencing the wonder of accompanying Dad on those windy trips across the Bay Bridge, thinking the moon above was following only us, miraculously being there every time I looked up at it, from any location. Angelica enjoys the ride now, and so we three—Junior, Vivian, and I—are left alone to wait for the absolute quiet so we can gather in the dark around the blaring TV like old times.

When Dad comes home later that night he finds us in front of the TV. And in one of his moods, in which he expresses his fears and stresses through being upset with us, he storms to his room to lay down sleeping Angelica, who is in his arms, and then roars toward us. He is edgier than normal, and I wonder at this display of force. Why this sudden attempt to structure this small free time of ours? It happens fast. The unplugging of the TV, the picking it up and struggling with it while trying to open the back door, the walking out the back door and coming back in through the front door some minutes later. I wonder if it's because Junior is back, if Dad's sense of control has once again vanished. He snaps, "I told you not to watch TV," and "Have you done your homework?" and "It's bedtime!" But I hear so many other things. I hear, *Why aren't you different? Why can't you be different? I want you to be different.* I ask those same questions of him. We wait a beat in the dark, the back door still ajar, before we move on. My siblings get up and we each slam our bedroom doors, one by one. It turns out we are the same family, just with new walls and fewer objects around us. We have more rooms now and more doors to close.

We all eventually forget the rage and move on with life without TV. In the evenings, Junior and I entertain ourselves by sitting on the hallway floor with the white pages and prank calling as many people as we can, using accents and ridiculous scenarios. We are hysterical, and Vivian walks in and out of her room shaking her head at our silliness.

One morning, Vivian and I sit on the deck and watch Angelica pet the rabbits we have in cages out back. We watch as she opens one of the cages and a bunny hops out and away. Vivian and I jump off the deck and we all try to catch the escaped rabbit. I get on my knees and look under the deck, and instead of the rabbit, I spot our lost TV, which Dad must have hidden there. I move my attention to the TV and ask Vivian to help me recover it.

It feels almost safe in the hills until, in the night, while we sit around the TV once again, we hear a pack of wild dogs, perhaps they are coyotes, in the backyard. Vivian, who loves our neglected rabbits more than anyone else, watches at the back window in tears as they ravage the bunnies. In the morning there are only patches of fur left, and the memory of barks and howls becoming more and more distant in the night.

It feels almost safe.

WHITE BOY. WHITE BOY. They taunt. White nigga. North Oakland white nigga. Punk. Bitch. They say all these things. And it reminds him of the bus incident in middle school where the boys tricked him into stealing and then bullied him. What do I have to do to avoid getting jumped? There is nothing to do. There are so many of them. White nigga. White ass. Bitch ass. North Oakland ass. Punk ass. All the insults. So many boys, black boys of all shades, coming closer and closer until he is on the edge of the cliff at that school on the highest hill where all the boys take buses from the not-good places and come to school not to learn but to brutally work out their infinite anger, on one another, with vengeance, without fear of consequence. What is consequence when you are fourteen? What is life at fourteen but the coursing of naked emotion through your veins, expressing itself in misplaced ways? What is life at fourteen and beyond but hurting people because you are hurt?

They surround him. They have him now. He is in the middle of a large circle of boys, like the kind that forms spontaneously at dance parties, but violent and deeply sad. Whoop his ass. And they do. One by one at first and then all together, fists and elbows, sneakered feet stomping on and around his head, his ribs. His ribs hurt so much. He can't protect them because both hands are covering his head and face. Why is it happening for so long? Is it still going on? White ass nigga comin' up in our school. Ain't no bitches allowed in this school. Bitch ass. White ass. Punk ass. This is East Oakland, bitch. He keeps his head covered and waits for it to end but it goes on and on. East Oakland. East Oakland, they jeer. He feels hands on his ankles, gripping hard. He feels his body being lifted from his feet, being swung around and around the circle of boys, all of them getting a last chance to take a swing at any body part that comes their way, the group anger morphing into something singular, mighty, and unstoppable. The pain in his ribs is intense.

He feels the ground beneath him again. They've put him down. Maybe it's over. Will he be able to walk? He looks up and sees their backs walking away like this was nothing. He peels himself from the ground, touches his various body parts to make sure they are still attached. His ribs. They hurt so much he can barely move. All his body parts are intact, it seems. He slowly peels himself up. It happens outside the school, on an actual hill, with a beautiful view, near the bus he'll take back home. He limps, painfully, to the bus stop and waits for his bus, taking what dignity he has left to look as if he isn't bloody, as if he isn't limping, to take himself home where it might be safe.

I HEAR THE jingle of keys in the front door. Junior is home later than usual from school. I jump up and run down the hall to greet him at the front door. "Finally!" Our energies clash immediately. His is tough and mine is that of a puppy awaiting its playmate. When he opens the door his eyes are wet, his mouth twisted in shame. "What happened?" I look closer as he enters, and I see the bruising around his eyes, the angry redness of his cheeks, the limp in his walk. He ignores my question and sniffles past me all the way to his room where he shuts the door. I hover around the outside of his room and listen for him to call for me but he doesn't and all I can hear are sounds of Snoop playing loud behind the door.

I knock on Mom's bedroom door and she yawns away sleep. "Something happened to Junior," I say.

"What happened?" She awakens quickly, sits up. "Where is he?"

"In his room. He has black eyes and he's limping."

"Oh my god." She starts to get up, puts a robe on. "Where is Daddy?"

I follow behind her as she makes her way to his room, knocks hard on his door. "Oh my god," she says again when she sees him. She takes his face in her hands, and he winces and turns away. "Oh my god," she says again and again. "Just look at you," she says in her sweet cooing voice. Then she switches to British. "Who in the hell did this to you?"

She has rapid-fire questions, barely giving him the chance to answer. He is so ashamed to admit: It happened near school. He knows who did it. He's afraid to report it because they might do it again.

When Dad comes home, he has different questions:

"Where are you hurt? Did anyone call the police? Do you need to go to the hospital?"

Mom and Dad take him to urgent care, where he is treated for bruised ribs and a police report is taken and charges are pressed against the boys.

Vivian and I wait at home for him to return, making ourselves busy, waiting for news. Finally they return. He is told to rest until his ribs heal.

That night Mom cooks dinner and clears off the table. We eat dinner as a family as we only do on holidays. Mom has prepared creamed rice, sautéed broccoli, and baked chicken. We fix our own plates and take them back to the dining room table and commence eating without prayer. Over the click-clack of silverware to plate, we listen to the silence that is Junior's face, wait for Mom or Dad to have an answer. Surely he can't go back to school. He eats with voracity, which makes me think somewhere beneath his bruises, he might be all right.

Mom looks at Dad and breaks the silence. "Chris, what should we do?" Sometimes she asks him questions, knowing he will not have the answers, using that time to think of her own solutions. *How in god's name will we protect our son?* Dad screws up his face and looks at Junior.

"You're not going back to that school. Not ever." Mom stops eating, her lipstick-painted mouth pursed seriously. "We will find another place for you. You hear me? A better place." She already has her work clothes on. Junior's eating slows. He nods in agreement. Dad is still quiet, his face still in knots. Finally he speaks, looks at Junior.

"I'll start making calls tomorrow."

We clear our plates, and I load the dishwasher and listen to the sounds of Mom getting ready to leave for work, Dad following close behind, nearly waiting on her as she frantically gathers her things, asking rhetorical questions that Dad always answers literally: "Where is my purse? Do I have my badge? Do I have a lunch?" Predictably Dad enters the kitchen where I am. "Can you make your mom a lunch, please?" I do, carefully arranging chicken, rice, and broccoli in a plastic container. Dad waits at the door restlessly, waiting for her. I bring the lunch to him, and then she comes out, somehow managing to look like a diva, even sleep-deprived and in her work clothes. In part because she makes a fuss as she leaves for work, and without asking, makes the entire house assist her in getting out the door, but also because she is lovely. "Bye, baby," she says, and I stand in a cloud of her perfume and watch them leave. She sashays down the stairs toward the truck, her post-office apron tied in a neat bow at the small of her back like a dress.

I find Junior in my bedroom, where the TV now lives after being salvaged from its hiding place underneath the deck in the backyard. Since Junior was beat up, I imagine Dad will be gentler, not so angry with us when he comes back without Mom. He flicks it on and gets comfortable on my bed. I join him.

"Does your eye hurt?" I ask, looking at him, going in to touch his bruising.

"Don't," he says, pushing my hand away. He is more subdued than usual. We stare at the TV.

"What are you gonna do?" It is the natural question. It

is not exactly that Mom and Dad will do nothing, but rather that they have no idea what to do. He is the one that has to return, maybe not to that school, but to some other school, and continue to face the boys on the verge of men. He is a boy on the verge of man. It is he who has to exist in the world of school, and it is indeed a different world where different rules apply. Mom and Dad know nothing of this world. We leave the house, leave this family, and become players in a game in which we are still learning the rules: Which roles are the most desirable, which positions the most powerful? How do you become powerful? How do you protect yourself?

"I'm gonna fight," he says finally, still looking at the TV, his feet swinging over the edge of the bed like a little boy's, incongruous with what comes out of his mouth next. "I'm gonna beat the shit out of them." He seems detached from the meaning of what he says. I am not used to such venomous words coming from him. This is social warfare. This is high school. This is becoming a man. I can feel the fervor in his words, but also the split: my soft brother Junior and the Junior who must survive. Not fighting is not an option. But how will he win against all those boys?

"But how many of them were there? Don't do it, Junior." I shake my head at him. "Don't go back there."

"I don't know, man."

"Didn't Daddy press charges? Doesn't that mean they'll go to jail, err, juvie?" I correct myself. Jail for boys.

"Yeah, and then I'm the snitch," he says.

We sit with the TV on, just us, considering this dilemma, Vivian in her room, Angelica on her thrilling trip to San

Francisco, and we hear steps entering the house, the front door shutting.

It's Cornelius. I wonder what he'll think of this new life, of who we have become in this new life. The identity I assume is one of hope, maybe wrapped up in naivete about some good future I imagine. Junior is painstakingly building his black boy shield, and for good reason—he's been brutalized. Vivian, too, builds a black girl shield in the form of Malcolm X quotes. My brothers and sisters are warriors in their imaginations, constructing personalities built to fight, built not to trust the world. They show me what it is to grow up.

We haven't seen Cornelius in a long time. In my dreams, I imagine everyone's life has improved since the fire, but it is not true. How badly I want it to be true. How badly I want for us to live in peace. I feel exhausted that, despite what we've lost already, we can't keep anything good going for long; everything must always fall apart and become ugly. I feel I am the sand inside an hourglass—running out of hope, losing my grip on the little scraps of happiness I had caught; I feel depleted for myself and on behalf of my family. Surviving is exhausting. I can't feel compassion for my parents—not yet—I am still too young. All I can feel is the downward emotional spiral of my siblings and me, my little tribe.

Cornelius is renting an apartment with some other guys, and in my view, though I haven't seen it, and even though I know better, in my mind it is luxury, high-class, better than anything anyone in this family has ever had. He drives a car—a lime-green Hornet—and has a pit bull named Ebony. When he comes in he is large, so much taller than me, his hi-top seems to be brushing the ceiling. He has come to empty the contents of our refrigerator into plastic grocery bags he's brought with him. We haven't seen much of him since the house burned down. When we lived in a hotel during the summer, and while Junior was in North Carolina, he took the opportunity to move out. He is back, also, it seems, to check in on the young members of his family. Dad must have told him what happened. Vivian comes out of her room, and we all crowd around the TV in my bedroom for his visit.

"Are you okay?" He looks to Junior first, letting a heaping bowl of cereal rest in his lap while he waits for us to answer. Junior shrugs his shoulders. "Man, they fucked you up good, didn't they? Who are those little fuckers? I'll go take care of them." He goes on, as Mom did, as Dad did, without letting Junior speak. "This happened at school? What kind of shit school did they send you to? Where were the teachers?" Cornelius hits his fist against the wall and makes a grunting noise that scares me a little. He is strong, physical, and has a tendency to let rage carry him away. "This shit makes me so fucking mad!" Junior looks overwhelmed; maybe he is holding back tears. "So, how are you guys?" Cornelius asks after a few seconds when he's calmer. "How's this house and everything? How is everyone?" And we know his question is so many other questions: Is Daddy hoarding? Did the mess come back? Is Mommy sleeping? Is everyone getting by in school? Is the baby okay? Are Mom and Dad okay? Is Junior okay? Are you okay? The immensity of that question gathers in my throat and produces a choking sensation. Am I okay? Are any of us? He waits for one of us to answer while shoveling spoonfuls of milk-soaked granola into his mouth, not taking his eyes off us.

"Well, just look at him," Vivian finally speaks, pointing to Junior. "We're doing great," she says sarcastically. She rests her head in her hand for a moment and then looks back up. "I mean, we're okay. Right, guys?"

I look from Vivian to Junior, each with a bit of a shell-shocked look on their face, each looking at the floor. I push myself back into the corner of my bed, hug my knees, and try not to look anyone directly in the eye. Cornelius stares at us all in silence. A child, an adolescent, and a teenager reacting with complete discomfort to a simple question. We are mutes. We are without language and without voice, unraveling under the harsh spotlight of adult human attention.

Cornelius stops chewing, swallows what's in his mouth, and takes a breath. He scoots in close. "Come here," he says, extending his arms as if to hug us. We are all uncomfortable. "Come here," he says again, motioning with his hands that he wants our arms. We open them out to one another, forming a human circle in the middle of my bedroom with *The Simpsons* blaring behind us, and we embrace one another. "We're gonna be okay," Cornelius leads us in his version of a prayer. "I love you all. We love each other. We're looking out for each other and we are gonna be okay." The words are affirmation; if we say it, it must be true. He chokes out the words, and it feels like I am being cornered; I shrink into the edge of my bed and try to become invisible. It is something like torture for me, the singular distress of this very foreign sense of conventional nurturing and love. It is hard work to look unaffected while jumping inside your skin, frantically looking for an exit. I peek to see what is happening in the faces of my family. Vivian stares at the floor; so does Junior. Junior is clenched up as though he, too, is looking for escape from his body. I know how he feels— the awkwardness of being touched feels good at first and then painful, like reaching for something hot and getting burned. His body probably wants to recoil the way mine does. I wonder if his throat is stopped up like mine, holding back tears. I watch him for a moment longer. His eyebrows in a frown, his lips quivering, his soft curls haloed around the little-boy skin of his face. I feel so inadequate. I want to give him something I don't have. I want someone to give me what I've never had. I want to take him up in big arms and tell him you don't have to be scared, I have you, I will protect you, you are safe, my boy. He will cry and convulse because the love will feel so strange, and with my giant hand I will stroke the curls around his face into place until he believes me, until he feels safe. But none of these things is true. I am small. It isn't safe. I say nothing and move my eyes back to settle on the floral comforter in front of me. I decide to believe Cornelius, even though somewhere deep within me I know it is a lie.

LIFE IN THE East Oakland hills is a dream for me and a nightmare for Junior. I have made new friends and like my new school. He hasn't been back to school. Some of the boys who jumped him have been found and are now in juvenile hall. He doesn't seem happy about it, but despondent and uneasy about where he'll be sent next. So am I. I watch my parents' movements, their attempts to protect him, with distrust. Their lives are so unlike ours, how could they know what to do? They advocate on his behalf but it's like they speak another language. One of the calls Dad made after the fight was to a group home. Another was to the psychiatric division of Kaiser. Perhaps Junior could live for a while, secluded in a group home for boys—for troubled boys. Perhaps Junior could benefit from talking to a therapist. Perhaps Junior is troubled.

While Junior stays out of school, time passes, a whole semester passes, and soon we'll move back into the old house, which is almost finished. Soon we'll change schools once again. I'll go to the neighborhood school near Piedmont, and he'll go to our neighborhood high school on the North Oakland side to repeat the ninth grade, which he's practically missed because of this incident.

Despite all the uncertainty, Junior and I take advantage of the neighborhood before we have to move again. On the weekends we explore the creek and follow it all the way up to Montclair, a small, wealthy town on the other side of the freeway. There are hidden treasures like this one all over Oakland if you know where to find them. The path is full of overgrown blackberry briars to one side, and we eat the sweet berries along our way. In the creek just below the path, fresh water greedily rushes over small stones, leaving the smooth tops of the large ones for us to use as steps. We hop from stone to stone, from one side of Oakland to another, with a lot of silence between us because I am, as usual, the slow one. My view is of Junior above me, hand in salute at his forehead, other hand on his straight hip, looking down at me. He stands above the gushing creek, standing on water it seems, enveloped by redwoods. Light splashes across his face. "C'mon," he encourages me.

"I'm coming," I say. "I'm coming." But he can't hear me. I am trying to keep up. Our ways are different. He is fast and I am cautious. I like to take my time, look at things, touch them, process them. He likes to ask questions while running and hope anyone fast enough can answer him. He is always in front of me, always my road map. Where do we go now?

I reach him finally at the creek's end, and only then do I remember we are in our city. The wonder of the creek has come to an abrupt end. Blocks of cement stairs accented in graffiti welcome us at the end of the creek. We climb them and see that the forest opens devastatingly to a freeway exit. Car after luxury car swooshes past us at the ridge of the forest. We wait in the shadows of the redwoods for an opportunity to flee across the busy street to the peace of a nearby park. Junior holds both arms open, preventing me from crossing until it's safe. "C'mon," he says when the road is clear, and takes off running. I follow mightily.

In a bustling park full of moms and nannies chasing chubby white toddlers, Junior and I head for the outskirts— the redwood- and oak-lined perimeter of the park—in search of long sticks, crayfish-catching devices. "You need a long one." Junior turns and shows me the one I need.

"What are we gonna do with them?" I ask. There is a small pond, which is home to many small poppy-colored animals, just beyond the playground. "I wouldn't eat one of them if you paid me," I say. They are squirmy and bug-like. Junior laughs and hands me his stick. Weaving around strollers, dodging toddling babies, we make our way past the park and to the pond where we sit and we wait. I lie across the cement, my legs extended out behind me, and stare straight into the clear pond, watching critters claw their way toward my stick. In this moment, it is just me and summer and my big brother. I do not think of the pain he's encountered or the uncertainty of life; it is just us against the sun, the city, the approaching changes.

"Is this supposed to be fun?"

"It's what you do when you want to think," Junior says.

"It's boring." My body is limp, the sunshine hitting my back. Only my eyes and lips and mind are active. I watch as the disgusting animals avoid my stick and go the other way. "What are you thinking about?" Junior shrugs. Perhaps he is also enjoying this moment together, enjoying being out-side with no responsibility other than to make the most of the day. Perhaps he doesn't have the language to express what's really in his heart.

The last time I had the chance to think in nature was on Lake Chabot, where we went camping as a family years earlier. Mom hurt herself on that trip. We hiked along the shore of the lake and she slipped and fell, cutting her shin badly on a rock. The shimmering redness of her bloody flesh shocked me. Mortality brushed against me possibly for the first time.

Junior and Dad went fishing on that trip. I did not know we were in possession of fishing rods, didn't know that Dad had the forethought to plan something requiring so many parts. I recall the day vividly in my mind: the brightness of the sun, all of us younger children in nature; before Angelica was here, running free, Mom and Dad, happy. Outside the confines of that suffocating house I could feel what it was to be part of this family, what it felt like to be next to them without also being next to a thousand other things, next to them and unburdened by anguish. I feel it now, this space, this air, my breath. Next to my brother. We are so simple—sister and brother. No walls, no house, no family, no outside, no world.

Soon he will go away again. A group home this time. He has decided to give it a try. Dad let him choose. They went to visit it and determined it was the best option for him until they could find a suitable school for the following year. I look at him and wait for him to answer my question. Like me, he is leaning over the pond staring face down into it, waiting. He answers me finally. "I'm thinking about what it'll be like," he says. Then he quickly switches topics. "I got one!" He gleefully brings his stick toward me.

"Now what?" I ask. Neither one of us knows.

We walk in the direction of home, back down through the forest and back into the mean city.

I repeat my mantra to myself, Do better, please do better. Just go to school. Go to the group home. Go wherever it is you need to go. Go and just keep to yourself. Avoid the boys. Run. Run as fast as you can away from them. Run for your life. These are solutions I offer and none are acceptable. He will not conform to any of them. The shame of being bullied is so crushing he must build a fortress around himself made of the roughest raw material he can find on the street, and no one is allowed in. He is the master of his own body; he is the only one who can protect it.

Group homes are for boys who are permanently suspended, boys who do not fit inside the walls of the school, boys who were bad before they could speak. This is where Junior will be, where Mom and Dad think he will be protected for just a little longer. Until what? Until when? They think this place will hold him for now. Perhaps this place will shield you from yourself, from who they think you are, just a little bit longer.

While my parents focus their attention on rebuilding our home and getting Junior into a new school, I am ready for fifth grade to begin. While Junior does his part to take all the attention, I am a good daughter and it comes easy. I do so consistently well in school that it's boring; no one looks at my grades. I make friends easily. I imagined Nellie would be my only friend because we share in having complicated families, and while she's still my best friend, it turns out that I am liked by other children. I am invited to birthday parties and sleepovers and to play on the weekends and after school. These people, my new friends, want to know me, want to see where I live. A whole social world opens to me; I am in it, not just an observer of it. I begin to see myself as someone outside of my family, someone who other people like and want around, someone who makes people laugh, someone whose ideas and opinions people want to hear.

Still, I feel different from other kids, like I'm hiding something. I want to say, "I used to live in a house where no one was allowed inside," but that would feel like only part of it. I want to say, "I was so quiet and shy for so long that you wanting to be my friend feels foreign and overwhelming, but I like the way it feels to be wanted," but that, too, would be only part of it. I want to say, "Neither of my parents has any emotional capacity, and I am an extremely emotional and sensitive child" and "My big brother is my idol, and I'm worried about him and stressed out that he keeps getting hurt and abandoned," but I am ten going on eleven, and have language for none of these feelings in my heart, and so I just pretend I am like everyone else and like I have always had a nice clean home and a normal family. I smile and accept invitations and write in my diary. Meanwhile, I am holding my breath a little, unable to fully relax into my own transformation.

I make friends with a girl named Ernestine. Not only does she have a different name, but I feel she is different like me and I'm drawn to her in the same way I was drawn to Nellie. Unlike the other kids, with their big houses and two parents with fancy jobs and their organized sleepovers, Ernestine lives in an apartment with just her mom who works all the time, so she's often alone. She has two identical twin brothers who are a lot older than her but seem to look out for her. She seems a little sad, and we spend our time listening to Smashing Pumpkins and the Cranberries on repeat, analyzing the lyrics.

We go on adventures after school and on the weekends for hours. We hike through the same creek Junior and I have explored, but we take markers with us and tag the sidewalks, trees, and rocks along our path with our mark— *XYU*. This tag makes me feel like a poet, like I have control of my experience, like I can name it. "XYU" is the name of a Smashing Pumpkins song that symbolized for me the conflicting sense of both darkness and hope I feel within, and writing it all over the neighborhood makes me feel like the city is my witness.

Besides Nellie and Junior, Ernestine becomes the person I spend most of my time with. One day on our walk to the creek, we stop in a convenience store to see if we can steal something, cigarettes in particular. "Buy something little," I say, "and I'll go behind the counter while they're helping you and take a pack." The store is very old-fashioned with no visible cameras, the plan is so easy. My heart races with adrenaline and while Ernestine finishes her gum purchase, I swipe a pack of Marlboro Reds and walk coolly outside. When she sees what I have, she's giddy. It turns out stealing is exhilarating; I feel powerful, admired, and in control. I add stealing to my own repertoire of things that make me feel better. Smoking will follow.

Ernestine and I find matches at the nearby pizza restaurant and continue on our way to the creek. We climb off the path to a secluded section, sit on a redwood stump, and share a stolen cigarette. This is the second cigarette I've smoked in my life. The first was the one Junior stole from an old lady neighbor, and we smoked it together when I was six and he was ten. Nearly five years later, I am stealing my own experience, what feels to me like growing up, like freedom.

SIX

Two years we spend in the house on the hill. I am nearly twelve when we move out and back to North Oakland. I am on the edge, facing womanhood. Two years we spend in the creeks and the parks and the Mormon temple. Heart palpitating, I think my chest will explode. I am ill from exertion, pedaling uphill with all my focus, just so I can come down and feel the breeze on my face and the effortless freedom of wind—this is what expansion feels like. This is just a taste of what it feels like to be big, and yet light enough that the wind alone can carry me. This is what has happened in the house on the hill.

I never want to go back. I never want to leave the house I now associate with presents on Christmas, sleepovers, having friends over, my brother at home. I have this urge to show people my life. "Look at me," I whisper shyly while hiding fiercely, hoping someone will hear. In this house, they've heard, they've come, they've seen; I want a witness so badly. For the first time I have a glimpse of what it is to be a social human being. But soon we will move back and all that will be lost. Here, the mess never came; here we are able to maintain some order, but other things have fallen apart. Junior is falling apart. He is coming undone. The shield he's building around himself is nearly complete. His edge sharpens as he grows taller—out of a boy, into a man.

But we have to go back. The old house is finished; it has been rebuilt. There are more bedrooms, including one just for me, a whole second floor we never had, a second bathroom. Perhaps now this house can hold us, perhaps now there is room for us to take up space and grow. Once again I can say to Junior: Look. Look at your room, look at mine. Look, we have fancy maroon carpets now. We have marbled tiles covering our kitchen floor. Look, we can see the wood on the floors.

When we move in, it is summer just before school starts. We transport my bed and my dolls to my new room. There are three windows in this room—two larger ones that look onto a giant cypress tree, and a small, rectangular one. I situate my bed below the small one. I like the shape of it, how it isolates my view of the church clock across the street. The unruly branches of the cypress dangle across it, creating a drama that pleases me. Eventually the walls of my bedroom become covered with magazine portraits of my crushes from TV and the tape-cassette art from my favorite singers. Jonathan Taylor Thomas, Romeo from Immature, and Toni Braxton pose above my bed. I have a small bookshelf with American Girl books I am starting to outgrow and Baby-Sitter's Club books passed down from Vivian.

Junior transports his collection of vintage sodas, his modest collection of sneakers still in their boxes, posters of some of his favorite artists: Snoop, Lil' Kim, Tupac. His bedroom windows look out onto the side yard and the young, quivering leaves of the carob trees Dad planted. The new upstairs floor has been assigned to the girls: me, Vivian, and even Angelica will get our own rooms. Junior will be on the first floor near Mom and Dad in what used to be the room we shared, now all his own.

We must become reacquainted with our old neighborhood. Two years is a lifetime when you are eleven and fourteen. We walk down the avenue we know so well and stop in our old favorite shops. Not a lot has changed. The convenience store has changed owners. What used to be called Hafiz's Cheaper is now a 7-Eleven; the price of a soda has gone up. The staff in the stationery shop still follow us around when we browse. I like to test the gel pens and practice signing my name in bright colors on the test sheets: *Melissa Valentine*, over and over and over in all shades of glitter. Junior likes to slip permanent markers into his pocket and tag messages across the city. His latest tag is *STRIP*. I know how it feels to feel something you can't explain on the inside and need to get it out for all to see on the outside. Whatever *STRIP* means, I know it is meaningful, just like mine was to me. He likes to write the *S* last and use the end of it to underline the entire word, creating a long and shapely loop below. I see his tag all over our neighborhood along with his usual *N.S.O.* for North Side Oakland. He is back on his turf. I believe he is the only boy this close to Piedmont claiming North Oakland, but he does so vehemently. North Side Oakland, the North Pole, the Pole for short—all of it belongs to him.

Just like when we were younger, Junior shows me a new

patch of wet cement outside our house. The roots of the carob tree out front raised the sidewalk, and so the cement needed to be replaced. Thick, wet gray matter in a perfect square beckons us. "Look," he says, and points to the ground. I shake my head knowing Dad will be livid, but I follow anyway. It is worth it to make your mark. He carefully writes the letters *N.S.O.* I look at his work and consider what I should write. *M.C.V.*, I write—my initials. And he takes his stick back and writes again, underneath his first tag: *C.C.V.*—his initials, Christopher Cole Valentine. Here we are again, marking ourselves, this time right in front.

But having our names outside does not make us more excited about the move. I am addicted to new, to hope, but this house, even though theoretically new, is old; its very foundation a symbol for isolation, for heaviness. Even though I'm older and I have my own room and I should be happy, the move has a disheartening effect on me. All I see are piles and piles of things and junk; it was slow to return, but it comes back. The only place I feel unburdened is outside or up in my room. So I stay out or up as much as possible. There's an upstairs now. At least now there is an up to go to. The upstairs and downstairs feel like two different houses.

Again, we change schools. I am to enter the sixth grade and attend the school in walking distance of our house. Junior is admitted to the school Vivian attends near our house. His stint in the group home didn't last long. He was pulled out quickly because there was more violence. The place was quickly deemed unsafe and full of bad boys who would be a bad influence, and so, instead of attending any school, any home for boys, Junior, again unsupervised, found other boys like him on the street. He didn't have to look far to find them. He just walked down to the edge, to MacArthur Boulevard where the line is drawn, and found friends in other kids who were not fit for school. There is a constant uprooting him out of environments and implanting him into new, possibly safer ones. The bullying incident from King Estates stays with us all and even though he may incite trouble—steal, talk back, puff his feathers—it showed us how vulnerable he is.

Junior's new room in the old, now new, house doesn't yet have his smell—it's earthy and crisp like the outside. The house still carries the lingering smell of soot beneath the new smells of paint and wood. The school year begins quietly, our problems only temporarily over. My exciting school news is that I must now wear a uniform to school. I am amused by having to dress like a doll every day. Junior's uniform consists of pants that are baggier and baggier, and loud-colored Nike sneakers. I am unsure of where he finds the money to buy his uniform, but I will soon find out.

It doesn't take long into the school year for more violence to commence. Junior has stopped going to class. His school calls every day around four o'clock in the afternoon with an automated voice telling Mom and Dad or the answering machine that "their son or daughter at Oakland Technical High School has missed one or more periods today." When probed, he finally and shamefully admits that a busload of boys from various East Oakland high schools have made a habit of getting off at his school and fighting any boy from North Oakland they see. Junior ran to avoid the fights. He ran to the gym. He ran to the other side of the school. He ran home. What he didn't say is that he is afraid he will be jumped again. He is afraid to return to school. Again, Mom and Dad must find a new place for him. This time it is a continuation school downtown where he will not be looked down upon for being behind, where—perhaps—he can be safe. He tries again.

On a rare day when we come home from school at the same time, Junior tells me he wants to show me something. Like every other time he's wanted to show me something, I suspect it is something illegal. "Come here," he says, inviting me into his room and looking around to make sure no one is nearby. Vivian is out still, Mom sleeping, Dad at work. He closes the door and dumps the contents of his backpack onto the bed. Onto the comforter spills a portable CD player, a leather jacket, a CD case, and a wallet.

"What is this?" But I know what it is. I want him to say it. I want him to say, "I stole from a person." But instead he says, "I thought you would like this." He's beaming. He opens the CD case and flips through it. "See? Look." He points to a No Doubt CD, then flips to Nirvana, and then to Pearl Jam.

"Cool!" I squeal. He looks pleased with himself.

"I thought you liked them."

I like them very much even though I know it's wrong to be excited about receiving stolen goods as a gift. But I also know the feeling of power associated with the crime when you feel powerless and confused. I think about the things I've stolen or have wanted to steal or look forward to stealing. I think about the cigarettes I took recently, the way I felt when I'd gotten away with it, the pride I felt when Ernestine was proud of me, impressed with me. I try and tone down my excitement and gratitude for all my new gifts.

Junior picks up the CD player. "And I got this for you so you can have something to listen to them on." He says it as if he's picked them all out from the mall for me.

"Did you steal all this stuff? Junior . . ."

"Don't worry about that."

"Junior." I don't know what to say but his name. The ground we're on feels shaky, the air thin. This is different from the little pack of cigarettes, and even though I can understand why he does it, the consequences for him seem to be stacking up, the stakes getting higher. This is not okay. If I object, he'll stop sharing his world with me; I know this instinctively. If I accept, I know I am an accomplice. I can't say no to my brother. So I say yes.

"Wow," I say. "Thank you." I try not to look at the wallet. I don't want to see the face of the person whose belongings these are. Junior is pleased again, proud of himself. I take the CD player and try the headset on. "This is too much. We should share it."

"Keep it here," he says, pointing under the bed, "so Mommy and Daddy won't find it."

I agree. We sit together for a while. He pulls money out of the wallet and a wad of cash out of his pocket and lays it all out on the bed. He begins to count, radiant, his gap-toothed smile beaming. The success of his scheme brings him such joy. This is the most successful he's ever been. Ripping off Mercedes emblems and selling one or two as pendants at his last school seems juvenile compared to this. Bubblegum and pens. Selling lemonade on the corner with me for a few dollars. Holly plants during the holidays. Stealing the cash drawer at the Quaker Harvest Festival. All business ventures before this one were child's play. This is real money, continuous money. This is easy money. It is better than fighting; he will never be a good fighter. It is better than being hard, the hardest—it is so much work to be angry all the time, to never smile. This is power. This is the ultimate shield. Stronger than angry boys on buses. He is armed now. If he must be an angry boy, he will be a powerful boy.

I have been adjusting to life at my new school. Sixth grade feels like the edge of something. Next year will be middle school and I'll have to change again. This year I learn to play the flute, earn the honor of Student of the Year, befriend a Filipina girl in my class named Serena, get my period, and have my shoes made fun of for the first time—a pair of boys' Nikes that were all black, so they wouldn't get dirty, and a size too big, in case my feet grew at all that year. Serena is the only person I tell about my period, and she tells me not to worry because she's had hers since she was nine and it's not that bad. But it is to me. I don't tell Mom for fear that she'll be upset with me. She likes me as a little girl, her "right-hand man," and I don't think she will like this news. I keep it totally to myself. I want the freedom of being a teenager, of having more choices, of being more confident, but I don't necessarily want this. No one told me about this, and I'm ashamed, disappointed, about this reality of growing up.

Out of East Oakland now, Junior is back on our North Oakland turf, closer to the flats and closer to his old friend he used to bus down to West Oakland with. He has collected friends from the various places he's adjusted to (or maladjusted to), and he's collected habits, new ways of being, a new normal, a new standard of crime. He has learned to break into cars, steal their contents, and is learning about the world of marijuana—selling it and smoking it. What he'd really like to do is drive, but he can't yet. He begs Cornelius to teach him in his green Hornet. "You're too young." Always the same answer.

I remember the time he stole Dad's rental car in Alabama. I imagine him as a boy there, begging our aunts and uncles to let him drive one of their cars. Finally one of them acquiesced and he was giddy with excitement to hold the wheel in his hand, to navigate, to be in control. I remember the way the back of his head looked as he drove our aunt's Cadillac down the dirt road away from Grandma's house. He was too short and he drove too fast. I could imagine what his face looked like in front: the mischievous gaptoothed grin that was infectious and made people want to say yes, hidden beneath the big steering wheel of the car. Who could take away that smile?

Stealing, it seems, is the key to making money, the key to having power. Mom and Dad think he's improving, but I know the truth. They think he is in a better place at the continuation school, but there is no good place, no protection from the quest for power once yours has been threatened. They are more than surprised when they receive a call from the juvenile hall in San Leandro saying that Junior has been caught in West Oakland for breaking into a car. He is released on probation and assigned an officer who will come to our home, ask him questions, and call him at any hour she likes to make sure he is not on the street. Dad has to pick him up and bring him home, awakened with the truth that the rich kids and the hills and the group home and now the new house and the improved grades have not been a remedy for the thing that drives his son—the ravenous and fearless thing that urges him to want more, more, more. He is awakened to the fact that there might be no good place; he is crushed by his inability to protect his son.

Junior has acquired enough friends from all these no-good places and they have all given him ideas for how to get more power. Money. Cars. Cars will be next. He used to build model cars. It was such fun to build the delicate little race cars piece by piece with glue. It took such focus and gave him such immense pride to see them finished. Dad would put the most impressive ones up on the mantel. That, too, was child's play. Again, always, the one let into his room with the door closed behind us, I am the accomplice. I am the witness to it all. I watch as his power grows.

The question now is: How do I steal at a higher level and make more cash? His friends teach him, not the rich kids, but the others, the ones also seeking power. The ones from the group home. The ones from juvenile hall. The ones in continuation school. The ones he travels to visit in West Oakland on a bike. He learns how to steal cars. He can't resist the fun of driving them once stolen, doing doughnuts in the middle of the street like a flower in full bloom: *Look at me. Look how beautiful, how powerful I am.* Sometimes he spins these beautiful doughnuts right on our corner as if hoping someone he knows will see him: Dad, me. And sometimes we do. But he is too elusive to catch. The adrenaline of almost being caught by family or police is too irresistible. He must bring the cars to us and into our view—IROCs, Mustang 5.0s—to our safe and white and residential neighborhood where things like this don't happen, where black boys ravenous for power in stolen cars don't happen, or at least not in view. But he demands: *Look at me*. He drives away in a gap-toothed fury and returns on his tiny BMX, the same one we sped down hills on. I watched him then, following closely behind, looking at him going full speed ahead, as I do now.

"What?" He shrugs past Mom and Dad when he returns, parking his bike in the living room and marching to his room with a new confidence.

"Whose car were you driving?" And he just smiles, basking in the power he feels, and closes the door to his room. The point of all this is cash. Cash and power and attention. He will sell the cars to someone who knows what to do with them. He will steal all the belongings inside the cars, sell those or keep them for himself. Only I know that underneath his bed is more stolen goods. Not candy. Not glittery gel pens, but leather jackets and briefcases and odds and ends that have no business there. These are things he thinks he might want, things that look worth selling. Things that belong to other people.

I knock on his bedroom door. When he walked past Mom and Dad, I recognized the look in his eyes—he was high. And suddenly I'm back in that moment: it is the same glazed redness I saw in the rearview mirror from the back seat the time he and his friend Steve and I shared a blunt, and then drove and drove and drove. "I'm gonna teach you how to smoke," Junior announced that day, matter-of-factly. "Yeah," he says, affirming the statement with a head nod, grinning at me. We had walked to Steve's house that day after school, to "run an errand," Junior said elusively. He often invites me on odd missions: *be my witness*. Steve is an unlikely friend—a thirty-five-year-old self-identifying gypsy, a business associate turned friend. He is a professional thief and black-market salesman. He has many identities. One day he is Tom, another day Tony, with IDs to prove it. The day we smoked he was Steve. Steve lives near Junior's high school. Steve can sell anything, and so I imagine Junior sells the stolen cars to Steve or Steve knows people Junior can sell the cars to.

Steve walks out and is surprised to see me, a frizzy-haired kid in front of his operation. He should be as surprised to see Junior, also frizzy-haired, also a child. He should be ashamed of himself but he isn't. Junior introduces me, giving me purpose and an implied protection. "This is my sister," he says, but what is communicated is: *Don't fuck with her and don't question me, she's cool*. In his presence I feel cloaked, protected. I walk with the cloak everywhere I go even when he's not introducing me to some shady character.

Junior opens the back door of a very old but well-kept Cutlass. I slide into the back onto smooth vinyl seats. Junior closes my heavy door and hops in front with Steve. Junior isn't old enough to drive, but by now he knows how, has taught himself. Before he closes his door, he spills out the guts of a cigar onto the pavement and begins crumbling weed into the brown paper. "You ready to get high?" Junior asks me as he rolls the blunt closed and licks it along the side to seal it. I feel shy in front of the old outsider in the driver's seat so I just nod. He lights it up and takes the first puff. I am curious and always ready to participate in whatever Junior is doing, whatever he will include me in. Maybe this piece of adulthood will make me feel better, powerful, confident, so I go ahead and try it; I'm excited.

"Here," he says, passing the blunt to me. "Listen to me," he instructs. He gave me similar instructions on the other illicit smoking occasions. Still I do it wrong—hold it wrong and smoke it wrong. This is different from a cigarette. "No," Junior corrects me, "like this." He pinches his index finger and thumb together. I follow and bring the smoking thing to my lips and inhale. "Okay, now hold it!" Junior cheers me on. I inhale deeper. I do not breathe. "Now let it out," he says. I blow out the smoke along with a fit of coughs. Junior smiles and nods. He's proud of me. "Yeah," he nods again. "Good," he smiles. "Now pass it." I pass it to Steve, who accepts it graciously. "Now you're high," Junior says with a wide grin. Unable to focus on any one thought, I just sit there in the back seat, my eyelids heavy, and let myself be driven. The engine roars and Junior gives me the blunt again and again until he tells me to "kill it." I take one more puff before he takes it from me and tosses the roach out the window as we accelerate onto the freeway.

We pass by glittering Lake Merritt, the blinking Grand Lake Theatre, the patch of freeway with tall palm trees that makes me feel like we're in Hollywood, past the exit we take for Nellie's house. We keep going east, past the Fruit-vale exit we took to get to our old house, past High Street, past what is familiar to me. I wonder where we are going but I can't form words. My body melts into the warm vinyl, and I let myself be driven. I don't worry because my brother is here.

Now, outside his bedroom door, I wait for him to let me in. "It's me," I say. He lets me in and I sit on the foot of his bed. Junior is sitting on his bed; his eyes are red and he's wearing a lazy smirk. He's growing out his hair, and the frizz around the edges of his short ponytail protrudes electrically. His skin is oily like he needs to wash it. I am aware of skin, aware of appearance now more than ever before. As if seeing a reflection of myself in him, I mentally examine him and take note of all the flaws we might share: greasy face, blackheads around the nose, pimples, frizz, too-big nose, not-good-enough clothing, red eyes.

"You're high," I chide, stretching the word *high* into song.

"You're a genius," Junior replies with a bobblehead smile.

I am unsure of what it is I'd like to talk about. I just want to be around him. I like to hang out in his room and touch his things. I pick up a cassette tape—Mac Mall—and touch the smooth, cold case, and look at the boys on the cover. There are other tapes stacked up next to the player: Scarface, Too Short, E-40, Devin the Dude, Luniz, Dr. Dre. Junior presses play on what's already in there. It's Scarface, the "Smile for Me" single he often listens to on repeat. I lie down on the bed and listen to the lyrics while Junior looks at the numbers in his pager. It's a lonely song. It makes me sad. Junior nods his head, reaches for the phone next to his bed, and dials in some pages.

"I want a pager," I say.

"You're too young."

"I was too young to smoke a blunt too."

Junior puts the phone down and looks at me sternly. "You're only allowed to smoke with *me*."

"Don't tell me what I'm allowed to do."

"I'm serious," he says with a look so cutting it erases all signs of intoxication.

"God." I shrug my shoulders to show him how little I care. "Okay, whatever." But I am secretly elated. I like feeling cared for. I want someone to care about what I do.

"This song is sad," I say, changing the subject. "I like it."

He nods in my direction. "Yup."

We sit for a while in silence and listen to the music—me lying down, Junior staring across the room. Mom and Dad can be heard calling back and forth to each other, Dad frantically trying to answer Mom's questions (*Do I have dinner? Where is my badge? What time is it?*)—the dialogue of our lives.

Junior pulls his wallet out from the back pocket of his jeans and begins counting money. He separates the ones from the fives from the twenties from the hundreds. I am equal parts impressed and afraid. I know what he's doing is illegal but I also know, as he does, that he is invincible. Being caught is not a concern. He has found his path to being big and visible and taking up space and having power in the IROCs and Mustang 5.0s, in the navy-blue Maverick he has been eyeing for himself. He will buy it before he is legally old enough to drive. That one will be for him and he will acquire it legally.

I want to detect him, detect the boy I know. Do better, do better, I repeat. It was his little-boy self, riding around in an IROC earlier that day, spinning doughnuts at the intersection by our house. It is him I tell to do better. He is in there, hurting, his ribs smashed; the boy who'd been beat up badly, the boy who was made a fool of, the boy no one protected. In the street one night, showing off in his stolen car, he made so much noise revving up gas and expertly applying brakes to make the perfect doughnut; all who were home and awake ran out to the front porch to see what accident had occurred. But there was no accident. It was Junior recklessly and gleefully spinning in the street. *Look at me.* And then he disappeared back to wherever it was he had come from. Now tall enough to drive, still not old enough, still too fast.

Cars bore me. Especially the old ones. They are about as interesting as the vintage soda bottles he collects: not at all. He seems to be obsessed with the old. "I don't even know why you like those cars," I say. Junior shakes his head to imply I wouldn't understand. Maybe I don't. "They're ugly," I continue. "How do you even steal a car?"

"Who said anything about stealing?" he asks with a grin.

"I'm not dumb."

"But you *are* nosy."

"Well, you ride around here like you want everyone to know."

"Nah," he says, putting the organized bills neatly back into his wallet. But it seems as though that's true: *Look at me. Look how powerful. Look how fast. Look how beautiful.* He is an elegant swan gliding through a mud pond, a fragrant rose among weeds. *Look how beautiful.*

"I like new cars. I like Lexuses. Or Hondas. They're the prettiest," I say, wanting in on some of the power, acting as if my desire for new has any relation to what he does on the street. I want so badly to connect to him, and we can connect in our desire for different, our desire for more. Each one of us is looking for something we don't yet have.

I remember myself as a little girl perpetually behind him, walking to the twenty-four-hour drugstore near our house. Neither of us has any money. I amble behind, the bounce of his curls my guide. When we arrive, he gives me no warning, he just walks through the aisles with confidence until he reaches the one he wants. He gently strokes the fabric of the shirts before taking them quickly and confidently off their hangers, putting them on as if they'd always been his. One T-shirt. Two, three, four. I watch in awe as he fearlessly dresses himself in Oakland A's and other sports teams' shirts. As quickly as we walk in, we walk out. No alarms sound, no police arrive, no angry manager runs after us. I look around and around for all of these markers of crime as I trot after him in fear, but no one comes. No one notices. We are safe outside, in the sunshine, and free.

But now I am no longer invited to come along. I am invited only to be the silent accomplice and witness as the something I can't yet name takes my brother, its long and gnarly fingers grabbing at him, little by little scratching away at his innocence and playing for keeps. Where is he?

I try to locate him inside his teenage face. Sometimes I can, inside a smile or smirk, a glimmer in his eyes, a corny joke, in the way he sucks his teeth and cocks his head. He is still in there—all boy—and I wait for him to reveal himself to me. I wait for my brother to return to me but there is no turning back from growing up. There will be no return. What is happening to him is also happening to me: we are two kids growing up. Nothing can stop it.

"You'll get your car," he finally says after the money is safely in place and back in his pocket. He says it with assurance, as if he will be the one to procure it for me, and I do not question it. Just as he has brought me CDs and coats and electronics, I fully expect that one day he will bring a car for me to drive myself away in. He begins gathering clothes and his towel that hangs from the back of his closet door. He smells like he looks—like someone who hasn't showered for a day or two.

"But, a pager first." I smile, and then say, "Ew, you stink." He shoves me gently and kicks his red-and-gray sneakers off near the closet, then carefully puts them on top of the Nike box they belong to.

"Are you going out again?" I ask.

"Don't worry about it," he says with a grin, which means he would like me to ask more questions; he would like me to know where he's going.

"You going to see Danielle?"

He smiles. "None of your business." And this means yes. It is our secret language, or my secret understanding. I can hear what is between the words my brother says, the gestures he uses.

"Well, good," I say. "Don't go anywhere else. Just stay there."

"Ye-ah," he says as if he is suddenly from the Deep South, or a rapper on one of his cassette tapes.

"When will I get to meet her?" I ask, and study his face to determine how much he cares for this girl. His eyes meet mine before he opens the door to leave for his shower. He nods at me in acknowledgment. I think he likes her.

"You'll meet her."

He disappears through the kitchen and goes upstairs to use what I call *my* bathroom so he can use all of my products because we have the exact same hair. When he returns he will dress himself warmly so he can ride a bike through the crisp night all the way to West Oakland to visit the girlfriend he now has in the neighborhood where he spends most of his time. The bike he'll ride will be mine because he destroyed his own riding too fast and too hard long ago. It will be pink and it will be far too small for his long legs. He'll ride through the streets, his long legs tapering off to the side as he pedals. He will ride out of our neighborhood and into hers, into the ghetto, as we know it, leaving a trail of a thousand flowers behind him. *Look. Look how beautiful.*

SEVEN

There's a knock on my bedroom door. Another knock, then the knob to the locked door starts wiggling. If you wiggle it fast and hard enough it will pop open. Only Junior knows this trick. I hurry to the door, exasperated. "What!" I shout. It's Junior, grinning at my door. I roll my eyes at him. What could be so urgent?

"Come downstairs." He motions for me to follow. My feet are bare, and I quickly scan the room wondering if I should put shoes on, if we will be going outside, but he is already impatiently bouncing down the stairs. "C'mon," I hear him say from the stairwell. I hope he's finally purchased the car he's been saving for and we are rushing because the engine is running, waiting for us to jump inside. I hope I'll find the beautiful blue Maverick outside. I decide to grab my shoes.

"Hold on!" I yell. "I'm coming," I whisper into my too-big boys' sneakers, slipping them on as fast as I can. I look for him downstairs. The house is empty except for Mom asleep in her bed. I peek into his room. Not there. I go into the living room and find him at the front door, all smiles.

He opens it and motions for me to join him outside. I step onto the front porch and find the smallest woman I have ever seen sitting on the top step, holding her knees. She sits among Dad's potted plants. She has long, shining brown braids. Her braids are the color of amber. She is wearing a gray sweater and light-wash jeans. The bracelets on her arm jingle as she turns her head around at the sound of us, and tucks some loose braids behind her ear. I size her up: tiny, compact, perfectly smooth brown skin, brown eyes, fat fingers, warm smile. I step over the threshold and walk toward her.

"Hi, Melissa." She speaks in a soft voice. She knows my name. "Your brother has told me so much about you." She is still smiling. "It's so nice to meet you." She never stops smiling. She doesn't reach for my hand. This is not a handshaking meeting. I both hope she does and hope she doesn't try to hug me. I stare at her for too long before finally speaking.

"Hi," I say, trying to hide my unease. She welcomes me in for a hug and I accept, taking in the fruity scent of her body spray. She smells like a Victoria's Secret store. Junior is standing above us, watching us interact. He likes this girl.

"I'm Danielle," she says, and then looks up at Junior and smiles.

I hate how quiet I am. I don't know what to say. I find a way to smile and loosen my body. I take a seat on the stair beneath her so I am looking up at her when I speak.

"I love your hair," I tell her.

"Thank you," she says, beaming. "I could do your hair like this if you want." I try to hide the delight in my eyes.

"Thanks" is all I can say.

Junior walks down and joins us. He is quiet too. We sit in silence for a beat or two. He can't invite her in because he's too ashamed. We both try and entertain her from the stairs.

"So, Melissa," she starts, "Junior says I can't come in. Is that true?" I look at Junior to know what to say. I don't know what he's told her, what kind of lies.

"You will," Junior says. "Just not yet."

She rolls her eyes and touches his face, smiling all the while. "Okay," she says, shrugging her shoulders. And I wonder if Junior will have the courage to ever bring her inside.

"I'm hungry," Junior announces. "Y'all wanna go eat?" We agree, and I am relieved we are leaving the house, the elephant in the room, so we can relax and talk about something besides why no one can come in. "Lil Danielle don't eat nothin' so we gotta go to Barney's. She'll eat fries though." We are all standing now, and he brings her shoulders close to him since her waist is too low; she can't be taller than five feet. We walk to the restaurant together, and I observe the way they talk to each other. I want to know if we can trust her. She looks inflated next to him, as if his protection and love are physically expanding her. She seems somehow less tiny. They are close, but nervous around me in public. Their conversation consists of pokes and the sucking of teeth and jokes and shoves and any way to touch each other. Junior is fifteen going on sixteen. She is seventeen already. I am twelve.

We order french fries and milkshakes. I learn that she goes to high school in Berkeley and that she loves to do hair.

She can do my hair in any style, she tells me. She tells me my hair is so pretty and she can't wait to do it. I can't wait either. We set up a date then and there: next weekend she will braid my hair. She laughs at my ignorance about hair: whether or not it's acceptable for me to wear a weave. How will I wash it? My insecurity: How will I look? She assures me it will look great, and I believe her. I can tell Junior is happy watching us. He pays the bill with cash and they walk me home. She hugs me, and I can feel the soft fabric of her sweater and smell her saccharine scent again. This time she smells like an older sister, like freedom, like expansion. She will help me transform, I think.

JUNIOR HASN'T BEEN home in a few nights. I know he's with Danielle. At least I think he is, but Mom and Dad don't know or don't care. Their fifteen-year-old son is not at home. Their son is missing. On the third night, even I begin to worry, but I don't agree with their solution. They have decided to call the police. It's almost as if he knows, wanted to test them, wanted to see how long it would take to be missed this severely.

On the third night I hear commotion downstairs. I leave my room to see what the fuss is. Mom, Dad, Junior, and a police officer stand together in the living room. The police officer is addressing Junior. "What do you think you're doing, son?" he asks bobblehead Junior, who I can tell is high and drunk by the heaviness of his skull. He has a bottle of brandy under his bed, and he's taken to drinking from it day and night. He also wants to be different, wants to transform, and has found substances that make him feel that way. "Your parents were worried sick about you."

He smirks at the policeman, looking him in the eye as he says very slowly, "What they worried for? They ain't gotta be worried." His tongue is Southern again, or from somewhere other than where we were raised, as if his grammar weren't corrected by Dad every time he said the wrong tense of any word. "What you doin' here anyway?" Junior continues. His head looks as if it will tumble off his body as he speaks. His smile is lazy. I want to go up to him and offer him some support, hold his head so he can speak a straight sentence. Tell him to take a seat and show some respect. But I do nothing. I watch from my post down the hall near the kitchen. He is reckless, invincible. The cold hard thing that lives inside my brother is growing larger, playing with fire now, taunting police officers. Dad's eyes are blue but have fire in them. Mom frowns hard and deep. "Don't you got some other shit you need to be doin'? Man, I'm just a kid." He looks at the officer again. Dad grabs Junior by the wrist and Junior rips his hand free. "Man, get off me," and suddenly his smirk disappears into the shape of rage.

Dad shakes his head, shakes off the shame he feels. They are the same height now. His son has become someone unwieldy and unknown to him. We all look at him and try to locate the boy. "You're breaking my heart," Mom adds. "You had us worried sick. You better not go out there again." *Out there* is a place beyond the walls of the house, beyond any protection they can offer, out of their jurisdiction. West Oakland is *out there*; it is a place that is taking their boy, pulling at him, luring him with its drugs and money, its power. But that is only partly true. He goes willingly, enthusiastically, a student. *Love me, accept me, teach me to have power, take me.* He softens as she speaks, and smiles again.

"I'm all right, Mommy." He holds her gaze for a moment and then marches down the hall to his room, nodding at me as he passes. He closes the door without a care, leaving the chaos behind him to settle. A whiff of him fills my nose as he walks away. He smells like *out there*, like the street as I imagine it: cold and high and dangerous.

It is late now. Before I escape into my own room I listen for a few more seconds as the cop leaves. I have heard stories about a cop in the house before. It was because I ran away when I was two. I got two blocks away and waited in line at a burrito shop. I knew how to walk to it because Dad had taken me there on his shoulders so many times. I had memorized the route. But I was obviously alone, and so the owner called the police. Responding to calls about a missing baby, he drove me home. When he asked me to sit in the back of his car and handed me an apple juice, I didn't drink it. He didn't seem trustworthy. The cop in the house now sounds like he wants to help us. It sounds like he wants to help protect Junior, but I am not sure. I remember not drinking the apple juice. My story hadn't ended well. The apple-juice cop came into our house, looked around and saw the mess, and threatened to call child protective services. He shamed my mother. "How can you have a house that looks like this?" he demanded. "How can you have so many children and not be able to care for them? Why aren't they helping you clean up?"

The living room is cluttered now—it looks like a tornado has come through it—but Mom doesn't care about the state of the house. They have let this man into our home for a different reason. I watch as this nice cop wishes Mom and Dad good luck in keeping Junior out of trouble, and congratulates them on having found their son. Mom and Dad walk him to the door and disappear from my view. I can still hear some low talk coming from the front door but other than that the room is empty and quiet again. The bass of rap music starts from behind Junior's closed door. The lock of the front door clicks, and Mom and Dad look as though they have barely escaped something terrible. I proceed back upstairs to my own bed. At least our boy is home.

I switch schools again. Junior and I play musical chairs, drifting all over the Oakland Public School District. One of us is looking for the most basic of needs: safety. The other: connection. I attend seventh and eighth grades at a school on a hill, the same school as Nellie. It is a so-called art school and seems like a good idea. I present a portfolio of my art—pastel portraits and landscapes mostly—in a giant folder to show that I am artistic enough to be there, and they let me in. The mural in front that gives the impression of a happy place—California College of Arts and Crafts across the street, the hill it is on, the surrounding rich white people—but it isn't good. Like all good things, it, too, is a lie. Inside its walls are kids in various stages of drifting. At school we are away from family, searching for ourselves in one another, feeling around in the dark for what a future could look like. Not belonging to the state, nor our families, and definitely not the teachers; here we belong to no one. We are all on the edge of adulthood and all the dangers the adults have warned us of: pregnancy, prison, murder. Which is it? Or do we prefer college? An honest job? We are asked to choose, but many won't. Some of us will not make it.

It is a K–12 school, so I mingle with small kids and high school kids alike. Some of the girls at my school have given birth several times already. They bring their new babies to school for us to coo over. On the other side of girlhood is fear. Mom has already warned me: my period means that I must never go near a boy. That was her only instruction, and it was stated severely with fearful eyes.

I take the weed Junior gave me and introduce my own friends to it. Just as Junior taught me, I teach my friends how to smoke. Now I get to be the teacher. I convince them to cut school with me, and we escape like prisoners through the side streets so as not to be seen by anyone's parent or by a teacher. We walk with our heads down until we reach the nearby freeway underpass, where the loud and constant rumbling of BART trains above makes us feel invisible while we smoke weed from a pipe. I am good at school but I do not like school. It is easy for me to get good grades, but I learn nothing that feels important to me. The most important thing to me is growing up. I must become old enough to take care of myself. This yearning is powerful. Getting good grades is easy, finding a good reason to care about school is not.

Soon I will begin high school. Dad has presented me with an option. Like Claire, I can attend private school on a scholarship program, or I can go to the same school as all my other siblings went to, where Junior went before the continuation school and where he's since returned. I cram and take the entrance exam, but at the last minute I choose public school. I don't like the private school women who interview me. I am afraid of them, afraid I'll be expected to be like them, afraid I am not like them, afraid that I'm not really smart enough, that my intelligence is a lie and only in comparison to the low standards around me. They sit on catalog furniture in sterile, scentless offices and ask me about what I like to do and what I like to read as they write things about me on notepads. Underneath their button-downs and straightened hair and slacks, I wonder if they think they are better than me. I am angry that the thought has entered my mind.

I become so mixed up in my thoughts, paranoid: How dare they think they're better than me! I could never be like them. I feel so out of place and begin to hate them a little for it. I am frustrated with myself for not feeling good enough, for having these thoughts and letting them get in the way of my interview. One of them asks me what I like to do in my spare time. "Write poetry," I tell her. She asks me who my favorite poets are, and I stumble and finally spit out Langston Hughes even though it's not true. I am too ashamed to tell her that my favorite poets are girls my age who perform after school at Berkeley High, where I like to watch poetry slams, where I'd like to share my poems if I could ever be brave enough. Being myself couldn't possibly be good enough for this fancy school. I don't feel good enough. I don't feel prepared. I stop the application process, choose public school, and I don't turn back from this decision once I make up my mind. It's what I know, it's where my friends are going, and it's where I want to be. It's where Junior is. Mom and Dad let me make this choice.

Oakland Tech is where all of my siblings went except for Claire. It is in walking distance from our house, and I know a handful of girls who are going too—girls that seem smart to me, like they are going to be okay. I convince myself that I've made the right choice, that I will also be okay. There's an advanced humanities program called Paideia that I will be a part of. Even though college is far away and I don't feel very academically inclined—I'm more excited about the prospect of working and making money—I have some vague idea that I'll probably need to go to college because my siblings did. And I am told that if I'm not in this program, my chances for college will be nonexistent. This is the program for smart kids, I am told. It's the program that Vivian and Cornelius did.

Located on the border between North and West Oakland, Oakland Tech has kids from both sides, and even many that bus out from East Oakland. The facade of the school is stately: large and white with giant columns and steps out front. It looks important from the outside and I start to feel all right about my decision. I will find out that, like Junior, there are many students who treat school like a part-time job, attending when they please and selling drugs and hanging out as their primary obligation. I will come to learn that Junior is known around the school by students from all different grades, by cops, and by teachers as some combination of cool and trouble. Girls like him, boys either respect him or want to fight him, the cops want to arrest him, and the teachers want him kicked out. I will come to find that there is a security guard at every entrance of the school and the school has cop cars patrolling all day long, a few parked outside each side of the campus. They are waiting to catch young truants, drug dealers, and those armed. I have heard of murders that happen to students off campus. I will come to know that "so-and-so got shot" is a frequent occurrence. One day so-and-so will be in class, and one day he will be gone forever. I wonder what my reputation will be in this new world; I wonder who I will be.

Junior has already been a student off and on for three years at Oakland Tech. He is seventeen now and I am fourteen. Not since elementary school have we attended the same school at the same time. When we were in elementary school together, he found me crying once because an older boy had accidentally hit me in the face with his soccer ball, and I'd been so mortified that I'd just sat on the bench in the yard, a small kindergartner, and cried. Junior ran up to me. "What happened to you?" When I told him, he walked quickly up to the boy, took the ball from his hands, and slammed it into his face. He walked back over to me, and I saw the boy holding his face, his mouth dropped open, speechless. "He won't do it again," Junior said. "C'mon, get up." He pulled me up and we walked home. Junior should be a senior in high school now, but he flunked; it is uncertain what grade he's actually in or if he'll graduate. But most importantly, we will overlap. I will have my brother with me my first year. He will protect me.

Junior has promised he will take me shopping for school. Looking good is the first step to fitting in. I am all nerves. My body has just developed, and suddenly I have a new shape that I don't know how to dress and would prefer to hide. Things I could have never worn now look the way they're supposed to: I fill shirts and pants out. I'm tall enough now that I don't have to roll up my jeans. Suddenly I am no longer chubby. My fat cheeks are now cheekbones. There are new kinds of eyes on my body and I want to hide from them, but I'm also curious about them. *Look how beautiful.* This is a kind of power I've never had. I still feel most comfortable borrowing Junior's clothes. I swim in his anoraks, his Eddie Bauer jackets, but it is decidedly time for new sneakers. Mine—the ones Dad decided I needed to grow into—remain creased and too big, with holes starting to form. I meet Junior outside the house, and we take BART to Niketown in San Francisco. We pass by the Skechers shop filled with pink and glittery sneakers, but I can't get distracted. Nikes are what I must wear.

As we enter the public sphere, I become hyperaware of who we are and how we appear. I observe Junior being a quiet and observant person. He looks at everything and everyone. He is taking in our surroundings like a hound dog, sniffing for unfamiliar smells, sounds, and people. He is watchful and looks everyone we pass in the eye until his fierce gaze makes them look away. We walk the three blocks from the BART station in downtown San Francisco to the Nike store. We walk uphill; San Francisco consists only of steep hills. I shuffle through the crowds of tourists, darting around them as they make sudden movements—stopping in the middle of a sidewalk to look at a map or looking around to read a street sign with squinted eyes. There are never tourists in Oakland. Our city doesn't attract, it repels, and I think to myself, what a wonderful secret. I hope they never come and swarm our streets, our lake, our hills. But today I must face the crowd with my brother, trying to keep up with him as always. He is always just a few steps ahead of me. Like a skilled boxer dodging a swing, I weave around someone and catch up to him.

"There it is." He points like we've reached some mecca. I have never been here. It is not a store I have ever wanted to enter. The only Nikes I've ever owned Dad bought me from a Foot Locker in town. The store is massive. It is a two-story glass castle with a giant image of the muscular, glistening arms of a basketball star I don't recognize. Despite the annoying bustle of touristy San Francisco, I feel expansive when I enter the store. I feel important.

"Okay," Junior says. "What do you like?"

I stammer, shrugging my shoulders. "I don't know." I don't. I know nothing about sneakers, about stores this beautiful, about being told I can have what I want.

"Oh man." Junior steers us toward a display. "These right here are fresh," he says, grinning, holding up a completely neon-green shoe.

"Whoa," I say with wide eyes. "No way, too bright. What the heck would you wear with those?" But I like the boldness of the color.

"All right, what about these?" He holds up a less ostentatious version of the same shoe—red and white with a sole made of their signature air trapped in a clear bubble.

"Getting warmer," I say.

While Junior asks for his size, I wander to the wall

of shoes for women and stare at my options. I feel overwhelmed by all the pink so I look for the men's wall. Junior finds me with his orange box of shoes. "Are you sure you have enough money for two?" I ask in a whisper. It embarrasses me to be spending this much money.

"I told you not to worry about it." I breathe that in and try to accept this gesture.

"I need help. I hate all the girls' shoes," I say as I scan the room looking for something that catches my eye. "I liked those crazy green ones," I admit.

Junior smiles. "I know," he says, and guides us to the men's wall, where there seems to be a cousin of that shoe. It is pearl white, a subtle sheen with electric blue and neon-green embellishments all leading to the pop: the neon-green bubble at the bottom of the shoe. They are beautiful; they are art—but most excitingly, they are the same style as Junior's. We will wear the same uniform. We will fight in the same army. It will be us against high school.

Our shoes ring up at over $200 total, and I hit him, a reflex, as he begins counting twenty-dollar bills. I hit him a second time—this time on purpose—before he hands the money to the woman on the other side of the counter. Is he sure? Should we be doing this? It feels wrong to spend this much money, to not buy them on sale, to not have a coupon of some sort, or several. Part of me feels like he won't have enough and the cashier will send us back to Oakland and we'll walk out and everything will go back to normal and I will wear my too-big and worn-out black Nikes until Dad elects to escort me to the sale in the already discounted basement section of Sears. But Junior hands her the money.

And she gives him back his change. And he puts it in his pocket. As we walk out, I look over my shoulder repeatedly because surely someone will call the police. Surely we have done something very wrong here. Surely someone will appear to take our things away from us. Surely we shouldn't have these things.

My heart is beating with real fear as we make it past the threshold and to the outside. No one catches us. Junior is still holding our giant bag of shoes. We didn't steal them. No alarms have gone off; no manager is chasing us. These works of art now belong to us. We bought them with real money.

"Why do you have so much money?" Surprised by my own exasperation and unable to stop it, I cut straight to the chase. Junior just smiles and becomes the silent, stoic man-boy he is when we are outside, when we are in the world. "I'm serious," I continue. "You can't just act like you have a job, like you work. You're not fooling anyone. Where did you get this money?" All the *things*, I clarify in my mind, all the money. So much; so many orange boxes of shoes, the plush coats I borrow regularly, an always-full pocket of cash being counted obsessively. It is my fear talking.

"You don't need to know." He pushes away the question, enjoying the power in the bit of mystery he is able to maintain. Then he looks at me. "You're welcome," he says.

"Man. Thank you, Junior. I love my shoes."

"Spoiled ass . . . can't even say thank you."

"Shut up," I tease. "I said thank you." And I am so thankful. I feel ready for high school.

We walk back to BART in our feelings. I'm feeling

proud to have a big brother who is nice to me and wants me to have what I need for my first day of high school, and he feels proud to be able to offer it. The crowd has either faded or has parted for us so that we may walk in our happy silence, the criminal and his accomplice. I already know what he's doing to have so much money. He doesn't have to speak it. I imagine him joyfully riding around, spinning in delightful doughnuts, showing off his fragrant blossoms in stolen cars. For some reason my mind doesn't permit me to imagine anything criminal beyond that, nothing concrete. *The street. Out there.* I work hard to conjure those abstract places. I try again. *The street.* I wrinkle my brows and concentrate. I will my mind to imagine it, to try and put him in it. Some vague, inconsistent dreamworld. As soon as the fog of it clears, the image that has begun to form disappears, and I am back here with him on this street. Not like *that* street—*the street*—which is so difficult to imagine us on, but on this good street, with a shopping bag, in the daylight, where no one is after either of us and we are safe. *That* street, when I can imagine it, is not good. The mind's fog is thick like on an Oakland day when you can actually see the physical moisture in the dense air; the air is heavy with it, and like the air, I become heavy when I try and see it. I can start to see things, scenarios, outlines of people beyond the fog of my very limited imagination and then they disappear. That's enough, my mind seems to say, a kind of survival. I don't want to see him there.

Back at the BART station, Junior turns and looks at me. "You wanna come somewhere with me?" I do. I always do.

"Where?" I pretend I will consider.

"Over to Mike and them's house." Mike is our cousin, the same age as Junior. Lina, Mike's sister, is my age, and Lorna, our oldest cousin, is Claire's age. Junior has recently forged a relationship with all of them, making frequent visits to the Fillmore, the neighborhood in San Francisco where they live. Our aunt, Mom's sister, owned a huge two-story Victorian before she died, and all of them inherited it. When he mentions going there, I think it odd, and I wonder if maybe that is where he stays when he doesn't come home.

"Yeah, okay," I say. I haven't seen our cousins in what feels like years. We are just across the bay, but Mom never encouraged us to know one another, so every attempt always felt unnatural and forced. But I want to go now. I want to know them despite what Mom has said over the years about their involvement in unsavory activities. By now I know there is no good place, no safe place. I go without hesitation.

"Cool," he says. "We gotta take the bus then. BART doesn't stop over there." And when he says this it becomes clear that he has not only been there before but has been many times. He leads the way to the bus stop. As we walk, the tourists vanish as if there is some invisible line, and soon we have entered a part of town that seems to be solely occupied by the homeless and the mentally unwell. People scream out and have lively and animated conversations with voices in their minds. People pull up at their deeply stained and loosely hanging pants, which threaten to fall with every movement. People huddle in alleys and corridors with sacks of stained belongings and signs asking for food or money. We wait on one of these corners for our bus. Junior seems unmoved by it and chuckles to himself. "You think this is bad? This ain't even nothin'." And in that moment, *the street*, that foggy place, fills in a tiny bit more in my mind. I am not afraid. These people don't scare me. But it is Junior's relationship to them. Who are you when you leave? I ask the back of his body as he climbs the stairs the bus driver has lowered for us. We find a seat in the back of the bus and watch a scene familiar to city dwellers. The city transforms from blight to beauty every few blocks, from derelict to dazzling, a reminder that nothing and no one can be beautiful all the time. The ugly of a city, of a person, is enmeshed in its beauty. Junior pulls the ringer. We have arrived.

The bus drops us off at Fillmore and Sutter. It feels like an in-between part of town, on the edge of what some, without knowing who lives on either end, might call good and bad. We jog across the street on a yellow light. Sunlight struggles to come through a thick fog coming in from the bay. The fog descends ominously on the city, but that ominous impression is false: though the fog is aggressive, demanding to be noticed, it is benign, even friendly, and it smells like rain; it cleanses.

A man appears seemingly out of nowhere. He is old, or maybe he just looks old. He seems to know my brother. "Hey man" is how he acknowledges Junior. His greeting is returned by a head nod. "Hey man," the man says again, and now it seems he is following us. "Hey!" he yells in our direction. "Man!" Junior stops in the middle of the street we are crossing. There is no traffic on this street so we are not in danger. He looks the man up and down. The man stops walking, stops yelling.

"Did I say you could speak to me?" Junior says.

"Hey man, I don't know what the—"

Junior cuts him off. "You do what the fuck I say. You hear me?"

"Nah, nigga, what you talkin' about," the man stammers.

Junior begins laughing, looks at me. "C'mon," he says, and he motions for me to follow him to the other side of the street. "You wanna see a crackhead dance?" I don't answer. There is no good answer for such a question. Of course I don't, but this is not the time for me to state the obvious because there is a man in the street who is too old to be spoken to the way my brother is speaking to him, too old to be taking orders from a seventeen-year-old, too human to want something from my brother as desperately as he does. *The street* is being filled in before my eyes.

"I want your sorry ass to dance for my sister. Give us a show, you sorry ass nigga."

I want nothing to do with this show. I want to hide, but there is nowhere. I barely know what neighborhood I'm in, and it becomes clear that Junior knows it quite well. He knows this man. We stand and look at the man as he considers the demand. And then he begins to move his body to some unknown rhythm, offbeat and inelegant; he bends his old knees up and down, up and down, his hands up to the sky as if in praise. To my surprise he begins to laugh. He continues his jig for what seems like minutes. Junior is cackling, rolling with laughter, and I am unsure of what to do with my body and mouth, unsure of how to label what has just happened in my mind: disturbing, sad, powerful, scary, entertaining, shameful. We are both children, and the only adult present is addicted to crack and dancing desperately in the middle of the street.

We continue on the journey to our cousin's house and leave the man there dancing in the street. I am ready for anything. I have to be, as an active accomplice. I work hard to shake off what I've just seen as we walk up the stairs and let ourselves into our cousins' home.

Lina greets us, and I am amazed and impressed by how friendly she is with me. I have only met her a handful of times, but she is gregarious and warm and I feel instantly absolved of having a mother who has limited our contact. I am grateful for her barrage of questions because I am shy. I let her talk while Junior heads upstairs to greet our older cousin Lorna. Lina and I follow shortly after. We all sit on her king-size bed. There are framed photos of relatives I have only seen once or twice but have heard many stories of: aunts, uncles, cousins, their children.

Lorna sits in the center of the bed like a true matriarch. The original matriarch is dead. Like the head of this household she assumes, we all sit around her. She is older, more powerful, more beautiful than all of us. We make small talk and casually watch music videos. Aaliyah comes on the TV, and I become mesmerized by the effortlessness of her dancing and the husky sweetness of her voice. Lorna is like that, I think. I dream of one day being such a woman, my mere presence a demand for power and honor. "I'm glad you're here," Lorna says as she strokes my hair. "Pretty girl." I'm sure my cheeks become red. "You're so quiet." I shrug and try to smile, try to make up for all I lack with grace. "It's good you brought her," she says, looking now at Junior. He knows them. He has found a new family, I think, feeling a combination of betrayal and jealousy.

"Where's Darnell at?" Junior asks. Darnell is Lorna's

boyfriend, the man posed next to her in photos on the walls. I am slowly piecing together that Darnell is who Junior most wants to see. He, I suppose, is not home because he is currently on *the street*, he is perhaps related to the desperation of the dancing man we just left in *the street*, and maybe related to the money we purchased our shoes with. Perhaps.

"Aw, he's out still," she says, and I think I see her shooting him a look. I imagine it's meant to be something motherly, sisterly, at least I hope it is: *Don't you dare, stop while you're ahead, don't get caught up, this life is not what you think*. But I don't know what he understands from it, or if I am projecting and still in shock from the dancing man. All I know is that it appears we will not leave until this man comes back from wherever he is and Junior gets to speak to him. It could also be that Junior has made a friend in him. Just like he found a friend in Steve the gypsy, he finds friends in older men. He, too, is looking for examples of who he can be.

We wait. I am nervous and quiet because I don't know them well and we are doing an intimate thing, sitting together on a bed. But Lorna and Lina make me feel at home, welcome. I relax into my section of the bed. We gather in this room as if there are no other rooms in this huge house. The light of the TV blares against the dark of the hallway that leads upstairs. The house is giant, an old Victorian, with a creaky staircase and many rooms I haven't seen. When we entered, there were two men in the kitchen smoking cigarettes, and I feel a bit of shame for being afraid of them. They are old enough to be uncles, but I am told they are my cousins. I have heard stories of these men from when they were boys, when they were sweet and innocent. When they became men I never heard anything good about them. I hear Mom's voice playing in my ear: *Crack, drugs, bad*, over and over again, trying her best to protect us from this very scene, but here we are. We are old enough to travel now.

It doesn't take long for Darnell to come home. I hear the stairs creaking as he walks up them. He enters the room where we are all gathered, kisses Lorna, and greets all of us. He is handsome, older, I suppose around Lorna's age—twenty-four or so. "What up, lil cuz," he says in Junior's direction, and they slap each other's hands, quickly embrace, and pat each other on the shoulder. Junior is beaming, the gap in his teeth on full display. They leave the room together and I hear the floors creak. Soon after, we leave and head back to Oakland.

SCHOOL HAS OFFICIALLY begun. I try and stay close to the friends I know, but we are separated throughout the school in different classes and different periods, and so I must make new friends in new classes. The time between classes is the worst. It is the time I feel most invisible. It is when teenagers swarm the halls to get to their next class and everyone has begun to claim his or her power. They bump it against one another, bump the weak ones, the powerless ones; they have started to grow a power inside of them they did not know they could have, a power to defend themselves, a power to be seen, to bloom. In these halls, in this school, and only here, that power belongs to them. It shows itself in these hallways, in looks and in nods and in hard shoves to the shoulder for those who stand in their way. This, I think, must be what happened inside of Junior, this fierce need to defend. I see it in these boys and in these girls, too. My survival strategy so far is to look straight ahead and dare someone to bump into me. I have not accessed my power yet, but I feel an anger brewing within me. Something about all of this seems so wrong to me, so unjust. In my Paidea classes I am with white and some Asian students; these classes are hard and the teachers expect a lot of us and even go as far as telling us we're better than the rest of the other students at school. In the other half of my classes, teachers watch the clocks and scream over rambunctious black, brown, and Asian teens until the bell rings. In one of my classes, the teacher plays a VHS of a recent campus fight that he had filmed, laughing and pointing when a student gets in a good hit.

My angst grows and begins to show on my body. People ask me "why you muggin'?" about my face, so I suppose I have a naturally mean look on my face. I must wear some of the shield Junior has built around himself. *Don't fuck with me, I am Chris's sister*, by extension, oozes from me. I'm not worried about my safety, and so I'm not interested in physically intimidating anyone or getting in a fight. I just want to be left alone. The anger inside me grows worse each day, entering the doors and greeting security guards, seeing how unjustly different my Paideia classes are from my regular gen-ed classes, I slowly lose my motivation to be there. Even though Junior doesn't attend classes, he is known by teachers and students, and thus I become known infamously as his sister, as "a Valentine." My other siblings who look less like me attended this school too. But Junior and I look like fraternal twins, and it's his immediate legacy I step into. He is known also by the police that patrol the school. "You're a Valentine?" an officer once asked flippantly, and I felt him watching me in an offensive way. The same cop ticketed me later for jaywalking near the school and repeated "a Valentine" like it was a slur as he cited me, stamping me with an identity: bad.

The way I must be every day is exhausting. I have to fight, and it exhausts me even in the first month. I don't want to fight. So instead, I fight my urge to fight. I resist it by not going to school at all. By the end of the first semester, there are only two classes I attend: Paideia English and Education Academy, a technical "major" offered at Oakland Tech for those who may be interested in teaching. In these classes I feel smart. In English I can write. I can show my intelligence with words, which I feel confident doing. I can read, and even though the reading load is heavy, I enjoy the books. Education Academy is taught by a woman I think I might want to be like, so I go to her class because I like being around her. She is black and pretty, smart, and speaks in a soothing voice, never yelling at any students or dividing the class into *smart* and *bad*. She commands respect quietly in a way I admire and seems to really enjoy teaching. I go because I respect her, and I would feel ashamed of myself if I cut her class and had to face her. In other classes, though, I can feel myself slipping away. In those periods I am too behind to ever catch up, and I am marked with more identities: *stupid*, *bad*, *ordinary*, *a Valentine*. Sometimes I come in through the back of the school to avoid security guards and pass by the day care for students who are also mothers and the empty football field that offers a sense of expansion before I enter the prison. I come in well after the bell has rung, returning from cutting the classes I am flunking out of. Mom and Dad don't know because grades haven't arrived yet. My choice to fail is still my secret.

My Nikes, however, are a hit. That year, I begin to discover what I like to wear. I have a part-time job at a gym doing childcare and with my extra money I buy clothing and shoes for the first time, dressing myself in a way that expresses how I feel. I discover I like platform boots. Nellie and I take BART and the bus into the city and go shopping in the Haight. I spend multiple paychecks on platform boots. They make me feel powerful. I buy ripped jeans and cropped sweaters from secondhand stores, and cigarettes with Claire's ID. On days when I cut school, I walk to the neighborhood near Oakland Tech's campus, drink lattes at cafés, and smoke cigarettes until I have to go to one of the classes I like. Some days I dress in vintage and platforms; other days, I wear dark lipstick, my hair slicked back in a tight ponytail, baby hairs gelled to my forehead, a silver Eddie Bauer puff coat, tight jeans, and the Nikes that Junior bought me. Suddenly I want to be seen. *Look at me.*

I am writing a poem in my journal at home, and I hear what I know to be Junior's quick steps as he flies up the stairs two at a time. He jiggles the handle of my doorknob until it busts open. "What!" I scream, even though I know it's him. "I could be doing anything!" I cry once more, defending my need for privacy. He looks at me with an innocence I haven't seen in a long time. He looks sad.

"What?" I say in a tone that asks for forgiveness for raising my voice.

"Darnell died." It takes me a moment to recall who this person is who has caused this sadness in my brother's eyes. And I remember Lorna. I remember San Francisco. I remember one of his lives he showed me. One of his families. "The funeral is on Saturday."

"Oh my god," I say, and put my hand on his shoulder. "Are you okay? How is Lorna?"

"I'm all right," he says. He is shaking his head. "It's fucked up." He shakes off the water beginning to form in his eyes.

"How did it happen?" But I already know the answer. It has begun to happen to us. The boys we know are beginning to die. Boys at school, boys in the paper, boys on the news. With frequency.

"He got shot." I put my head down. We put our heads down together and stand in silence for a moment. "You want to go to the funeral with me?" Yes. Yes. I nod my head.

On Saturday I dress for the first funeral I can remember. I was a little girl when my aunt died and I have no memory of it. Someone else dressed me; my emotions were too undeveloped for it to matter to me. This one matters. How do I dress? I opt for a lime-green dress with a delicate floral print and my platform boots. I am showing my arms, my legs; I feel exposed, but pretty, powerful. I walk downstairs to meet Junior so we can go to the funeral. Dad meets me at the bottom of the stairs. He and Mom are uneasy about us attending this funeral, about us spending time in San Francisco. He blocks me at the bottom of the stairs. His eyes become large and then turn into a squint. I can see he is turning angry. I can't imagine why. We are going to mourn our cousin's boyfriend. To him, we are going to mourn a thug, honor it, make an outing of it. "Where are you going dressed like that?" he spits. I see Junior out of the corner of my eye. He is looking at us from the living room at the other end of the long hallway.

"You know where we're going." I have begun to talk back. And I begin to push past him.

"Get back here," he calls after me. "You look like a goddamn whore!" I stop. I am unable to move, physically weighed down by what he's just said. An ugliness and a shame come over me, preventing me from moving.

"Man," Junior cuts in. I hear him but I can't look at him because I can't yet move. "Why you gotta be like that?" All my bodily energy is now focused on not crying. I finally turn around and face Dad.

"Fuck you," I say, making sure to look him directly in his eyes. "I hate you!" I think I scream this but it feels more like a howl, or like a bark or a growl coming out of my body. I feel like what he thinks I am: I am on display. I am an animal. *Look at me. Look how ugly I can be.* And I follow Junior out to the navy-blue Maverick he has finally bought and stare straight ahead into the street as we drive, my arms folded in front of me, trying to hide my ugliness. I have to save my tears for the dead one we are going to mourn. Junior respects my silence and just drives, only occasionally glancing at me. We start over the Bay Bridge and finally I begin to relax, the expansiveness of the sea moving beneath us, allowing me some space away from home, to exhale.

"You look nice," Junior says as we fly over the bridge, the old car engine roaring as we pick up speed. I look out onto the blue-green water, the perfect light. Even with the clouds as heavy as they are above it—their darkness is the reason for the magnificent color of the water. I don't say thank you to Junior. I just nod my head in acknowledgment. I am grateful for him. We drive the rest of the way in the silence of his sadness and mine.

We get lost on the way, and we're late for the funeral by the time we find parking. We see the last bit of the service—a sea of black people wearing black. It reminds me of church, but everyone is crying. I am struck by how young everyone is. Swarms of mourning black children. Junior and I join them and look for our cousins. We reach them just in time to squeeze them before they are scooped into the back of a limousine that will take them to the cemetery. Outside the funeral home where the crowd has begun to disperse, we walk back to our car a few blocks away. On the way I spot more than one tree or street sign with teddy bears, candles, and photos collected around it in remembrance of black boys we don't know who died in the streets we walk on. I pray for them in the only way I know how as we pass their unofficial graves, offering them some form of *I love you, I'm sorry, may you find peace*. They are no different than Darnell, who we are about to bury.

We follow the procession up and around hills, briefly onto the freeway, and finally to the gloomy cemetery. It's cold, and I wish I'd brought a jacket or a sweater. I don't know where we've driven, if we're even in San Francisco anymore; the land is flat and green, the sky dense with fog. I walk toward our cousins with my arms folded over as much of my body as possible. I want to keep myself warm and also to hide my certain ugliness. I feel out of place in my green dress but I march on, next to Junior, to pay my respects. We find a place to stand next to Lina, who stands next to Lorna, and we follow everyone's eyes to the freshly dug hole in the ground that Darnell will be lowered into. His casket looks as if it's hovering above the hole, as if in death he can levitate, like he is an angel. The people closest to him throw their roses on top of him before he is lowered down. As his casket is lowered into the ground, I say some version of the prayer I wished for the boys on the street to Darnell—*I love you, I'm sorry*. Next to me Lina collapses, cries out, is uncontrollable, while Lorna stands and cries silently. I have never seen this kind of spectacle, this outpouring of emotion, so loud. This man was loved. I look around me at all the crying people and the people next to them and behind them and all the people who must carry this, who must walk out of this cemetery holding this, and walk back into their lives with it. And suddenly I am swollen with emotion, beyond sad. I look at my brother, who is looking at the ground with tentative tears. All this sadness.

EIGHT

Dad's eyes have begun to take on a sunken look. He works during the day with plants and trees and soil and roots. His hands look like sandpaper. He does another kind of work at night: worrying about Junior. He cannot sleep when Junior is out on the street, while Mom is out in Hunter's Point, San Francisco, sitting on a stool in front of a conveyor belt, sorting badly addressed mail, and also thinking of her son. He tries to sleep on the couch, waiting up for him, but often he doesn't come at all. When Dad does sleep it is fitful, jumping up at every sound, looking out the window, out the door to see if maybe it is the sound of his son. But it is often just the wind knocking over a tool or a plant. Sometimes it is someone lurking, trying to steal one of his loose tools, and he jumps out of bed to scare them away. It is rarely Junior.

Sometimes he gets in the truck, starts it up, and drives to Thirty-Seventh Street on the border of North and West Oakland, where he thinks Junior is. He is unafraid of *the street*, unafraid of the fact that he is the only white man and out of place as they come, driving his brown pickup truck around the hood asking people out on the corners if they've seen his son. I have seen him do it, wanting desperately to hide myself, to disassociate from him. Around Thirty-Seventh and Apgar; 3700 is the number Junior claims. It is one of his homes, one of his families. That's where Dad goes to look for him. "Have you seen my son?" he asks anyone young and black. He describes him: "He's about my height, has a ponytail." He talks about how he used to ride a pink bike, but now drives a blue Maverick. They know who he is. On a good night someone friendly will say, "Ah yeah, White Boy Chris," and Dad will become bewildered by the nickname, but he will agree. "Yes, then, White Boy Chris. That sounds right." But no one says a word. No one is a snitch. On a bad night, he'll be met by the aggressive stares of young men who communicate with a cold blank gaze, who are not snitches and not friendly. But Dad doesn't quite understand that language, or doesn't care, so he continues to wander around until finally he comes home, defeated, setting himself up to sleep on the couch at the front window so he can always watch for him, so he can be the one to open the door when Junior arrives, to lock it when he is safely inside.

One night Junior escorts me to and from a late-night hair session with Danielle. The part of West Oakland we go to feels like an island, detached from the rest of the city and deserted except for one Yemeni liquor and convenience store and train tracks that lead to a lot of empty warehouses. He drops me off at her house and immediately leaves, not wanting to come up. He tells us to handle our business, and he speeds off down the street, screeching around the corner before Danielle and I are even inside.

We walk up the steps of the small blue house, and across the street from it seems to be the freeway; I can hear the zooming wind beyond the barrier. I am nervous to enter her home. Her mother, who is wearing a nightgown, sizes me up before finally deciding to greet me politely. Her brother is walking with urgency toward the door as we enter, and I'm comforted by the fact that I'd seen him once before in the hallways of our high school. "Oh, hey!" I say, and wave. He nods at me and says, "Oh yeah, hey," remembering my face with a smile. He asks if I'm liking school.

"Not really," I answer honestly. We talk in the doorway while his mother watches our encounter from her post on the couch. He is derailed by the way I've answered his question and so our chat ends abruptly. He is not interested in knowing why not and so we agree to see each other around school.

Danielle takes me to her room all the way in the back of the house. I inspect it with great interest, and when I get to the wall with taped-up photos, I am surprised to see Junior's face among the other faces of people she loves, mostly small, smiling children. More evidence of his other life. Yet again he is inviting me to see it. The photo is of them at what looks like a school prom. She is wearing a long black gown with a sheer side panel. Junior is wearing a tux with a turquoise bow tie, a pink corsage, hair tied back in a ponytail, with a serious look on his face, his jaw clenched. Danielle smiles next to him. A banner at the bottom reads "A Night to Remember." All dressed up and proper, he looks like a person I've never seen before, yet he looks uncomfortable, his discomfort and possibly his rage threatening to come undone beneath the fancy costume. It looks even more uncomfortable than the one he wears every day: tough, mean, strong. How do you look tough when you have a pink flower pinned to your breast, a pretty woman by your side? You look at the cameraman like you will kill him. You make yourself look like a killer. You become a killer.

"Wow," I say. Danielle sits on the bed as I look around. I can tell she is observing me observing her; I can feel her eyes on my back. "You look gorgeous," I say.

"Thank you," she says from behind me.

"But what was Junior so mad about? Jeez." She comes over to look at the photo with me.

"That's your brother," she says with surrender in her voice, shrugging her shoulders as if I know the answer, as if we all know the answer to that question, as if I have met, and know intimately, my brother, the killer. And the truth is I have. I remember the time he slapped me when I was twelve. I felt so betrayed. It was the early days of his transformation, when he had just begun to have an identity out of the house and it was clear he was doing dangerous things *out there*, and doing dangerous things to his body, drinking brandy and smoking weed as if they were together keeping him alive. He hardened before all of our eyes, but I thought he'd always show me his soft self. I thought I would always be shown a way in. He was heading out the door, to "go out." Something came over me and I jumped on him. I threw myself into him. "Don't go out," I shouted. *Out* is such an unspeakable place. "Just don't go," I demanded.

"Just don't." Wasn't it that easy? I wiggled in front of him, and blocked the doorway with my body, spreading my arms out. "You're not leaving."

"Move." I did not move. "Move," he said again. I would not move. He waited. I watched his face turn as he waited, growing angrier, into someone unrecognizable. "I'm not gonna ask you again." And he waited a moment longer before slapping my face with the front of his red-hot hand. I could smell the liquor on him as he walked past, not looking back and not apologizing. How I wanted to forget that. How I wanted to blame his behavior on the gallon of brandy beside his bed. But Danielle's response reminds me: "That's your brother." I hate it. And so I shrug off her comment and convince myself I do not know that brother. I look for him. Just like Dad. Now it is me in West Oakland: Have you seen my brother? I ask this to the angry, unrecognizable man in the photo. Where are you?

I love the way Danielle's fingers feel on my scalp. It's as though I haven't felt closeness before now. I want to close my eyes and let my head dangle; I'd like to fall asleep like this. But I stay awake to keep her company. She takes tiny sections of hair in her fingers at a time and clamps a flat iron over each one many times until it is straight. The slight pull of my scalp as she does this is so wonderful that I lose track of time.

The pager that Junior got for me has been buzzing on my jeans. It's Dad repeatedly paging me 9-1-1, abusing this privilege. His version of an emergency is asking if Mom has a lunch or if the laundry's been picked up. Really, he just wants to know where I am. I know it's not truly an emergency, so I don't call back. I don't tell him where I am; I don't want him to know. I want to feel free—and I *do* in this unknown house with this unknown person in this unknown part of town with a brand-new hairstyle. I can't let Dad take this from me with his worry. I can't be reminded of home during this experience, so I continue to ignore Dad's pages. I want freedom so badly.

I touch my straight hair in complete shock. I have never had this style before. We had decided on it because of time. Danielle said braids would take longer. "How does it look?" I ask eagerly as she finishes the last bit.

"You look so pretty," she assures me. When she announces she is finished, she takes me to the mirror on the other side of the room and together we look. I am looking at myself, at my hair, and at both of us. At just five foot four, I am taller than her, but there is room enough for both of us in the mirror. I look at our hair together, her long braids hanging next to my newly straightened strands, and then I look into her face and she smiles. We both look through the mirror again. I am looking at myself, trying to get to know the person I see.

"I look different," I say finally.

"Do you like it?" She strokes my hair and tosses it playfully, trying to help me adjust to it. I tell her I do, but I don't know if it's true. This, like Junior's face in the photo, is a costume. I am deciding what kind of character to become, what texture to make my shield.

It is a long time before Junior returns. Danielle and I fall asleep awkwardly on her twin bed. Her mother comes in twice to see if I've gone yet. Finally Junior comes back and we drive home. In the late night the neighborhood feels not only isolated but sordid. The people out at this hour, in this neighborhood, are on drugs or looking for them. I can see Junior making eyes with people, and witness his familiarity with the streets as we drive up and around and turn, Junior madly shoving the gearshift around, crossing Broadway and going up a hill toward our side of town.

When we enter the house, Dad jumps up from the couch, where he's been trying to sleep. "Your mom was worried," he says, even though it is invariably him that was worried. Mom is not home; she's at work, scratching out bad zip codes over a conveyor belt. When Dad feels emotions, as if possessed with her, he expresses them through her: "Your mom wants to talk to you" (*I* want to talk to you); "Tell your mom what you did this weekend" (tell *me*); "Your mom was worried" (*I* was worried).

Danielle had asked me about all the pages I was getting back at her house. She wondered if my parents were worried about me, if I thought I should call home, or if I had a boyfriend. I laughed, not because it was funny, but because I didn't know how to say that my dad is the kind of man who follows me instead of asking me where I'm going. He is the kind of man to listen in on the line instead of asking who I'm talking to. He is someone who turns off the water for the whole house because he thinks I'm taking too long in the shower and not respecting his siphon system that takes bathwater and feeds it to the plants. He is the kind of man who is more in touch with the weather and the needs of plants than those of his children. *The dirt is so dry. How badly we need rain.* The kind of man who is happiest when it rains because then the plants thrive. A man who knows the names for every flower and what kind of environment will make each bloom. So I ignore his pages and show up past midnight because I feel somewhere in my heart that, though he'd named me (after the medicinal flower known as lemon balm, *Melissa officinalis*), though he'd named all of us, I was still not blooming, none of us was blooming—and for that, deserving or not, I punished him. This is what some people call rebellious. I don't want to be bothered with the burden of being a daughter; for a moment I just want to be myself. This was too much to express to Danielle in the moment, so I just laughed instead. "Everything's fine."

I feel like a criminal when I slide into the house with Junior. A true accomplice. I have two offenses against me: not calling home and straightening my hair. Mom will make me pay for the second in the morning. "What's up?" Dad asks coolly, after neither of us answers his first comment.

"Nothing," I respond, trying to breeze by without notice. But he isn't done.

"Where been?" He drops the *have* and the *you*, hoping to speak the language of his black teenagers.

"Nowhere," I say mysteriously and unfairly. "Just out."

"Out with your brother?" He walks over to the foyer and flips on the lights, looks at us and tries to imagine what we could have been doing together. Then he sees my hair.

"Oh!" he shouts. "Out of sight! You look like a movie star."

"Thanks," I say, feeling the need to look at him or let him look at me before I try and disappear again. I can feel him relaxing into knowing his children are home, into the possibility that we were doing something wholesome. He rustles and locks the front door and turns off the foyer light, then follows me into the kitchen where we will separate: I will go upstairs, and he will turn left and find his bedroom. Junior has already found his way to his bedroom and closed the door.

"Your mom was worried about you," he says again in the dark.

"I know," I say before heading up to my room. I pause at the edge of the stairs. "I just needed some privacy." This is my way of apologizing for both me and Junior. *I'm sorry I ignored you. We're not bad, we're just angry. I'm sorry.*

"Well, I'm glad you're back." He stands in those words for a few seconds and then heads to bed. His flowers are home. He can rest now.

The house is much quieter without Vivian. She received her associate's degree at the local community college and then went off to Smith College. Massachusetts may as well be outer space. I send long letters to outer space with photos and stickers and collages, and ask if I can come visit, tell her how much I miss her. Cornelius is still in his apartment, working and trying to finish college at UC Berkeley. Claire, too, is working and finishing her studies at San Francisco State. It is just Junior, Angelica, and I left in this castle of junk. Angelica is still young—six now. Junior is gone so much of the time it feels like I am here in this big house alone, except for Mom and Dad, who are exhausted and constantly worried about Junior's whereabouts. Between caring for Angelica and worrying about Junior, they haven't yet noticed that I've stopped going to school for the most part. I try and stay out for as long as possible, usually at friends' houses. But I'm sure to be home around 4:30 p.m. on days when I've cut, to answer the automated call from my school: "Your son or daughter at Oakland Technical has missed one or more periods today." Though that call could be for either me or Junior: we're both failing, he is just failing louder. Still I make an effort to answer those calls so they won't end up on the answering machine for Mom and Dad to hear.

Walking toward or through the house feels like quicksand, and my room is the only place in this structure where I can shake it off. When I'm home I stay there with the door locked, writing poetry or sitting on the roof outside my window where I can smoke cigarettes in secret. The only person who knows how to get in is Junior. Across the hall, Vivian's bedroom is still full of her things, and the upstairs has a feeling of being haunted. I always think I hear something or someone, but there is nothing and no one else there.

I stay out later and later, not doing anything bad, really—just having dinner with friends, sitting around talking, or listening to music—but still I don't tell anyone where I am. I seem reasonable—another costume—so my friends' parents assume I have permission to stay for dinner or to sleep over. On school nights, I either walk home alone or a friend walks me halfway. One night my friend Vanessa walks me home, and as we approach Broadway, we see a man crouched, walking sideways, expertly and speedily below the windows in the side yard of someone's house holding a gun, on his way to break in. He's an older guy I've seen around campus before, maybe about twenty-one. He makes eye contact with us, seeing that he's been seen. Vanessa and I hold hands and look at each other. "Run!" I whisper-yell loud enough so she hears the urgency, but quiet enough so he doesn't hear me. I run home and she runs the opposite way to her house. I call her when I get home to make sure she's made it.

The next night I fall asleep with my clothes on and sleep fitfully, my newly straight hair splayed over my pillow like silk threads. I dream there is a man knocking on the other side of the small window I sleep beneath. The man's face is so clear in the window. His mouth is moving, but I can't hear what he's saying. I can tell it is urgent though. I startle out of this wake-dream state and see that there really is a man there. I wasn't dreaming at all. The man is Junior. I snap awake, shake my head at him through the glass, and raise my hands up in confusion: *What? I can't hear you.* He shakes his head back at me, looking exasperated, and makes a circular motion with his wrist. He wants me to crank open my big window on the other side of the room. Why is he on the roof? How long has he been there? I stumble out of bed and move toward the window to let him in, not knowing what I will find when I do. I push a button on my pager near my bed to see the time. It is past two o'clock in the morning.

I yank the blinds up and wind open the window. I can see him coming around the side to get in. He has to move carefully around the window I've just opened so he doesn't fall off the roof. I hold my breath and watch as he throws one leg over the window toward me, his hand quickly following and slapping the windowsill for support. He makes it without falling. I can breathe again.

"What the hell are you doing?" Junior takes a giant step over the windowsill and into my bedroom. He's wearing baggy jeans and a windbreaker jacket. I step back from him and the cool air he brings in. "What the fuck," I say.

He brings his finger to his gnarled mouth, showing teeth. "Shh!" He shushes me aggressively. "Be quiet," he says. I switch to a whisper. "You scared the shit out of me."

"Sorry," he says. "I need your help."

I start to shake my head. I don't want to be involved in whatever it is, but I know I will say yes. What could he possibly need my help with that he couldn't just come through the front door like a normal person? But I know the answer. Mom and Dad told him that if he was going to use the house as a hotel, then he could stay out wherever he was and not come back. They told him he couldn't come and go as he pleased, worrying them to death. So lately he just goes out and doesn't return. They are still worried to death. I size him up, wondering where he's been and if he's showered, eaten. He looks all right, his hair a bit frizzy around the edges. He looks like he's just woken up. I wait for his announcement. What help does he need from me at two in the morning?

I look away briefly to click on my bedside lamp so we can see each other better. When I turn my head back he is drawing a gun from inside his pants. I step back, sit on my bed, and cover my mouth so I won't gasp. "What is that? What are you doing with that? Get that away from me."

His face remains neutral. He doesn't answer my questions. He looks at me with no expression except for his chronically clenched jaw. Then he hands me the gun, the barrel facing him. "I need you to hold it for me," he says.

In the dim room on my floral-covered twin bed, I take the gun into my hand and inspect it. It's warm. It's heavier than I think and I nearly drop it on the floor, making my heart jump with the fear of it accidentally going off and hurting one of us. This is ultimate danger in my hand, and ultimate protection. The thing looks almighty in my small hand, and I think maybe I can understand the appeal of such power, but then I return to the moment, look at my brother who has just handed me the first gun I've ever held. Surely this is not his. With masks and anger and toughness and now with guns, he believes he is protecting himself. I am filled with sorrow. For him, and for all those involved, on every side of every gun.

"Is someone chasing you?" I ask. He is quiet. "The police?" I ask again. "Someone else?" He takes a breath. For some reason he cannot tell me the truth, does not want me to know all of it. Another kind of protection. And perhaps I don't really want to know it all either. Perhaps I prefer to see truth in these small glimpses of my brother that allow him to be just my brother and not all of his other names: criminal, thug, monster, animal.

"I just need you to hold it," he pleads, avoiding my questions, and begins looking around the room for a place to put it. He begins opening my dresser drawers.

"Junior." I believe the sound of my voice is the same as begging him to stop. "This is a gun." I state the absolute obvious, but what I hope he hears is my plea: *You better not use this. You better not have used this. This is not you.* But he continues rummaging in a drawer he's decided is the right one. It seems he's in a hurry.

"Here," he says. "Put it here." He ignores my words and takes the gun from me. He places it at the bottom of the drawer where he's pushed aside my clothing to make room. He covers it up carefully with a heap of shirts and closes it.

"Junior, what's going on?" This feels different from buying shoes with drug money, different from accepting gifts of stolen goods from stolen cars. I've gone too far. I am complicit. This gun is as much mine as it is his. I feel that I, too, am killing and have killed. I am just as much a criminal for saying yes. *Yes.* I agree, once more, to look the other way, because, once again, I choose to have a big brother. I know what lies on the other side of no. *No* means not having a brother, not being invited in.

He looks at me. "I gotta go." Where is he going? Why must I have this gun? I have so many questions and he gives me nothing. "Thanks," he offers.

"Why don't you just sleep here?" I don't want him going back out into the night. Perhaps just the right question, just the right suggestion, will make him stay. "Where are you going now?"

"Out," he says. Outside is a dangerous place, like the street, the place that pulls him, the place I don't want to see. "Don't worry about me."

"Be careful," I say. It is the kind of thing you say to someone who is about to board a plane or drive a long distance at night, but Junior is going to step out onto our roof, scale down the giant cedar tree that grows up past the dining room, past my bedroom, into the sky; he will climb over

Dad's tools and planters, and dogs will bark in the distance. He might come across a hissing raccoon or an opossum. Once he makes it to the edge of our backyard, he will climb Dad's compost mound that leads right to a high wall. He'll jump the seven or so feet to the ground and land on cement with both feet, making a loud thud. When he balances himself, he'll take off running through other backyards. The police will be on the perimeter of the block; he is on the inside of the block, moving as if the block were his own body and he is blood, following along the veins of it, to the organs, the heart, someplace he will be safe. *Stay here. Stay*, I want to say. But with all the tricks he knows for getting in, he knows just as many for getting out.

"I'll be all right." He steps out of the window and back onto the roof. I believe him. In him I see someone above the law. Though he's nearly eighteen now, I still see a child; I see my brother. He clutches the window for support and walks sideways along the roof until he must use the stucco for support, until he makes it to the cedar tree. I see his hand let go of the edge of my window. He's gone. He disappears into the darkness. I stare off into the trees and listen before closing the window. He is so quiet. He is so good at hiding. He makes himself invisible. I shut the window only when I hear leaves rustling below and I know he's made it to the ground. Now he is *out there*.

I see him in bursts, but mostly I just hear about him in whispers in the hallway when I'm at school. "That's Chris's sister," they say, and the words echo through me. I should feel protected by the fear/respect he incites in people, but I just feel numb. I can't yet know that what I feel is abandonment. He's left me for the street, my other siblings have left me for college, but I don't yet know that this is one of the reasons for my dwindling motivation to do anything. And so I am in this school, this prison with guards at every entry and exit, failing slowly and quietly. No one expects to see the Fs and Ds on my report card. But once the teachers deliver my grades, they stop looking at me as a quiet, harmless girl with potential, and start looking at me as just another delinquent. It feels like we are hated. I am a young monster in training. I come from nothing and will carry on my legacy and grow up to become nothing. I'm sitting in the back of my English class, where we are discussing an Octavia E. Butler novel, *Parable of the Sower*. I devoured the novel and let it wholly satisfy some unnameable sense of longing and doom inside of me. I am listening to my classmates talk as they raise their hands one by one to make observations I think are simple-minded, but I am too afraid to raise my own and be heard. I watch them from the back. I have the perfect view when Junior bursts through the classroom door.

He sees me immediately and nods. I nod back. I enjoy witnessing my classmates react to his presence. I watch as they look around and at one another, trying to figure out who the tall upperclassman is, the one they have heard whispered about in the hallways. "Melissa," the teacher calls me. "You have a visitor." She motions for me to come to the front of the class so he and I can go out to the hall and talk.

I feel all eyes on me as I walk for what feel like minutes to the front of the classroom. It is uncomfortable to be looked upon, but I feel a sense of pride, some sort of power in this being shown up for, in someone checking in on me. I walk with my head high, believing I matter, believing I am important, as though I am walking on some fantasy red carpet, and not to meet my delinquent brother who has a greasy bag of fast food for me. I fully allow myself to feel like royalty beside him, allow myself to feel good that he cares for me enough to find me and bring me nourishment. Let them see thugs if that's all they can see. I am royalty.

I am wearing my favorite platform boots with bell-bottom jeans and a windbreaker, my hair slicked back in a tight ponytail with my baby hairs framing my face. We are dressed almost identically save for my shoes; even our hairstyles match. He looks clean, his hair is wet, and I wonder, as I do regularly, where he's been. He hands me the greasy bag. "I brought you lunch." I thank him and ask if he's eaten.

"Nah," he says. "Don't worry about me. Get back to class."

"Man," I say, beaming. "Thank you."

"And do good," he says, and walks off. "I gotta go." He nods a farewell from down the hall and I slip back into the class and back down my red carpet.

A few weeks later, Junior asks me to meet him on the corner of Broadway and Pleasant Valley so we can have lunch together. He does not attend school anymore and I feel, in a way, envious of that. We walk to what we believe is the nice fast food restaurant up the street, Wendy's, which is just a few blocks from our school. School is out for lunch break and so there are patches of kids all over the streets—boys wearing baggy jeans and puff coats, waddling like little penguins to keep their pants from falling to their knees; girls in tight jeans and too-snug shirts, holding books tight to their chests, trying to disappear and be seen at the same time. I am somewhere in the middle, toying with the idea of having a body, of being a woman, of wearing clothes that women wear.

Junior is standing on the corner waiting for me. I wave and he nods, then flashes a new smile, gold teeth, sparkling in the sun. "You like 'em?"

"Oh shit," I say, "let me see." I walk up to his face and inspect his mouth, the top row now gilded. "Those are tight."

"What's up?" he says, sizing me up, holding his eyes at my feet. "Where are the shoes I got you?"

"I can't wear them every day."

"Those look like straight-up roach stompers," he chuckles, covering his mouth with a loose fist. "How's school?"

"Eh." I answer with a shrug. "Bullshit. You know."

"I'm tellin' you," he says. "Don't be like me. Please." He says the words slowly. "Do not be like me." I have heard this speech many times and so I roll my eyes.

I bring my fist to my mouth to cover a fake cough. "Hypocrite," I cough out.

"Whatever, man. I'm trying to help you out. I ain't even graduating. You think I want that shit?"

"Seems like it to me."

"Get the fuck on, man."

"I'm starving," I say, changing the subject.

"Man, it's hot," he says, and begins taking off his jacket.

He asks me to hold it while he adjusts his pants, which have fallen down too low. While he shimmies next to me, waiting at the red light, I take the jacket in my hand and almost drop it. Its unexpected weight surprises me, and instantly I remember the night in my bedroom, the gun hidden in my dresser. I carefully feel the outline of the object under the nylon of his jacket and I look at him.

Why, Junior? What is this for? Why do you have this? There are a thousand ways to ask the same question, to make the same plea: Stop! Stop before you are killed. But I just shake my head and look for the right way to say what I am feeling. The light has turned green, and so we walk across the thoroughfare with what feels like a thousand cars and eyes and witnesses looking right at us because we are a spectacle. Aren't we? We are two young and fearless thugs on a red carpet, stopping traffic in all directions. I walk carefully, slowly, trying not to agitate any part of the heavy metal object I hold. We walk in silence, and when we reach the other side of the street, the cars start zooming past us as if we were never there. I stand for a moment on the corner, gun in hand through Junior's jacket pocket, cars swirling around us like we are the nucleus of a tornado, heavy with the knowing that we stand before so many, being looked at yet truly *seen* by none.

We walk again, just one more block to Wendy's. I am not hungry anymore. My stomach has turned on itself. "Take this." I push the jacket, the gun, at him to show him I reject this protection and I try to walk ahead. We enter the restaurant and wait in line to order items from the ninety-nine-cent menu. Students are all around us counting their change to make a dollar so they can buy french fries or a sandwich. We are silent among the chipper gossip and small talk; neither of us cares about them or their conversation.

In my silence, I slowly begin to forgive him; my protesting self leaves, and I slowly return to stand next to my brother again. I look at the menu. I have no money. What a luxury to be able to choose more than one item, to be told I can have whatever I want because Junior will pay. I let my big brother take me to lunch and I order three whole things and he orders three whole things, and we find a corner to occupy and sit there together, me and him and our gun, protected. We don't know anyone here. And no one knows we have a gun. No one can even see us.

THE DAYS BLEED into one another. I am in the tenth grade now. I am almost sixteen. What day is it? When you stop going to classes it is much easier to lose track. I am walking home from a friend's house, dragging my feet, not ready or wanting to go home yet. Junior is living back home in spurts; Mom and Dad can't stick to their rule so he is back as he pleases; they take what they can get of him. I'm not sure what I'll find at home, mostly I'm unsure of what state I will find Junior in. I cross Broadway where it divides two North Oakland neighborhoods, Mosswood and Piedmont. It is dusk and I am alone, but there is an added sense of danger I am detecting. I look over both my shoulders. Nothing. A few seconds later I look again and see a man on a bike. He smiles at me and I know better than to respond. I keep walking, peering over my shoulder every once in a while to see if he's still there and he is, waving and now a little closer. I look long enough to make sure I don't know him. I don't. When I cross Broadway and close in on our neighborhood and he is still behind me, close and trying to engage with me now, my concern turns to fear and I address him. "Are you following me?" He looks happy that I am finally addressing him, his smile becomes large and stupid, revealing his very bad teeth. He speeds up close to me, now walking his bike.

"Hola," he says. He adds more words in Spanish that I can't understand.

"I don't speak Spanish—no hablo español," I say. I am sure not to smile so he doesn't misread me. "And you need to stop following me." He continues to grin and I continue to speed up, trying to create a safer distance between us. I look around and there are far too many bushes, no other people, the sun is going down. It registers. I am afraid. I feel threatened. "If you follow me home my brother will kick your ass," I offer as a final threat. But he just laughs and keeps speaking to me in Spanish, and now he's begun to use his hands as he speaks, seeming to express some urgency. I mean what I've promised the man, but it is clear he doesn't understand. For all I know he could be asking me for directions, but I don't think so. I walk as fast as I can without running so as to look unafraid of this small man, but I am. Just two more blocks and I'll be home.

As I am about to cross a quiet residential street close to ours, a blue Maverick turns the corner. It's Junior. This is the way home. He's on his way home. Thank god. He must sense my fear because he leaves the car running at the stop sign. Leaves the door open. He walks in a way I've never seen, with an incredible limp as if one of his feet is injured; this is how you walk when you are tough. His fists are in red balls and his face is in a shape I have never seen. It reminds me of the face he had when he was a boy and was being punished for misbehaving—fuming and scowling at the same time. But this is the rage of a man I have never seen. There is no pause between question and action. No waiting for answers. Does he know I'm afraid?

"Who the fuck is that?" he asks, but doesn't look at me and doesn't wait for my answer.

"I don't know who he is. I think he was following me. I don't know . . ." My voice trails off. He isn't listening to me. I am not sure he even sees me anymore. He has not taken his eyes off the man. I am afraid for another reason now. What will happen next? And what happens next happens so quickly I cannot process it. Junior is now before the man, towering over him. He punches him once in the jaw. The man falls to the ground holding the place where he's been hit. He gets back up and backs away and puts his hands up to gesture surrender. Junior hits him again and he falls down. Junior kicks him now. I don't know if what's happening is right or wrong, if it's too much or just enough. I don't know if I'm being protected or if someone else is being abused. Just as fast as he's acted on the situation, he's finished.

"Come on," he says. Now he is looking at me. There he is. There's my brother. "Get in the car."

I do as he says. I get in and we are silent for the two-block ride home. There is a sense that I must let him come back before I address what's just happened. Even with this big show of strength, I feel so vulnerable and still afraid. It's not just me. The car is full of both of our fear—afraid of each other and ourselves, afraid of *out there*, afraid of what can happen to our bodies. Afraid of no one and everyone. Knowing deeply the fear is legitimate: it isn't safe. We both know that. I look at his profile. His long dad-nose, his thin lips, his greasy skin, his hands fiercely gripping the wheel like someone is after him—but we are just going home, we are just in Piedmont. The man next to me gripping the steering wheel is the one who once slapped me. And now I've seen him do it to someone else. I look at him and I know that I am not the only person who has met this man. I think of Danielle. She knows this man. And the separation I have made in my mind, the different men inside my brother I believe to be there—the boy—begin to dissolve before my eyes. They are all mixed together now. One allows the other.

I fix my eyes on something else, release my own hands that have been in fists. The tree-lined street we drive along is quaint. Dusk is my favorite time of day. The time of day you can look into people's homes and see them living their lives with beautiful soft light and pillows and throw blankets and lamps and studies and family dinners. The fear in this car is incongruent to the street we drive along—our street, our trees, our home, our safety. Inside this car we are terrified and uncomfortable. Perhaps I have just been saved from a dangerous situation. Perhaps I have just been offered one more life. Who will save *him*? Who will offer him one more life?

Walking through the threshold to my family home gets harder and harder. The outside and the inside of my life grow more and more distant from one another. I have begun to stand taller. I have begun to wear my fear as apathy. Junior is home less and less, and I am lonelier than I know how to recognize. Dad has punished me for staying out late by tossing the contents of my drawers onto the neighbor's roof. Thank god the gun wasn't there when he did it. Across the window are all my clothes mixed with overgrown ivy, thrown up there just like trash. When I enter the house I am thankful to hear C-Bo playing from Junior's room. I'm surprised he's home, and I go straight to his room and knock. I wonder what new arrangement he has with Mom and Dad. Miraculously, Mom is sleeping over the bass pounding right next to her bedroom. He turns the music down. "What?"

"It's me." I hear some things shuffling around and he finally opens the door for me. Dad has taken the lock off his door so he can't hide whatever it is he's doing when he's in there, but he has figured out a way to keep the door closed. I can see his finger fiddling with a metal clasp and the door opens. He seems to be in good spirits. I take a seat on his bed and he closes the door behind me, turns the music back on.

"Mom's sleeping, turn it down," I say. "Gosh." He turns it down a bit. I don't like C-Bo. He loves him. Whenever he's home he's on repeat.

"Thank god you're home," I say.

"Why? What's up?" Junior gives me his attention, smiling. He smiles more since he's gotten gold teeth.

"I'm going crazy living here." I put my head in my hands and start to rub my eyes, take a deep breath and compose myself. "I'm all alone here. It's just me and Angelica. You're never home. Daddy threw all my clothes on Mr. Cramer's roof."

Junior starts to laugh. "What the fuck?"

"Don't laugh. I'm so fucking pissed. I can't even go up there. It makes me so mad. And I have nothing to wear!" He continues to laugh, in his special gap-toothed way, wind vibrating through his teeth. He holds his belly. "Are you done?" I ask.

"That's hella funny. I'm sorry. Stay in here and keep me company."

I relax onto the bed, letting myself plop back and listen to the music.

"This dude is fake," I say. Junior shoots me a look.

"What are you talking about?" He dismisses me and gets on his knees to get something from under his bed.

"You really think this guy has murdered all these people? That's all he talks about. It's so boring. He probably hasn't killed anyone. And what the fuck does 187 even mean?"

"It's police code for homicide," he says.

"How do you know that?" He shrugs, focused on his activity. He brings out one of our dinner plates, which is covered in crack. Then he pulls out sheets of plastic and puts tiny portions of crack into them, twisting them into microbaggies that look like the firecrackers kids throw into the street and pop like fireworks.

"Wanna help me?"

"No!" I shout. "I wish you wouldn't do that. What do you think is gonna happen to you?"

"Nothing's gonna happen to me."

"What if the police catch you?"

221

"They won't, first of all. They can't. All you gotta do is swallow it. And run."

"Swallow it?" I ask, horrified. "Junior," I admonish him. "Have you smoked crack? *Do* you smoke crack?" He starts to laugh at me.

"Man." He laughs. "Hell nah, I don't smoke crack."

"Well, don't swallow it. Ever." He laughs again. He's almost done making the tiny bags, and now the plate is empty with just a powdering of the drug left on the plate. I look at it as if it is diseased.

"What are you gonna do with that?" I ask, backing away from it. "Do something with it," I command. "Get rid of it." He finds my concern amusing and laughs again. He brings the plate up to his face, sticks his tongue out, and licks the plate clean. He got what he wanted, a reaction out of me.

"Junior!" I scream.

"Quiet!" he shouts back, and brings the plate down. "Don't trip."

"Don't trip? You just did crack!"

"Melissa." He looks sternly at me. "I'm fine." He smiles. He is so many things. He already has so many names. *Crack-head* and *drug addict* cannot be added to the list. I worry. I have never seen him bag up crack before. I didn't know for sure he sold crack, but now I know. He showed me crack, like he showed me a gun, like he showed me cash, like he showed me weed, and stolen cars, and gifts and lunches and dinners and clothing and funerals. He wants me to see. I want him to be my brother. I don't want him to have the other names. I don't want him to be of the other places. I want him to be of this house, of this street, with our names outside, of this home, of this family, not the others he's found, or the ones he still looks for. I act cool. Crack, no big deal. Weed, I'll smoke it with you. I am so damn cool. Gun, I'll hold it for you. I will bear witness to who you are in your masks, so I can be there when you return; I must be willing to see it all if I am to see you. What would happen to you if you didn't wear those other names? Who would you be? I sit on your bed, I open windows, doors, accept gifts, waiting for you to arrive, to return.

I am complicit again. Now it is crack I am okay with. That man you made dance. The other men. The time I paged you and you called back and I told you my bike had been stolen because you are my big brother and because I knew you'd know what to do. You found it instantly and I thought you were magic. But it was because you knew the crack addict who likely stole it. You knew where they waited to buy more crack. You saw the things they had: my bike, other people's bikes. Dots connect and *the street*, once again, that abstract and terrible place, becomes just that much more filled in and then I see your smile, the crack plate before us. I want so much for us to be brother and sister—not a thug and his sister, a drug dealer and his sister, a monster and his sister—so I sit with you on this bed and I say nothing and I believe you when you say they can't catch me, they won't catch me, I will be fine. C-Bo echoes around us, the violent and doom-filled lyrics, 187s and us, on a bed (a nice bed), in a house (a big house), on a street (a nice street), so far from *that* street (it makes no sense), the words envelop us as we are: boy and girl, sister and brother, son and daughter. In that space without labels when I can't hear the soundtrack, when I shut out the crack, the guns, the murders, the failing, the chaos—we just *are*. We are not good or bad, no walls nor shields have been built around us, and we have no names because here we are far too brilliant, far too bright for labels. In this space we are transcendent; here, we bear the names of all the flowers. In this space, we are free to bloom—to be big, fragrant, joyful, radiant. It is in this place where I wait for you. You are not a thug or a delinquent or a monster. I am not stupid, a whore, or a fuckup. This is the place I like to see us, the space I want to make for us.

"What are you about to do?" I ask.

Our eyes meet for a moment. "I'm about to go out," he says, almost apologetically. "Got to make this money."

I don't plead this time. I don't beg. I'm so tired. The crack brings a new level of exhaustion over me, a new level of numb. It is all I can do to lift myself from his bed, to leave this room, and to drag myself to my own. He grabs his towel hanging over his closet door and heads to the door and we walk upstairs together.

"Don't use all my conditioner," I say. He smiles at me.

"I'll get you some more." He winks.

From my room I can hear the shower running. When he's finished I smell the flowers from his hair. He showers and dresses like a man going off to work at an office. But it is night and his office is the street. He taps my closed bedroom door as a hello or a goodbye as he often does before he heads back downstairs to dress and go off to work.

"Bye!" I yell from behind the door.

Junior doesn't come home and doesn't come home and doesn't come home. Every time the phone rings there is terror in our hearts. We all know what happens to black boys on the street. We know what happens to black boys. This knowing is felt in the way we move around the house. In the way we move. In the way we sleep. In the way we breathe. In the way we speak. It is felt when I walk through the door of this house. It is felt the most when the phone rings. Mom is the only one brave enough to say it out loud. "I'm just waiting for the call," she says, and she says it often now. We all know what call she means.

The phone rings one day and there is news. Mom grabs her heart. "Junior is in jail." She exhales. "He's alive. He's alive. My boy is alive."

PART THREE
DISAPPEARANCE

Oakland, CA
1999–2016

NINE

Poof. He's gone.

You can live on a hill. You can live on the good side of town. You can live among white people. You can even have white relatives. You can leave. You can return. You can have opportunity. You can be loved. But you will still be vulnerable.

My brother is in prison, along with too many other black men. The street I didn't want to see is now illuminated. There is a funnel that begins at birth, it begins when you are first labeled *bad*, a degrading pipeline through school and all the way into a hopeless future. Junior has made it through to the end of the tunnel. He is in good company with his brothers, each with different stories of desire and hunger, all distorted and gone awry, each a human and a monster, fully grown now. He's become a monster now— eighteen years old, a man.

There is a new silence that rings through the house in his absence. It's piercing like a siren whose call you can still hear after it's long gone. We must catch our breath and ease it back to a normal rhythm, whatever normal is, and occupy the hours and minutes and seconds that were filled with worry and dread. Some sort of PTSD daze comes over us, especially Mom and Dad, who look ill. Which is worse, prison or the street? Knowing or not knowing? I go on with my days, entrenched in a new kind of denial. He'll be out soon, they'll reduce his sentence, when he's out he'll be reformed, he'll get a job and go to college. He is different from the rest—I believe somehow our love makes him different. But this is not what happens when you go to prison.

He said he couldn't be caught. He lied. He lost. This is the biggest loss yet. It can't be good in there, I think to myself, not wanting to believe the reality, whispering, "Do better, do better," to an empty house, his empty room. I am angry with him for not being invincible, for losing. All those secrets I kept. All the things I witnessed. I was a good accomplice, a good witness. I was a good sister. All of it was my investment in some future I imagined for us. Some future where we could be free and happy, where we could have what we wanted, where we could exist without protection, where the possibilities for who we could become would be endless. I try and hold on to my denial, this idea that he is different, the idea that maybe he'll change, but his being in prison is evidence against this vision. His being in prison is proof that we are losing this game. Hope is not enough. This hopelessness begins to creep into my very being.

This special sight his story has given me is a superpower I don't want. My special ability to see humans in monsters, my belief in monsters, my love for monsters, and now the certainty that aligning with monsters makes me on the losing side. It's mine now and all of ours—this knowing that there is a design for our destruction. I become this knowing. It is in my cells. My brother being in prison now lives in my cells. We couldn't keep him away from the street. We couldn't protect him. We are all losers. I try and push away the feeling of abandonment that threatens to show and keeps me from visiting him. We don't know how long it'll be. There was jail and now there are courts and prison and soon there will be a different prison, one much farther away from us where they will hold him until his hearing, where he'll finish out his sentence. California is full of prisons. He is just one out of millions.

A letter addressed to me has been slid under my bedroom door. In the return address corner is Junior's real name, Christopher Valentine, followed by a long number. His handwriting is of the precise, practiced sort that has never written much except from prison, as if his life depends on it. It is now the only way he can express himself. For many days I do not touch it. It lies on the floor in the heap of my teenage life: graded papers, torn-out sheets of glossy magazine pages, photos taken with friends, books, clothes.

He mostly writes to Mom and Dad, promising things that make them boast for a week, that he'll get his GED in prison, that he's reading one of the books Dad sent, that he plans to go to college when he gets out, before they go back to their ill state, the state you exist in when your child is in prison. But one day there is a letter with my name on it. I crank open my bedroom window and step out onto the roof. With a cigarette, a lighter, and the letter, I sit on the warm shingles and stare out over the neighborhood into a sea of rooftops and trees. I light up a Marlboro Red and look at the stick figure drawing he's included in the margin of the thin paper. A boy behind bars with the caption: *I want to come home*. Seeing it melts my angry facade. I'm angry because we lost. I'm angry because we failed. I'm overwhelmed by this. We couldn't keep him safe. I'm angry because I can't unknow what I now know about the world and what it does to my brothers. I'm angry because I'm a teenager. I'm angry because I'm alone and undirected. Who can I trust to show me what I can be? Who will show me how to be? I stew inside these questions; I'm intimate with them. I let them inside my body through cigarette and marijuana smoke, alcohol, razor blades, whatever destructive thing I can find. I ask cigarettes and weed and alcohol if they know the answers. And my anger is also simple: I miss my brother.

Dear Melissa,

What's happening with you? Do you like Tech? You better be going to all your classes and doing good in all of them. If I could have the chance to do everything over, I'd probably be in college right now, but instead I'm in San Quentin. Who knows where they'll end up moving me. Everybody used to say if I ever ended up in jail or prison, I'd end up being somebody's bitch. I'll be damned if that happens. Look at this shit, I know this should have been two or three paragraphs, but I don't know how to do that shit. I know you're not a boy and wouldn't do half the things I've done. But look at me and ask yourself, is this any kind of a life? It may look good on the outside, but I'll tell you. It feels like shit on the inside.

I look out above the trees, numb. This is my spot. On the roof I can think, just be. I can taste what it might feel like to exist apart from my family, outside of this house, outside of the way I feel. Prison produces a different kind of death. It is an insidious, poisonous kind of death that kills not only the prisoner but the family too, especially the parents, especially if the prisoner is eighteen and mostly a child. I take another drag from my cigarette and continue.

> *Mom and Dad don't know what to say about me. I don't either. I feel discouraged to try and go to community college. Look at me. One big ass paragraph. I can't even write a letter let alone get past ninth grade algebra. There's a reason for everything, but for a person who always has a reason or excuse for everything, it gets old. This shit in here is degrading—taking showers with thirty other boys. There isn't much a person could do or say to make me feel worse than I do, 'cause there aren't too many things worse than being in prison. I can't think of many words to tell Mom and Dad except I'll be home soon.*

For a few more lines he scolds me for doing poorly in school. Not seeing any irony in doing so, he demands I improve my GPA. He has heard I'm not doing well. He bribes me, telling me he'll buy me my first car when he gets out, a Lexus. *Love, Jr.*, he signs off. My cigarette burns away between my fingers. I take in the last drag of smoke and toss the butt onto the neighbor's ivy-covered roof. I throw the letter back inside my room, onto the floor, and stare out above the rooftops. I trace them all the way up to the cemetery at the top of the hill where our street ends and meets the dead—one line, one tiny speck of map that expands and expands and expands until I see just how *nothing* we are, how nowhere. The absence of Junior takes the life from me.

"You need to see your brother," my parents say again and again. They see him once a week and are in constant communication with a public defender. I know they have told Junior I'm struggling, and so when he calls and asks to speak to me I walk away and decline to speak because I know what he'll say: *Do better.* I am unable to hear it through my anger. I am a failure, and so it only feels right to let myself fall deeper into this place where I feel I belong, a place beyond salvation.

The truth is I do want to see him. I want to tell him I love him. This love is conditional; it is needy and desperate. *I need you to show me who I can be.* I might say, *Do better*. I might say, *Come home already*, but no matter what I feel and what I might say, I know the thoughts will fail me; they will not verbalize. I do not yet trust myself to speak, to voice my silence both learned and inherited.

When I finally decide to join my parents and make the trip to San Quentin, it is not because they make me; it is because some primitive, cellular part of me knows that what is happening to him must be seen—it must be given a name; it must be spoken. What is happening to him is also happening to me.

Dad drives because Mom doesn't know how. She is the black breadwinner and he is her white chauffeur. It is easy to find both darkness and humor in the unlikeliness of their love. When they married in 1972, miscegenation had been legal for just barely five years, and in Mom's home state of Alabama, it was still technically banned. While my mother picked cotton in fields outside Selma, my father practiced yoga on the manicured lawns of his private high school in Philadelphia. Just as it is necessary to see my brother in prison, it is necessary to know the truth and context of their story. These are the stories that make me. What has happened to them happens to me.

Not in some story, not in history, not in my head, but in real time, I get in the back seat of our new car—a champagne-colored Nissan Sentra—and decide to leave the bubble of my feelings and offer myself to my family. Okay. I am here. I am alive. I will go. We are in this story together, because of one another. We pull ourselves together and we go and we visit our son and our brother in prison.

My father's sandpaper claws clutch the steering wheel. His skin is so peppered in sunspots, the dry cracks of his hands so deeply veined with dirt, a baseball cap always covering his messy hair, that you can barely make out the details of him—his orange hair, his many freckles, his blue eyes. My mother is dressed in her nice clothes—a muumuu-style navy dress with stockings. Her gaze out the window, her eyes fixed on the bay below us. We inhale and exhale her thick perfume. No one speaks.

The San Quentin sun is unexpected. It is an island almost exclusively dedicated to the prison. The parking lot of the prison is a dry and flat desert. Mom and Dad exit the car quickly and look at their feet while they walk. Still, no one speaks. Junior did not graduate from high school this year; he is instead being tried before a court not for drugs but for kidnapping and assault, and will probably be shipped to some other, more remote prison.

As soon as we enter, I am cold. The sun does not follow us. The room where we must check in and show ID and empty our pockets is barren and icy. Guards look us over; some of them leer at me. I cross my arms to cover myself from their gaze. Where is Junior? I try and picture the cells and imagine him hunched over on a cement floor writing me a letter, begging me to do better. I am his sister. I want to scream this to the guards who screen us through detectors, pat us down. That's my brother in there. I glare at the men as if they are the reason I find myself at a prison today. He doesn't belong here. He is only a boy.

I imagine that my parents want to shout similar things about their son. But the weight of their grief and mine locks our mouths closed. Our only armor against what swells inside us are these labels: sister, parent. We walk in wearing them, as strong as we can. And we wait to see our loved one. A line of men in orange suits comes marching out. There are others waiting as well. Women dressed as if for a night out, full faces of make-up, some wrangling children. I look for people like us: My pale, eagle-nosed father, crouching as if in apology for his height. Mom, short, round, and deep bronze, at his side, a look of concern carved permanently between her coarse black brows, the only hard feature on her otherwise soft, unwrinkled skin. Me, fifteen, protecting the woman's figure I now occupy under my crossed arms.

When he enters, the first thing I notice is his hair, a buzz cut in place of his long ponytail of curls. His smile is the same. He grins when he sees us. "Valentine," the guard calls, directing him to a flimsy wooden table, allowing us to visit across from him, one at a time. I let them go first. They visit every Saturday and come home in a haze, then they go to Quaker meeting on Sunday and pray for him. They wear strong and dedicated parent uniforms, but I can see right through them, how they've shrunken, gotten older, don't sleep. Mom goes first. I can see her tearing up before him. It makes Junior cry too. I remember the letter on my bedroom floor, his drawing of the boy who wanted to come home.

Finally it's my turn. "Did you get my letter?" Junior asks me.

"Yeah," I say. "I'm waiting for my Lexus."

"So, you're fucking up?" he asks, getting serious. He sits upright and his smile turns straight.

I roll my eyes playfully. "You realize you're in prison, right?"

"Oh, I know where I'm at, trust me," he says. "That's not the point. The point is you're younger. There's still hope for you."

"Oh, okay, this is what we're talking about? Cool. I'm leaving then. I don't know why I came here." I pretend to get up, but quickly sit back down and smile. "You're a fuckin' trip, you know that?" I shake my head at him and watch his body loosen up. He's happy to see me. "What the fuck are you doing in here? Hurry up and come home." I say this as if he is an exception, because he is my brother and their son.

237

"I know, man. I'm going to be out soon," he says with a confidence borrowed from some unknown place.

"I came here to lecture you, but you beat me to it." He smiles. "But seriously. What are you gonna do when you get out? When *are* you getting out?" I have so many questions, all of them unanswerable.

There is one answer in particular I am looking for, one question I cannot ask: *Why?* Why did you do it? Why did you attempt to rob a sex worker in San Francisco? Why, when she said no, and your friend got out of the passenger seat so he could push her into the back seat, didn't you stop him? And why, when she fought back and escaped into the street, did you drive the car? Why did you drive the car over her limbs?

I look around suspiciously at the guards. I wish there weren't ears and eyes on us. I wish he could tell me why he'd done it. I want to ask my brother if he hates himself. He must, to have treated someone this way. I want to know how and why. I wonder if I hate myself too. I look at him across from me—we look so much alike. I search his face for answers.

And then I remember another part of the report, the part that said Junior had been so intoxicated during the incident that he drove the car very slowly down the street, away from the woman, and was found easily and immediately by the San Francisco police. And when they handcuffed him and sat him in the back of their patrol car, he immediately passed out.

The photos of the woman's body live in a manila envelope on our dining room table. I think of these photos of the woman as I look at him across from me. The angles captured by the police camera made her bruised and bloodied body parts look large and detached: a leg, an arm, the side of a face, a few strands of blond hair covering an ear. I look at her white skin made whiter against the purple and red. I do not want to see her name at the top.

I try to reenact the scenario that I've been told, that I read in the police report, place Junior in it in my mind. Two nameless boys, a sex worker, a pimp, and a drug dealer. The car is tan in my mind, like the one Dad used to drive in the old pictures from a time before I was born. When he gets out of the car, my mind goes blank. I cannot make him beat this woman. I cannot make him run her over. Though I make myself look at slivers of the evidence of her bruised body, just an inch out of the manila envelope, I cannot make them do it in my mind. Every time my mind tries to push the woman into the back of the car, I skip forward. I gently pick her up and place her on the cement of the street behind the car, where the men look at what they've done. I lay her down in the street and place her limbs in a position to be photographed. The men look at the body and are full of remorse. They turn away from her, close themselves up inside the car, and drive away because they don't know what else to do. They have low-cut hair, wear white T-shirts and jeans with pistols tucked into the waistbands, the metal warmed by skin.

The car takes off down the street. On this street is nothing and no one; it is dark and silent except for their breath, and the rhythm of their hearts. I like to imagine them with hearts. It is a two-lane highway in the wilderness where I imagine them. Only in the wild can my mind even picture her body. The woman is alive and her crawling body is discovered by the next passing car. The police take photos of her limbs. They end up on our dining room table, where no one dares pull them out all the way. Only a sliver of flesh. Please no name.

But this cannot be what happened. Still, I cannot make Junior do it. I look at him before me. My mouth is moving and he makes gestures before me, but nothing is said. It is so hard to look at the whole picture. I am answerless. He was blackout drunk and only one or two blocks from the scene when the police found them. And he fit the description easily, the only one with a long ponytail of ringlets.

He is finally old enough for prison. In Junior's face I see a boy who is ten. Here is a ten-year-old in prison. A child, a man, a child, a man, my mind goes back and forth. Then I see him as he is—just barely eighteen. His thin, dry lips move, the gap between his front teeth has narrowed, his usually polished brown complexion is sallow under the harsh light above us, against the orange costume he wears. Small talk circles us. He talks about how much paper they can have and how it's fucked up I haven't written, how the other inmates think he's a pretty boy.

I listen while thinking a thousand other thoughts. This is it, I think, looking over my shoulder at Mom and Dad sitting in the waiting area. They are nothing more than warm bodies going through the motions of the living. I look at Junior's moving mouth, the colorless air between us. I want to say something. I want to do something. I want to go to my parents and offer them comfort. I want to make Junior change. I want to heal him. I want to heal myself. I want him to say something different from the nonsense coming from his mouth. I want him to promise to change. I want him to say how hurt he is. I want the barrier of air between us to vanish so I can say the thing that no one will say, do anything besides slouch and watch, motionless and numb as my brother speaks. I want to do something that will make them all feel something. I have never needed Junior to say something else more than I do now. I want to slap his face and tell him, *Do better, I need you. Please, don't you dare leave me.*

But the exterior me feels small and powerless and overwhelmed, so she does nothing and says nothing. When our time is up, I float back to where the bodies of my parents sit and we walk out as we came in: separate and shrunken. Once we're out, the sun coats my body with its warmth. Junior won't feel this sun. As I watch Mom and Dad ahead of me, hunched over with their heads down, practicing tomorrow's prayers, I am overwhelmed with the desire to be big. I want to be so big, big enough to fill every silence and lift up even the heaviest of bodies. I let this idea comfort me.

My brother is a bad guy. He hurts people. And yet I still want to love him. I still wish for our healing. I still believe he's good and worthy of life.

THE SPACE OF our lives begins to fill up inside his absence. When Junior was home he was all anyone thought of, and so my grades fell without anyone taking notice. My parents' existence was one big effort to keep him away from the street and out of prison. Suddenly my report card is posted on the refrigerator and Mom wants an answer. "What is this?" she asks, referring to my two-point-something GPA, to the Fs I received in a number of classes. In his absence, I am noticed for the first time in a very long time.

After her prying, I finally admit to Mom that, after being late to chemistry for the last time, the teacher told me I couldn't come back unless I brought a parent with me, and so I stopped going altogether. After hearing this, Mom sighs and puts her hand over her face. "Melissa," she chastises me. I have always been good, and she is faced for the very first time with the damage that has been done, with what she has missed over the last year and a half. "I'm going with you to class tomorrow."

There is nothing to say, and so the next day Mom escorts me to school. On the walk, I notice things I don't usually: how each blade of grass on the neighbor's lawn is individually dewed, how the morning light pierces through the fog, how the sound of my rubber heels hitting against the concrete is calming to me. Her scent creates a vortex around us. She is so good, and next to her I let myself feel cared for, I let it feel good, but my criminality is ever present. I feel ashamed for what I've done, how I've failed. Ashamed that this is the reason she is coming to school. Not because I won the Student of the Year award like I did in the sixth grade, not because I am receiving the award at the Kiwanis Club or participating in the spelling bee or because I have a flute recital. Those days are over, and I am falling further and further away from my mother, away from our home, and closer to a pit of apathy, the same pit that Junior got lost in.

We may as well be walking to prison. It is what comes next after failing in school. I feel unworthy of her presence. All of her goodness in my nose and in my peripheral view. I become hyperconscious, hearing every sound and seeing every thing for the first time. I feel like I have superpowers, but I don't; it is the heightened awareness of my inadequacy before me, in her presence. Junior is the bad one. I am supposed to be good. But I don't value good anymore. All I want is to be big, to be powerful and loud. I am bigger than Mom. Especially in my platforms. I can see straight across the top of her head.

As we cross the border that separates Piedmont from North Oakland, we begin seeing other kids making the journey up Broadway toward Oakland Tech in small and scattered groups. My shame transforms to a sudden sense of pride when I see them. I have a mother, I remind myself. I have a mother. And I let that reminder seep into me. Someone cares about me. And suddenly I want them all to see me next to her, in her good clothes, proud. Someone cares.

Mom hasn't slept all night. She took off her work clothes, her badge, and she changed into what look like her Quaker-meeting clothes: a thick gray cotton long-sleeve dress that goes down to her ankles and black kitten heels that clack femininely as we walk up the stairs to the school. "Oh Jesus," she says. "I remember the last time I was here. Same reason." She looks at me with disdain, and my shame returns. I say nothing. "I simply could not believe it," she goes on, her voice making the adjustment from Southern to somewhere between British and too loud. "I went to your brother's class because his report card came back looking pitiful. I wanted to see for myself. So I went and I observed a class. I surprised him. I came in and found him sleeping in the very back of the class. Just doing nothing. Asleep. Broke my heart." She looks at me. "Don't break my heart too."

I am filled with some emotion I don't recognize; it has been so long since I've felt anything like it toward myself. For the first time all year I have the desire to improve. I think it's love or maybe desire itself showing up. Before Junior went to prison, all everyone wanted was for him to be better. All the love in the whole family was sent to him, all the prayers, all the hope and desire—it all went to him. There was none left.

I am speechless. Out of my body. Who is the girl she's talking to? Certainly it's not me. Who is the bad girl? Who is the one who will break her heart? I show her to the class, one of many I am flunking, and watch her walk in. I have never been to school this early. There are some kids I recognize from my classes, good kids. I lean into a corner near the lockers with my arms crossed, and I passively observe the few students and the openness at this time of morning before the bell has rung. What will happen to me? I wonder, as if all life itself is out of control and certainly out of mine. Mom walks out of the classroom and the teacher follows. He looks at me with different eyes: *You come from somewhere. You come from someone. Someone cares about you.* Mom motions for me to come forward, and I walk, one foot in front of the other, slow and steady. She scoots out of the way so I can enter. "Go." She points to a desk near the front of the room. I go. "You're early now. Sit." I don't remember what it feels like to have someone command me like this. She continues speaking as though she is a hypnotist implanting ideas into my mind. "You will be early every day and you will sit in the front of the class just like this and you will make up your assignments just like he tells you and you will pass."

But it is hard to change, even harder to care. I slug along, remembering, in fragments, that I am capable; but it is much easier to forget, to let go of the idea altogether that I can be anyone other than who I am in this moment. I still haven't written Junior back. His letters pile up.

Things have changed at home. Cornelius has returned. For one lost brother, another returns. It turns out he was also failing, and he couldn't afford to live off campus anymore. Vivian is still away, and she's getting ready to go abroad to the Dominican Republic. Claire has moved to Oakland with her boyfriend because they both work here now. She is inching her way closer to us, and perhaps for one sister lost, I will gain another.

When Cornelius moves back in, he is changed. He takes up in Angelica's room, and she is displaced to any part of the house she'd like now that there are so many empty ones to choose from: Junior's, who is in prison, Vivian's, who is in college; or she can share with Mom and Dad. Cornelius doesn't bother to clean up any of Angelica's toys; he just begins occupying the room as it is. He sleeps in her twin bed with floral covers, puts his history books on the floor among the dolls. He spends long periods of time in there and doesn't make a sound. I often forget anyone is upstairs with me until I hear a cough or a sneeze or some kind of angry outburst—"Fuck!"—from a stubbed toe.

One morning, I get dressed as usual, defeated and coming to accept that it is already ten o'clock and I have missed chemistry again. I have made a mockery of Mom and I know it. It's as if my blood is heavy with sand or I am made of lead when I walk; I feel old, hobbling around from one place to the next with no direction or urgency. I can't muster up the energy to care about anything. I want nothing. Perhaps this is depression, but I don't know that word. Perhaps what is happening quietly to Cornelius in Angelica's room is also depression, but we don't know that word. He made it, didn't he? Got out and went to college. But it is hard to change. It is difficult to remember you are capable. Easier to let go. Perhaps what is happening downstairs in the bed Mom fitfully sleeps in, the now-empty couch Dad no longer sleeps on, because, for now, he knows where Junior is—perhaps all that, too, is depression. But none of us know that word so we move about, we live, and we try to keep ourselves and one another alive with the energy we have left. It feels that dire. Perhaps we don't have a word for the grief of surviving, for the cost of staying alive.

I pretend to get ready for school in the upstairs bathroom. Forgetting anyone is up here with me. Forgetting Cornelius. I stare at myself in the bathroom mirror beyond splatters of dried toothpaste. I'm surrounded by trash. The toilet doesn't work. The bathtub is full of still gray water with a foam of dead skin and dirt on top that is meant to be repurposed for the garden and used to flush the toilet.

A collection of empty shampoo bottles are scattered around the floor, waiting for someone to recycle them.

Going through the motions of getting ready for school, I brush my teeth like the animal I feel like, suds dripping out of my mouth and down my chin. I brush harder and look at myself in the mirror. Snarl-faced and intense, I take in my crooked face, my thin, freckled lips. I'm concentrating so hard that it takes me a while to register there is someone at the door.

"What are you doing here?" Cornelius asks.

"What are *you* doing here?" I manage to garble the words out, leaning over the sink to spit.

"Why aren't you at school?"

"Why aren't *you* at school?"

"Don't play with me," he says, and enters the bathroom, where I continue to brush.

I turn the water on and then turn to face him before rinsing my mouth. "What do you want?" I ask. But I know what he wants. He wants to warn me to not be like him, he wants to make me go to school. He wants to avert another one of us from failure. I expect him to leave now, but he stays.

"Go to school," he says in a tone that's more like a growl than a command. "You have no business still being here."

"I'm getting ready."

"Go to school," he says again.

"I'm trying to," I say, and I go to rinse the suds from my mouth. But before I can touch the water to my face, I am on the floor. Cornelius has thrown me on the floor with a powerful blow to my face. He stands over me, large and gnarly, and I do my best to defend myself, remind him that I am alive with the meanest stare I can manage, my eyelids twitching with anger. I get up as fast as I can and throw myself into him, fighting without thinking, raging and punching against his bullish mass. I push and kick and punch at him with all of my strength, but he is like a tree; he will not move.

He points to the stairs. "Go," he orders, ushering me down the stairs on his worthy mission to get me to go to school.

"What are you doing?" I ask again; I still want him to answer. I need a language for what is happening. I want it to be named. His face becomes animal-like. He raises his hand, and I feel heat and force meeting my cheek once again. Now blood with the tears and toothpaste. I topple down the stairs. He follows. Lying at the bottom of the stairs, where the back door opens into the kitchen, I see Dad. I am on the floor like a defeated animal. I watch Dad's bright blue eyes dim. His face is screwed up in a look of shock, but he says nothing, does not offer to help me up. Cornelius stands over me on the last step, panting like an ogre. I look at Dad for confirmation that he's allowing this to happen. Confirmed. He is. In his look I receive disturbing information: he, too, is afraid. He is afraid of what will happen to his children. He is afraid of what will happen to me. And he has developed a singular fear of his boys, who have grown up to be bigger, stronger than he is, and perhaps most frightening of all, black. Before my eyes flash the violent years. The bits of memory where I see a bloody hairy gash on a scalp, a head hitting a cabinet door, terrible words, slurs. I thought they'd kill each other. And what caused the fights? Manhood, presumably. Grotesque and deeply insecure and willing to do anything for an ounce of power, an ounce of respect.

I look up at the men and their sorry manhood. I get myself up and run out of the house and away from the coward men. Cornelius follows me in his blue Trans Am. I walk up our good street with my blackening eye, with toothpaste still on my mouth. The street is tree-lined and clean; our neighbors are intellectuals and have serious professions and push expensive strollers containing important children. With no school bag, just the clothes on my back—platform boots and a floral knee-length skirt over my jeans—I march, feeling important only in my conviction to never return. Let them see the blood dripping from my nose, the dried toothpaste on my mouth. Let them see a thug. Cornelius is creeping on me, driving very slow, his neck craned out the window. I yell at him to go away, to go fuck himself, to fix his own broken life, and finally he takes off, gunning the engine.

I'm alone now. This is a very different way to be escorted to school. Vanessa is waiting for me in between the two large columns at the steps of the school. "What happened?" She covers her mouth when she sees me.

"Cornelius," I say. We sit on the school steps together; everyone is already inside, settling into homeroom. Pretty soon a security guard will ask us what we're doing. "I'm not going in there."

"Let's get out of here before the security guards find us," she says. We leave campus and walk two blocks to her house.

She is quiet, as if she's at someone's funeral and doesn't have the right words of condolence. "I'm so sorry," she says.

"I'll call my dad," she says when we reach her house, because when things are wrong or confusing in her life, she calls her parents and they help. I let them help me. I don't want to go back home. I don't want to go to school. I'm lost. I have no one on my team anymore. Junior is gone now and his letters are piling up and they sound just like Cornelius, Mom, and Dad: disappointed and completely hypocritical. I can't bear to send him the letters I write that say, *You don't belong, come home, you are better than that, it's not the same without you, the system is so unjust.* They don't feel like the truth. The truth is that there is no separation. He isn't in there while we're out here. We are all in the same place. We are all the street, we're all prison. We're all criminals. We're all him. None of us is free. We are all locked up, whether our shackles be made of manhood or violence or our families or our schools or the color of our skin or our bodies.

Vanessa holds the phone on her shoulder while she repeats to me what her father is saying on the other line. "He says because he's a teacher, and you're a minor, by law he has to report the incident."

I wash the blood and toothpaste off my face in the bathroom while she waits. Her father has agreed to let her walk me to the hospital. Then, he says, she has to go back to school. Her father doesn't want her missing an entire day of school so that I can have someone with me as the police take photos of my body parts.

At the hospital, I lift my shirt to reveal bruises on my side where I landed on the stairs. A photo of my swollen nose is snapped. My feet dangle on the doctor's table, my platform boots hanging like weights. Perhaps I will become a girl in a manila envelope on a table in a house. Perhaps my photos will be part of a thick file of other girls, on a desk. Perhaps someone will find me.

The cell phone Claire bought for me sits in my pocket silently. I do not call home. I do not call and warn Cornelius that when the police asked me if I wanted to press charges I said yes. I do not tell anyone that when the police asked me if I was afraid to go home I said yes, even if I did mean it symbolically.

"Are you afraid your brother will harm you again?" the emotionless officer asks.

"Yes." I look at him blankly, my big eyes not blinking, and he probably thinks he has real crimes to solve, better things to do than sit in a hospital with a teenager who's got a grudge against her brother.

I do not call home when the police officer leaves me with no words and another man enters the hospital room and asks me to come with him. The system doesn't speak in symbolism.

"Where are we going?"

I do not call home when the man opens the door and signals for me to get into the back seat of the black unmarked government car.

"Where are you taking me?"

I do not call home when the man does not answer my questions and gets on the freeway and drives us to East Oakland, farther than I've ever been. Ninetieth Avenue. Ninety-First, Ninety-Second, Ninety-Third. Liquor stores and groups of teenagers at bus stops, teenagers also not in school. We turn left onto Ninety-Eighth Avenue. We drive and drive until the avenue becomes a hill and the man stops the car in front of a big house with a long, empty porch and a sparkling-white rock garden in front. The man leaves me in the car and I watch as he hops onto the porch and rings the doorbell.

A fat brown-skinned woman that could be my aunt in Alabama opens the door. She's wearing a shapeless nightgown but it's only three in the afternoon. She doesn't smile. They exchange words, and the man points to the car and she looks at me. I try to hide my face. Where are we? What is this?

The man takes sweeping steps to the car, perhaps relieved to be getting rid of me. He opens my door and finally says something. "C'mon."

"Where are we?" I ask. He doesn't answer. He simply delivers me to the door where the woman has gone in already and then he leaves me. I watch him get back in the car, start the engine, and disappear without looking back.

I should turn around and walk down the hill toward MacArthur Boulevard with all the liquor stores. I should wait at the bus stop with some of the other delinquents. But I don't. I have no money. Where have I been taken? I let the slow, squeaking screen door shut behind me, and I approach the woman's house as if it is a museum, slowly, looking carefully at everything. Is this house better than mine? The living room is dark and the woman is nowhere in sight. Her couch is covered in plastic wrap and her dining room table is covered by a crisp crocheted tablecloth. I go toward the light, what looks to be a bedroom with a blaring television. The local news. I peek my head in the doorway, not wanting to be seen, but I'm caught.

"Come in," she says. I tentatively enter the room. The woman is lying in bed under the covers watching the news. She barely turns to look at me. "So, what happened to you?" she asks, looking at the TV. I guess she means why did the man bring me here.

"My brother beat me up," I say.

"Why did your brother beat you up?"

"Because I was late for school."

"Why were you late for school?"

"I don't know," I say, annoyed and feeling the need to protect myself. Then it all comes spilling out, all in one breath: a frantic retelling of everything that happened that day, from seeing Vanessa to getting in the government car with that man. When I'm done, I search her face and wait for a reaction. "I don't know why I'm here."

The woman chuckles and faces me. I'm not sure which part of what I've said is funny.

"Your room is upstairs, the first door on the right. Ask the others to show you."

My room? The others? I stay in her doorway for a moment, horrified. What is happening? Why is no one telling me what's happening? I feel fear sink in. I back away from the door, but before I leave, I say, "So, am I supposed to stay here?"

She looks at me now. "Do you want to stay here?"

"No," I say. "I made a mistake pressing charges against my brother. He's not going to do anything to me. My parents

253

are going to be so worried about me. I really should go back home." The system did not understand my symbolic cry for help. I wanted to make a point, not get myself thrown into foster care.

She smiles at me and says nothing. She has gone from motherly to witchy and strange. Why won't she tell me what's happening? When she says nothing in response, I finally give up and resign to stay the night.

The stairs feel different from the rest of the house, which is covered in plastic and protected. The stairs are not protected. They're creaky, wooden, and dry. I walk slowly to avoid the loud creaking, so as not to disturb anyone, or surprise one of the others, whoever they are, but my slowness makes the floor creak even louder.

The top floor of the house is sparse. The wide hallway is bare except for a few scattered toys: a yellow plastic tractor and a race-car track for tiny cars. A little boy who looks about five leans against the doorway to one of the rooms and stares at the visitor in her platform boots, her printed skirt. I am as afraid as he is. Snot runs down the little boy's brown face.

"Hi." I wave. He only stares back, watching me. "Do you live here?" I ask, trying to understand through him what this place is. He says nothing.

A teenage girl emerges from another room. She looks like she's getting ready to leave. "Yeah, we live here," she answers for him. Now it's my turn to stare. "What are you here for?" she asks.

Here for? As if this is some prison for children. "My brother," I stutter a little. "My brother, he hit me."

"Sorry," she says. The little boy doesn't move, he just keeps standing in the doorway staring at me.

"It's okay," I say. "I don't really think I'm supposed to be here."

The girl laughs as she zips her jacket. "Me either," she says. "I can't wait until I'm eighteen."

"Where are you going?"

"To my friend's house."

"You can leave?"

She laughs again. "Yes, you can leave."

I am utterly confused. I'm here in prison but I can leave and it seems people stay here until they're eighteen. She walks down the stairs and I look after her, not wanting her to go. Now it's just the snot-nosed boy and me. Or are there others? What have I done?

I go into what I suppose is my room; it's unoccupied, bare except for an empty bunk bed. There is one window. I look out of it into the neighbors' yards, over the tops of houses, at the pink sky. The sun will be going down soon. I cannot be here at night. I wish I could call Junior to come and get me. I sit down near the bottom bunk on the wooden floor. I hug my knees and start to cry. In my fit of tears I pull out my phone. No one is worried about me yet because they assume I've gone to school. I dial my sister Claire's number and get her voicemail.

"Claire, I need help," I say to her voicemail. "I made a report against Cornelius, and then I guess when you're a minor they can't take you home, so a man took me to a weird house, and there's a weird lady downstairs and she won't tell me anything, and there's weird kids here who keep staring at me," I say, blubbering. "It's on Ninety-Eighth and Mac-Arthur. I can't stay here. I'm so scared. Come and get me."

I stand and get my bearings, walk around the spare room, listening to my steps creak under me. I repeat affirmations to myself: *You don't belong here, you don't belong here.* But here I am. I approach the doorway of the room, each one of my steps causing a clamor that I imagine will get me caught. Get me caught from what? What am I doing? I am escaping. The little boy appears in his doorway opposite me, looking at me as I walk noisily down the hallway toward the stairs. Part of me feels bad for leaving him even though we know nothing about each other. Who will care for him? The woman downstairs? I hold his unblinking gaze for as long as I can before I must focus my eyes on the steps before me.

At the bottom of the stairs, I take a deep breath before entering the woman's room for the second time. I don't have a plan. Her TV still blares, the only sound in the house. I pat my eyes and feel their puffiness, take a deep breath.

"Excuse me," I announce myself, knocking softly on the edge of her door, my heart racing inside my chest. I poke my head inside the room and repeat, "Excuse me." She looks up at me. "I was wondering if I could borrow $1.25 from you so I can go to the corner store and buy something to drink." It is a bold request. I look deeply at her, into her. I try to communicate my message: *C'mon. We both know this was a mistake. Help me out.* I silently plead. From the way she raises her head I think she's understood me. I feel myself getting stronger, bolder. This woman, I feel, could be my mother. Her bedridden existence comforts me in a strange way. I go all the way into the room, walk up to the side of her bed, and sit next to her the way I would my mother. We look at each other.

"Hand me my purse," she says, pointing to the other side of the bedroom where her tan handbag sits on her dresser. My heart flutters. I hand her the purse and take my seat next to her while she counts change. Soon I'll be free. "Here," she says, placing exactly $1.25 into my palm.

"Thank you," I say. I squeeze the money tight in my fist and approach the door again. I turn around at the doorway and face her once more. "I'll come right back," I lie. My legs move fast toward the front door. Time stops as I make my getaway.

The world looks new to the escaped prisoner. I hurry down the hill I rode up in with the man, passing by town-houses with grass yards, trying desperately to get out of sight of the woman's house. I want to be at the bus stop before she can waddle out of bed and to the door to call my name. Does she even know my name? I suddenly remember my black eye and my shame returns. I head right to the bus stop I saw earlier with all the truants. Am I a truant?

The bus takes me all the way down MacArthur Boulevard, which spans across all of Oakland—North, West, and East neighborhoods. I ride it all the way to North Oakland where the streets are no longer numbers, and get off at the Piedmont stop near the border where I live. I am home now.

With my head down, I walk home taking the side streets. I don't want anyone to ask me what happened to my face. I pray Cornelius won't be home and that Claire will be. But when I get there I find the house empty except for

Mom snoring in her back room. No one had any clue where I'd been. I feel a surge of protective emotion as I make my way through the first floor. I don't know what I'll do if I see one of them. Upstairs in my room I open both windows, cranking their handles and removing the screens. On the maroon carpet near the bookshelf lies a torn-open letter from Junior. I think about its contents, him begging me again and again to go to school. He's in a prison in someplace called Susanville now. My mind cannot put him in prison, so I picture him in the forests or deserts of the California-Nevada border. Danielle will visit him there. She will take a Greyhound bus for fifteen hours. I imagine him in a forest on the very top of a winding mountain road where he sits in repose writing letters, growing wise, reading books, earning his GED. He will wait for Danielle on the mountain. Wherever he is, he is becoming a man.

I leave the letter where it is on the floor and climb out of the window and sit on the rough black roof a few feet from the edge. I light a cigarette on the roof. My view looks north, facing other black tar rooftops. The sweet gum and oak trees start to resemble green lollipops the farther up I follow them. I trace them until they become small, their colors bleeding into one another and meeting at the hilly cemetery, the farthest place in the distance.

Back inside, I fall asleep. I wake to loud banging on my bedroom door. It's Claire. "Melissa!" she screams from outside my door in her shrill voice, an octave she only reaches when she's truly upset. I stumble out of bed and go to open the door.

"Jesus fucking Christ," she greets me. "Where the fuck

have you been, and what happened to you?" She pulls my chin toward her to inspect my black eye. "I called and called, and I looked for you. Why didn't you pick up?"

"Sorry," I mumble.

"Sorry? You can't call me like that and then disappear. I was so worried about you." She pulls me close to her and hugs me. I drink in her smell and allow myself to be held. It feels nice. I don't want her to stop. "Come down here," she says. "Mom wants to talk to you. She's up." She takes my hand and guides me toward the stairs, but I don't move.

"Is Cornelius here?"

"No."

"Dad?"

"No."

I want to feel wanted by her and Mom, so I follow her to Mom's room, where she's sitting up in bed waiting for me. I am reminded of the woman in East Oakland, but this woman is my mother and this truth fills me with gratitude. I lie next to her. Claire sits on the other side of the bed. Mom starts. "What in the world happened?" She winces, then becomes British: "What is this?" They both wait for me to speak.

"Cornelius beat me up."

"What is the meaning of this?" Mom cries high-pitched.

"I was late for school, so he thought he would hurry me up by knocking me down the stairs."

"Why were you late for school?"

"Mom," Claire interrupts her line of questioning with a cutting look, and then looks at me. "Tell her where you've been."

259

"I gave a police report at the hospital and then this guy took me to East Oakland, I think to a foster home. And then I escaped."

Claire cuts in. "But before she did that she called me acting like she was going to die and scared me half to death. I went looking for her."

"You escaped?" Mom says, looking from me to Claire, wanting the whole story.

"Yeah," I say. "There was an old lady there and she sent me upstairs to my room. There were two kids who lived up there. One was a girl my age and another was a weird little boy who stared at me the whole time—"

Mom interrupts my story with laughter. "Now, wait a second. Tell me about the little boy. How was he weird? Was he black? How old was he?"

"He looked like he was about five. Yeah, he was black. I don't know, he seemed lonely and no one was up there with him and his nose was running. He had snot dripping down his nose. I said hi and everything, but he never responded."

"Lord have mercy!" Mom cries. "What did that old woman look like? How come she didn't clean that poor baby's nose?"

"I don't know. She stayed down in her room the whole time."

"How did she look? Was she black?"

"Yeah, she was black."

"Was she *real* black?"

"She was pretty light."

"Light skinned, eh?"

"Yeah, and fat."

"Fat, huh?"

"Yeah, so I was up in my room and I was really scared that I was going to have to live there. That's when I called Claire."

Mom is unable to stop herself from cackling. "You thought you were going to have to live there?"

"Well, yeah, because the man took me there and it seemed really official and I'm a minor, and—"

"A man? What kind of man?" Mom asks, cutting me off.

I don't pretend I don't know what she means by the question. "He was black."

"Everyone was black, weren't they? Were the police black too?"

"Yes. So I was scared that I was going to have to live there in that bare room with the boy across the hall, and no one told me what was going on, so I assumed it was my new home and I didn't know what the rules were. So I went back down to the lady and asked her for money to buy a drink and I took the bus home."

"Damn," Mom exclaims; she has become Southern now. "Easy, wasn't it?" She looks at us, both her daughters. "Well, damn," she says, with a softened voice. "Well, you're lucky. Serves you right. Calling the police on your brother like a damn fool. You have no business calling no police on your brother. We have enough children in prison."

"Where is Cornelius anyway?" I ask.

"Probably staying away from here so he doesn't get arrested," Mom says.

"Are you on his side?"

"Look," Mom says sternly. "We don't need police involved. Look at what happened to you. You hear me?"

"The police came here," Claire says.

"Really?"

"They didn't do anything, it's just going to be on his record. He's pissed."

"Why didn't they arrest him?" I ask.

"Because, Melissa," Claire says condescendingly, "plenty of little sisters get beat up by their big brothers and nobody is getting arrested for it. Okay?"

"Fuck that," I say.

"Hey!" Mom says. "Watch your mouth."

I look at Mom. "And your husband watched the whole thing."

"Watch your mouth," she says coldly. "Be careful before you end up at that old woman's house again." She can't help herself. She starts laughing again and Claire joins in.

I return to my room and listen from up there to the sounds of them living below me. I hear Dad come home. I hear Claire leave; she screams goodbye up to me from the staircase. I hear the clanging and yelling of getting Mom ready for work. I smell food, then I smell her hair being pressed. I never hear Cornelius come home. There is a sting to the silence when they leave. It's piercing. Someone is missing. Junior is missing.

I start and stop, start and stop letters to him. I have not sent him one. He is so disappointed he hasn't wanted to talk to me the last few times he's called. I begin writing:

Dear Junior,

I'm often scared that one of us will die while we're on bad terms. I can't tell you how many times I've cried myself to sleep thinking about how my older brother gave up on me. I can't fool anyone anymore. Now everyone will have to know that I'm human, I make mistakes. I'm sure you've never done anything you've regretted. I'm sure you're proud of everything you've done in your life . . .

I don't know who I am either, but I care about who I become. I'm not afraid of myself or afraid to find out who I am . . .

The life you've chosen scares me so much. I think about you dying, getting murdered, ruining your life. For what? Ask yourself for what. I hate seeing it happen to you.

The *it* happening to him is the monster of the street. *It* is the one with long fingers and deadly talons that summons him. The one that lures him with money, tells him that this is how you become powerful. This is how you become free. It tells him all of this in exchange for just one thing: You must hand over your freedom. And you must hand over your body. But the trick is so flawless that you think the life you have chosen is an expression of your freedom. It is an imaginary world. Where black boys and girls with mouths of gold are kings and queens. Where they fight to protect their throne. Where, underneath the robes and the gold and the armor, they are all kings and queens in search of themselves.

TEN

He has been away for a little over a year. He had his nineteenth birthday in prison. He moved far away to Susanville, California, where only Danielle visited him once. That was where he finished his sentence. There were men from the Oakland streets there. He had to fight and defend, and he did solitary more than once to pay for it. Prison was another version of the street. He will be home in time to celebrate his twentieth birthday. It is autumn and it is hot, a typical Indian summer in Oakland.

I have changed schools of my own volition. Another school year has already begun. I'm sixteen and a junior now. The summer was a reflective one. I have written and written to Junior all of my revelations, and sent nothing. I want to tell him in person when he's home. Better yet, I want him to see for himself.

I decide to make up the classes I've flunked. I decide I will clean up the mess I've made. I suggest a new school for myself, and Mom and Dad enroll me. The school is tiny and there are art classes; I know this because my two best friends go there and because it is the same school I attended for middle school. With good friends and with art and with fewer kids, I believe that maybe I can do better. And I do. After school I walk through Piedmont to the adult school where I make up my classes. The giant houses and beautiful gardens calm me. Inside the cozy homes I witness what I believe to be good lives taking place; they soothe me, and at dusk on my way home from night class, I stare unabashedly into them.

Our home becomes a little calmer despite the chaos that led to this moment. Violence keeps us all moving around one another like a game of musical chairs. One incident after the next. Cornelius moves back out and Claire moves in as if this is some kind of rehab center for broken people. Claire had called for help. Cornelius went to her rescue as her alcoholic boyfriend slammed his own head into their living room wall until it bled and she didn't know what to do. So she moves in, and I finally have an older sister with me again. Despite the violence that led us here, there is a sense of peace, of better things to come.

Mom begins a cleaning frenzy for Junior's arrival. Dad has framed Junior's GED certificate that he earned in prison and put it on the center of the mantel. His room, which had been occupied by various found furniture and books and pitchforkings, is cleaned out. The things that are Junior's are unearthed: his vintage soda-bottle collection, his CD and cassette tapes, his sneaker collection, his posters. We make his bed for him.

This is an event, a holiday. Dad blows up a photo of Junior to poster size and has it laminated at a nearby print center. It is a photo of Junior in front of one of Dad's jobs right before he went away. I know Dad was the photographer because of the scale of the photo. Dad gets low to take photos, finding the angles where the subject looks large. Junior is tall, a giant, smiling, with his hands on his hips in superhero fashion, as if he is about to take off flying. The poster is unrolled and showcased on a chair in the living room.

We complete the finishing touches on his room. Dad pulls some books off the shelf: *Crack in America* edited by Craig Reinarman and Harry G. Levine and *The Prison Industrial Complex* by Angela Davis. These are books he believes will help Junior understand his situation, books he must have also sent to him in prison, or books like them. I wipe the dust from each soda bottle in Junior's collection and place them gently on the side table. I help Mom make the bed. While we clean, we infuse the room with our hopes for him. *Change*, we imbue with every move of our hands, *you can do it, we will help you*, with every wipe of the towel, *this is where you belong*, with every tuck of the sheet, every fluff of the pillow, *you can heal here*.

I am nervous on the morning of his return. Dad goes and picks him up from the bus station and we wait. Mom continues to clean and put things away with an energy I haven't witnessed in a very long time. Much like when she is in a garden in the sun in Selma, she is beaming, she looks rested, and she hums a tune under her breath as she flits from room to room, organizing until the last moment. Her boy is coming back and things will be different now.

I carry with me a nervous energy for his return. He'll

be different. Who will he be? Who have I become? We will have to get to know each other again. I also carry guilt for having written him so many letters but not having sent any. I wonder if he'll be upset with me. But I'm excited to tell him about my plans for improving my grades and how things are already going well at my new school.

His return brings with it a lightness none of us has known since he left. Since before he left. Since long before. Since he was a boy. We remember our boy. It is that boy we imagine is returning from prison, the boy we knew, so full of potential. It's he who will walk through the front door beaming with his mischievous gap-toothed smile. For that boy, we see a future: college, a job, a life, and it fills us with hope we haven't had in a very long time. His well-being is tied to the well-being of the entire house. What happens to him happens to us. We have all been in prison. Before that we were all lost, we were all chased, and we were all monsters. Now is the time for hope. The house is full of it.

Danielle is on her way. We haven't seen much of her. Dad has communicated with her, but for the most part she's been as gone as he's been. But they stayed together; she waited for him, and now she is on her way to his arrival party. It will be one of the first times she'll be allowed into the house. It will be the first time I'll have seen her since he's been gone.

Claire is home now too. Angelica is running around. Whenever we clean, she seems freer. With more space, she runs in circles around all the parts of the house that have just opened up, spreading the goodness we all feel. Soon our boy will be home.

Mom calls to me from downstairs in her singsong way when he arrives. When I open the door to his room, he's in it. For so long the room has been empty. Mom is hovering over him, holding and kissing his face. When she is done, there is maroon lipstick on his forehead and his cheeks. She has worn lipstick for this occasion. He looks dizzy, overwhelmed, doesn't say much, just sort of shakes his head in disbelief to be back in the world, in his old bedroom, in his old house, surrounded by family. He's filled out, the angles of his face are more pronounced with his short haircut, his nose has broadened, his smile is even more confident. "I know I got fat," he says, almost in apology, smiling. His face is oily, its vibrant shine renewed. I observe him; I look for the ways in which he's changed. Danielle goes to him. It's the first time she's seen him since she took that long bus ride to Susanville a few months ago. They hug awkwardly in front of their audience. Angelica jumps up and down continuously as if the ground is made of rubber; her little-girl self cannot hold in the excitement the rest of us have learned to hold in. She's brimming with it. She hops over to Junior and throws herself onto him. I join her. I hug him, not yet knowing what to say but so relieved he's home.

"Man, I'm so happy to be out," he says.

I want to tell him I missed him and I had to fend for myself all this time and I felt abandoned. I want to slap him and let him know just how stupid I think he is for making the choices he did. I want to tell him he better not be mad at me because I can't stand one more hypocrite telling me to do better. I want to tell him do better. This is life or death. But I say none of it. "Welcome back," I say and I take in his familiar sticky skin smell for the first time in over a year.

The ceremony continues for a while, and then Mom says, "Okay, let him rest," and we leave him there with Danielle, the door opened a crack. We make ourselves busy but in the back of our minds we wonder what his next move will be. We pray he has transformed into a good boy, that he won't call anyone from the street, that he will stay right here for as long as it takes.

Junior is being good. He has been home. We all walk around on eggshells, not wanting to break the spell. Not wanting to upset him or fight or make too many demands. We are gentle and watchful: "What does Junior need?" "Is Junior okay?" "Go check on Junior." When he is gone, we hold our breath, waiting for him to return.

His blue Maverick is in the garage, and it's in need of a tune-up so he can't drive it yet. He's got no money. So many things cost money. I worry about his need for money. How will he get it? Danielle has a very old red Honda she bought while he was away. He begins driving it, mostly just taking her to work at her new job at a mattress warehouse in San Rafael.

"Come take a ride with me," Junior says to me one day. We haven't had much time to talk alone. There is so much tension to be cleared, but now that he's back it feels it is dissolving effortlessly, our presence confirming what we needed to know about each other for the last year: you are okay, you are here. There isn't a need to talk about anything but right now. What will the future be like? What will we do with our second chances? I welcome the time to ride with him over a bridge, let the water below clear out any residual drama. He seems different. He's quieter than before, calmer. We drive to San Rafael, me in the back, Danielle in the passenger's seat, all in relative silence. Just the whir of the old engine and the highway wind.

When Danielle gets out of the car, something eases between us. I can relax with my brother. I hop into the front seat. I put my feet up on the dashboard and lean back into my seat. The sun feels warmer. I close my eyes. I've never been to this city, and when I open my eyes, we are driving down a windy hill with beautiful houses on either side, overlooking the bay. The water twinkles. I feel rich. I feel like a tourist. I feel light for the first time in a very long time.

"So, what now?" I ask. Junior is quiet for a little too long, so I fill the space with questions. "You can go to college. You have your GED. Are you going to college?"

"Yeah," he says. "I want to."

"Good," I say. "That's good."

"I can't go back." I don't know if *back* means prison or the street, but I am so glad to hear it. I am still on eggshells. I don't want to push. I am affirming.

"That's good," I say calmly, but inside I am panting with relief like I have just been given water in a scorching desert. When I look at him driving, against the sunlight, his hair short, his fattened face, I think I can see a father; I think I can see a student; I think I can see someone's employee. I can see some future for him, and it makes me smile. I look out the window as we cross the San Rafael Bridge again, this time just us, and we are quiet and content.

IT'S BEEN JUST over a week since his return and we are all uplifted. It's hot out, and Claire and I decide to walk to lunch in Rockridge, the adjacent and more upscale neighborhood. We are feeling celebratory. There is a sense of newness in the air, making the sun hotter and brighter, seeming as though it is shining right over this family, following us and only us wherever we walk. Vivian is now in the Dominican Republic, studying abroad. Cornelius has finally finished his last rough semester and will be the first of any of us to graduate from college and walk across a stage. Claire has moved in temporarily, and it's like I have a new sister to share my life with. She is back in school and starting over after her breakup. Junior is downstairs in his room, filling it with his new self. There are job applications and community college applications and books scattered on the desk with his small, neat handwriting scrawled on each page in black ink. Mom continues smiling like I've only seen her do in Alabama, when she feels at home and at peace. Dad seems lighter. When he comes home, he makes sure Junior's GED is in its right place, front and center on the mantel. The sun follows us all in these early days of fall. Our boy is home.

Walking is peaceful. I love looking at the gardens in the big front yards of the craftsman houses Claire and I pass by. We point at the prettiest ones. "Look at those," I say, pointing to a house surrounded by blooming rosebushes and rose vines draping from the archway. We stop to smell some and then we get distracted by the house with even more dramatic draping purple wisteria, vines of fragrant jasmine, lavender, and honeysuckle. It's as if every garden reflects back to me the hope I feel beaming from my heart: for my sisters and brothers, for my parents, but especially for Junior. The flowers themselves are prayer to me: *You will be okay.* I want to embody the blooms, the beauty of them, and transfer them to my family, to Junior and to all the boys like him, to all the ones in prison, to the ones in the street who believe they're free but are not, to the mothers and the fathers and the sisters and the brothers. *You are beautiful. I see you. Look how beautiful you are.*

We follow the flowers until we reach the main street that connects our neighborhood to the better one. This is the same street I once crossed with a pistol in my hand. When we cross over, the houses will be bigger, the gardens more spectacular. I want it. I want to go to that better place.

I feel so big, like the sun itself is in me—like I can bloom too, like I have a magnetic power, like I can make people stop and notice, like I can create desire, like my very existence could be a prayer. We opt to sit outside on the patio of the restaurant we choose. I sit up straighter in my chair as I peruse the menu, as if I have always been perusing menus on patios. I peek at Claire. I wonder if she feels the way I do. She is absolutely beautiful to me, her curls hanging in her face, her glamorous sunglasses hiding her concentrating brows beneath. She looks like she deserves to sit on a patio, like she has always sat on patios. I don't tell her how beautiful she is to me. I feel this sense of beauty radiating from me. I can barely contain it. We order, me the ravioli and her the pesto. We coat our dishes in parmesan and slurp up the excess sauce like it is our birthright to eat parmesan. She crosses her legs and the tiny tattoo on her ankle faces me. It is a sankofa symbol with the infinity *8* inside. Eight, for our family—six kids and two parents, forever. The waiter comes over and asks if we'd like dessert. We both decline, and sit back and let the sun beam down on us. We don't know what we're celebrating. Peace, finally. New beginnings, perhaps.

The ringing of my cell phone takes me out of the dream state I've entered, basking in the light of this okayness, allowing myself to believe it. It's Danielle. I think it's odd she is calling, and pick it up with interest. Perhaps she wants to be closer again now that Junior's back.

"Hello?"

"Melissa." She says my name with urgency. What in the world could it be? "Melissa," she says again. Claire looks at me for information. *Who is it?* she asks with her hands, and I squint my eyes in her direction.

"Melissa," she says again.

"What is it?"

"Your brother was shot." Time stops. I pause for what feels like an hour, but it is in reality so fast. It's like I've been shot. It's fight or flight now. We must act. But first I float. I rise up over the table, over Claire, over the restaurant. Held up by the breath inside me I won't yet release, I ask for time, I ask for what she will tell me next not to be terrible. I ask for him to be safe.

"Where?" I ask. I need to know where he has been shot. A leg, an arm? I float and I brace myself for the answer.

"His head, Melissa." Her voice, which has been trying to gently deliver this information, cracks now.

"Oh my god." The blood, the cells, the bones, the matter inside of me, whatever I am made of, all I am made of gets up. I tell Claire. Junior has been shot in the head. And together we begin moving our bodies, trying to make our way out of this place and to him. The phone is on my ear still but my body parts are separate: a listening ear, a moving body, an active brain, a heavy heart. "Where is he?"

"He just got picked up by the ambulance and he's on his way to Highland." Everyone knows Highland is the homicide hospital. Highland is where people from the street go to die. I push that knowledge aside and I move.

"We're on our way."

I don't know how the bill is paid. I don't know if it's paid at all. We take off running down the fancy street with all the restaurants and shops, past the cafés, past the patios, past the gardens and the houses. We run thinking one synced thought, a mantra: *Be alive, be alive, be alive, be alive.* One of us calls Dad. One by one we all find out like a game of telephone: *Junior has been shot, Junior has been shot, Junior has been shot.* Dad picks us up at the halfway point. Mom and Angelica are already in the car. We drive fast. The fastest. I don't see anyone. Not a car, not a person, it is only us on the street. Claire holds my hand. No one speaks. No one breathes. A breath would mean this could be real. A breath could mean being dropped hard from the safety of suspension, this place of uncertainty where on the other side an answer awaits. We drive, breathlessly. *Be alive, be alive, be alive.*

I pray for life. *Alive, alive, alive, alive.* As if by telling all the parts of me to focus on this one goal, I could achieve life. I could make him live. I could remove the bullet from his brain, rapidly heal his wounds, send the bullet back into the gun from which it came, send the boy who did it back to where he came from, change his mind, give him some other goal. And we'd have Junior back. *Alive, alive, alive. Be alive, be alive.* I chant this unceasingly, feel it on a cellular level, as I follow my family through the visitor parking lot, through the revolving doors of the hospital and into the blue waiting room where it's quiet, where families are sent to wait for news. I don't know how long it takes. I am too busy: *be alive, be alive.* And eventually someone enters the blue room. A man, a doctor. He asks us if we are the Valentine family. We say that we are. He introduces himself.

"What I'm about to say . . ." His voice becomes part of my heart, echoing, beating. How is he speaking so loudly? How has his voice gotten inside of me, echoing through me with such violence? I hold my ears to protect myself from the sound of his voice. "What I'm about to say isn't easy." The words ricochet painfully inside me, bouncing from one eardrum to the other and down, through my body and landing heavily at my feet. It hurts. "Your son took a bullet pretty hard . . . affecting an area of the brain that"—he pauses—"that is fatal. Now—" He pauses once more. "He is still alive. He's conscious." *Alive, alive, alive.* I perk up. "But his level of consciousness is . . . basically that of a vegetable, and sadly, we are forced at this stage of head trauma, to pronounce victims . . . dead." *Dead, dead, dead.* The words fall to my feet. He keeps talking. "I'm so very sorry to have to tell you . . . your son did not make it."

Mom faces Dad with a look of horror, her mouth open. She throws her hands up, so angry with God. Dad shakes his head and they come together to hold each other in the first moment of losing what they created and tried so hard to protect. I must be floating because I feel so light I could topple over, like I am made of nothing. I am stunned, taking in short, gasping breaths. Claire takes me, she grounds me in her arms. I feel her hands on my head; I am unstable and grateful for the support. She sobs into my neck and holds me. I am limp in her arms. I have nothing left. I used everything to make him live, and it didn't work. Angelica is still so little she doesn't fully understand what's happened. Claire moves away from me and goes to her now, takes her in her arms and sobs. I start to pace around the room. I walk outside. I need evidence that I am real, that the world is real, that objects are real, that there is a sun in the sky, that there are trees, that I am alive, that what I've heard is real, that I now live in a world without my brother.

In the evening Junior is on the news. Dead boy. Dead black boy. Shot. Murder. Homicide. Killer. Killer unknown. Victim. West Oakland. And then it quickly moves on to the weather. The sound bites are devastating. *That's my brother!* I want to shout, but who will hear? It would change nothing. The others who saw the ten-second news clip, his picture, will go on about their lives. They will go on making their dinners. They will shake their heads and go on with their evenings. "Black-on-black crime," they might say. "What a shame. Kids just killing each other." They will not have seen the life that led up to that moment. They will not have seen the boy who, upon learning he had no power (very early), began building a shield to protect himself. He built it painstakingly, every day growing up, getting stronger and stronger until he felt he finally had a bit of power. When a black boy is born, he quickly learns the word for himself: *bad*. When a black boy is a child he quickly learns a new word for himself: *dangerous*. When a black boy is a teenager, he quickly learns he is feared. He learns where his place is: in the back of classrooms, in juvenile hall, in prison. You must make yourself mighty. You must protect yourself. You cannot let yourself be powerless. To be powerless is to acquiesce to a system built for your destruction. You must say no to it. You must find a way to have some power. You will sell drugs. You will intimidate others just as you have been intimidated. You will humiliate others just as you have been humiliated. You will be a player in the game of power, not knowing that the very power you seek is the power that was designed to kill you. The same power that protects also kills. And when you die, they win. I say this inside myself, to the people on the other ends of all the screens, to the "black-on-black crime" people, to all the people who don't know what I know.

My grief is political. I don't care to know who did it. I know who did it. It was some other wounded black boy. Of course he won't be found. He will be shot by some other wounded black boy, and it will go on and on. I know my grief belongs to other sisters and daughters and mothers. These things that I know about his death swirl within me. You got suckered, I think angrily. Why you? You're smarter than this. You let them win. You let them kill you. This was the plan. This is the plan! More and more and more black boys. Endless black boys will die, chasing some kind of power. We failed you. We couldn't save you. I say this to the television, to Junior who cannot hear me, to the people who can't see how I've changed, can't see what I know, to the people who affirm that knowing this changes nothing, that in a world where black life doesn't matter, certainly knowing that in fact it *does*, doesn't matter. But still, I feel I have a powerful secret. I feel I have the key that will end all the death.

What happens over the next few days is a long, blurry procession of *dead, dead, dead*. My body moves without me telling it to. I imagine my parents are the same. They start to float. Uncontrollable bursts of tears. All the cells of my body chant a new mantra: *dead, dead, dead*. How defeated we are. We couldn't keep him safe. This failure rings through the house like the sound of that doctor's voice. *Your son did not make it.* One of you did not make it. There were six, now there are five. One of you is missing. One of you did not make it. His absence is devastating. His GED, the laminated poster Dad made of him, and other blown-up photos of him are placed around the house to make him here, to bring his presence back into the house. We fill the house with him.

Though I had been excited about a fresh start at school, I stop going again. During the day, I float. My body does things. Danielle has returned to our lives and it is me she clings to. The days leading up to the funeral are foggy. The brain doesn't fully work. The body moves around without effort. The body stops wanting. It doesn't want food. It doesn't want sleep. It doesn't want joy. It wants only to remember Junior.

On the days leading up to the funeral, Danielle especially wants to be near us, near me. Vivian has flown in from the

Dominican Republic. I am so grateful to have more sisters. Vivian doesn't stop hugging me. I don't stop hugging Danielle. Our bodies do this without us telling them to. Danielle sleeps in my bed. She doesn't talk much; none of us do. We begin the night as separate as possible, looking for space without falling off my twin-size bed, but once we are deep asleep, she moves closer to me and I am awoken several nights in a row by her sobbing. She tells me she is dreaming about him. I tell her it's okay. My body doesn't want sleep. It wants memory. "Tell me about the dream." I am jealous. I want to see him too. "Tell me."

The funeral will be soon. The next day we are told we can see his body at the coroner's. *See him.* The words penetrate me. It is presented as a good opportunity, the last chance we will be able to see his body alone before the funeral, say our goodbyes. But just as I cannot make myself want sleep or want food or want joy, I cannot bring myself to want to see his cold dead body be pulled out from a drawer for us to sob around.

It is the day before his funeral, the day of the viewing. "Let's get your hair done," Danielle suggests. I let myself be pulled like a balloon to a hair salon with Danielle. We wander there on foot, looking for the first place that offers the service we seek: to be changed. The salon is near the high school I just switched out of, near a familiar bus stop where kids gather in groups waiting for buses to go home or cut school. It is on the Oakland side of the dividing line that separates the city from Piedmont. We walk over the hill and cross the threshold. Neither of us has ever been here. There is a liquor store on the corner that I've been to many times and all this time I never knew there was a tiny salon tucked away in the back. We are the only customers. A woman greets us and asks us what we want. I am in a dream state and let Danielle speak for the both of us.

"Just a press," she says. "For her." She points to me, and the woman invites me to sit in a chair. She tells me what to do in between sips of her sweating beverage. I smell alcohol on her breath as she talks. "Come here, put your head back like this." She washes my hair, and for the first time in a while I remember I have a body, I remember joy, until I am pulled back from the sensation violently and brought back to the knowing: *dead, dead, dead. He did not make it.* Like being slapped or having freezing water thrown onto you, I remember. Danielle sits in a chair next to the door and watches us. All three of us are reflected in the mirror. One of us is drunk, two of us are floating; one of us is trying to have a sense of control, one of us being altered by a pressing comb. While the woman sips and combs and sips and combs, attempting to transform me, Danielle and I look into the mirror at each other, at ourselves, past the reflection. While we look, we both know that everyone else is viewing Junior's body. That he is now being pulled out of a drawer. That his head is wrapped up in cloth to conceal his head wound, that his body will be empty of him, that he is gone. The woman sips and straightens, Danielle and I stare into the mirror, and in between every second it returns: *dead, dead, dead.*

The woman announces she is finished. Danielle walks over to me. She strokes my hair. "Do you like it?" We look into the mirror again, this time at me. I look like someone beautiful. I look like a normal person. I look like I could have a brother who is alive. I look like I could be happy. I look like someone who could want things.

"I look different." Still we stare into the mirror. Neither one of us can smile. Neither one of us knows why we are here. We are the blind leading the blind. The mourning trying to remember being alive. We are two women who have lost. What are we looking for? Some sign of change. Some physical representation of what has transformed inside us. Some acknowledgment that we are different now, marked. All I can say as we look is "I look different." I'd like to look different. I'd like to look into the mirror and see someone bigger, someone more powerful. I'd like to look so different that when people look at me they could know the secret I carry. But I look the same. I look like a girl. I look normal. I look unharmed by my knowing that boys like my brother die every day, and families like mine must try and go on living. No one will know how different I am, how traumatized I am. No one will know my secret.

I wear my straightened hair to the funeral the next day. I wear the only appropriate dress I have. It is a long black dress with a white floral motif that I wore to my eighth grade graduation. I catch glimpses of myself in glass doors and windows, and I don't recognize myself. And that feels right—Who am I without my brother? How did I get to this chapel? Who drove me here? Did I walk? I am pulled places. I have no control over my body. It moves. It goes here or there. It wants nothing. When I walk into the chapel I see a bulletin board filled with pictures of Junior from his whole little life: baby, child, teen, man. I stare at them and then I stand back and watch as more and more people fill into the room. Black people, white people, Quaker people, street people, kids I'd seen around our old high school. One by one they pull my limp body into theirs and squeeze me, tell me, "Hey, we're so sorry," tell me, "You will get through this," tell me, "You will survive."

And in the seconds between death, when a thought enters, I think, I don't want to survive, then. If this is something to be survived, I don't want to survive. If this is something to get through, I don't want to make it to the other side. That thing in me that's changed wants to let itself be seen, wants to let itself be changed by the part of this death that is universal, that is more personal even than family, the part of this tragedy that can be described as an epidemic, the part of this tragedy that is so old it has been written in books, the part of this death that is all of ours. Every single person walking into this chapel is part of it. I haven't been spared and I won't survive. None of us will. You and you and you. You're all as dead as me, and you're all in as much danger, because as long as we are dying in the streets like animals, each one of us is a little bit dead, each one of us in danger. The anger and the secret and the death and the love all mix together now; they come in swarms. Then a new thought enters: God, how loved he was. How many different kinds of people loved him. And I sit back, outside of myself, and watch in awe.

A girl I've seen at school before comes in with a camcorder and films the entire event, narrating while she films. Other kids come in baggy pants and oversize sweaters, leans in their gaits. They nod respectfully. Quakers next to his friends from *the street* next to wholesome-looking folk who watched him grow up around the neighborhood. Each looking around the room and seeing the complexity of his identities, seeing his photos, seeing his life as they'd perhaps never seen it before. One of his childhood friends enters with wet eyes, he comes to me, brings me in for a wordless hug. I feel the metal shell of his bulletproof vest on me as we embrace. How many others wear these? And in the seconds in between the blinding cloud of death, another thought emerges: You'll be next. I don't want to think it, and I am ashamed as soon as I do. I look around. And then you, and then you. And more and more and more black boys. More funerals like this one.

I find a seat in the front row in a long line of my family. Dad goes up to the podium and talks for a long time. Many words are said but I cannot hear a single one. Just *death, death, death* radiating from my bones, my blood, my cells— all the things I am said to be made of.

Next we are driven up many steep hills to the top of the cemetery where he will be buried. This is the most beautiful place in Oakland. You can see a panoramic view of the entire Bay Area—every bridge, every peninsula, every city, every lake. The cemetery is on the same street we live on, on the same street we were born on. There is the bridge we drove over together, there is another. Right there is the hospital you were born in, all the way over there is the hospital you died in, there is the house you lived in, there is the school you went to, there is the prison you lived in, here is the place you'll be buried. I can see them all from point to point; I can touch them with my fingers. *Life, life, life, death, death, death.* Baby, child, boy, man, death. School, prison, death. Point by point, all roads lead to death, the ultimate disappearance.

His body is lowered into the ground. I remember going to our cousin's boyfriend's funeral with Junior. I remember watching my cousin lose herself. Now it is my turn. Whatever life has gone dormant in me, I somehow find it and summon the energy to run toward his casket. I break away from Vivian, who is holding me. "I'm getting in there!" I scream. Vivian pulls my hand, grabs hold of me, but I am strong too, and I pull away. With my one freed hand I reach toward him, I scream again, the entire crowd watching me, just as I had watched my cousin. "Let me get in!"

After the funeral I stand and stare out into the gorgeous view as I had stood in the mirror at the salon—blankly, wanting something to appear different. When I finally bring myself to walk up the hill where our car is, I pass by Danielle. She is looking out at the view, beyond the view; she is surviving as she, too, has been advised.

After the funeral, the only thing I want is to not forget. Danielle doesn't sleep over anymore and with my room to myself again, I am free to have my rituals of remembrance. At night I talk to him, I scream at him: *How stupid you were. How abandoned I am. You cannot fix this one. You fell into their trap.* I crumple up and throw the letters I never sent to him across the room. Maybe if I had sent them, I think. I find every photo I have of him, and at night I place them around me and talk to them by candlelight. While I remember him, while I try and hold on to every memory and store each one in a safe place, I find unlikely solace in a box cutter. The first night I cut a little bit. The next night I cut a bit more. I am surviving.

WHAT A SHORT time it's been. He returned from prison and within a week was killed. He is buried, and what now? Not forgetting is a commitment our family dedicates itself to. Dad commissions an artist we know to draw his face. He has it printed on a T-shirt. He has another shirt made—a photo of Junior on my pink bike, smiling. New and larger photos of him are blown up and hung up on walls around the house. Junior as a boy. Junior as a baby. His whole life on all the walls.

Then we find a bigger wall. Until now, none of us could bring ourselves to go to the place. The details of his death told to us by witnesses could not be comprehended all at once. He ran. He was chased. He had run through a few backyards, hopped over a few fences. He was shot in the head on Thirty-Sixth and West Street in West Oakland along a freeway exit. The killer disappeared quickly, and Junior fell to the ground against the giant wall and began bleeding onto the street. A neighbor in a house across the street saw him lying there and ran outside. He looked dead or dying. She was a religious woman and so she asked him, as she believed him to be dying, if he accepted Jesus. He said yes. She held his hand, called an ambulance, and waited with him, as blood and life left his body.

There is still blood on the ground when we arrive at the wall where it happened. We are here to commemorate him. The cement on the ground doesn't look big enough for a body to have lain there. I imagine his legs and torso splayed out on the street close to moving cars, his head here on the cement close to the wall. This is not a place meant for humans. Cars swoosh by, exiting the freeway at high speeds. They don't notice us. I imagine Junior lying here and the cars passing by, no one seeing. Just as so many times before, we stood, marched, and died in the streets, and so many times, no one saw. No one looked.

Here, in this place, next to the blood, lie teddy bears, flowers, a bottle of Rémy Martin, and a picture his friends put there. *RIP Chris* in thick letters on the wall.

The cars driving by is too much; the wind they create leaves me feeling weightless and flimsy. The invisibility is too much. I reach into some unknown place and find a way to anchor myself there—here. His friends have made a grave for him here. So many graves on the streets, below the eye level of most, low down to the street where they die—freeway exits, gutters, alleys, in the middle of busy streets where it is easier to look away. The invisibility is piercing. The desire to be seen is so strong. I pull out a thick graffiti marker and join my family. Dad is writing a Bible verse along the wall. *Today you will be with me*, he writes, and I watch him as he completes the sentence with determination: *in paradise*. He proclaims, boldly and for all to see, that his son's place is in paradise. Mom watches him with her head in her hands; it has become her permanent pose. The woman who asked Junior to accept Jesus comes out of her house across the street and stands near her. Their lips move and they nod heads, hold hands. I join Dad and Cornelius and Claire and Vivian, and I write as big as I can, *Come back, come back, come back.* I write in as many ways as I can and as large as I can. I want everyone to see that someone died here—that people are dying here. I make them look. We bring blown-up pictures of him and tape them to the wall around our words as high as we can reach. *Look. See.* It is dizzying. And people do look. We don't see them; we are so involved in our activity, in our grief, that we haven't noticed. We have caused such a disturbance that someone has called the police on us. No one wants to see this public grave.

I continue to write. I draw a rose. One of the cops comes close. "What is this shit?" he asks. He is white and small. I want to spit on him, but I continue to draw the petals on my flower instead. Cornelius walks up to him and tries to get him and the other officer to understand what is happening. The small white one isn't having it. "You know you're defacing state property? I can have you all arrested." He and Cornelius get into it. Cornelius is provoked by this man; he's raw and angry, and it escalates quickly. When I turn around, he is in handcuffs. Claire runs over to them and screams, "Arrest me! Arrest me!" But he's not interested in her. Suddenly another police car rolls up and another man emerges.

"What's going on here?"

"Look, man," Cornelius begins with the new cop. The cop is black, so he can talk to him that way, call him *man*; he thinks he will sympathize. "My brother died here. Right there." He nods in the direction of the teddy bear next to the blood.

The cop shakes his head. He looks at all of us, standing frozen on the side of the freeway wall, markers in hand, bleary-eyed. He looks up at the wall. "Jesus," he says. He looks at Cornelius in handcuffs, at the small white man who holds him, at Claire heaving next to them. "Jesus, let him go."

The small cop protests. "But he's defacing state property . . . and resisting arrest."

"Let him go!"

He reluctantly lets Cornelius free. Cornelius looks like he's resisting very powerful urges to strike the white cop.

What is this shit? The cop's words reverberate in my ears as if my inner speakers are broken—*shit, shit, shit*—as if my auditory system is permanently set to the injustice channel, set to feel grief like this. It is all I hear. All I see. I'm left with this fight or flight, this hypervigilance, this anxiety that will not quiet. I feel desire emerge for the first time. My desire is clear. I want everyone to know what happened, to know what happens. I am told it is a crime to suggest that we see.

Converging right here on this street is one giant crime. I couldn't write big enough. There aren't enough walls to fit all the names of all the lost ones and all the poetry they incite. The streets aren't big enough to fit all the people who love the ones who die, not big enough to hold our regret for the world not being a nurturing one for them, for our failure to protect them, protect ourselves.

My secret is that, even as I am traumatized, I am filled with love. This love has changed me. I can't unsee what I've seen, and what I now know about the world and my anger, my grief—it has all morphed into love for the lost ones, love for children, love for myself. This love feels subversive; it will be the thing that heals me. Even though I will be traumatized and I will act out and I will grow up and become a woman just like I always wanted, it will be my invisible power that will live inside me. I will talk about this love, I will write about it, I vow to tell the truth that only I can tell through this particular hurt heart of mine. I loved him, and because I had that privilege, my heart is now huge. This is compassion; this is the gift in all of this, if there is one to be had from the trauma of losing him. I stand, shaking, bearing my secret: I am changed, but I still have love.

ELEVEN

We return to what is left of our lives. We were focused on trying to keep him alive for so long, and so there is emptiness where everyday life used to be. I walk around numb, floating along, because when I tune in, the reality is so brutal it knocks me out. We do not recover; none of us do. We become islands within the walls of the house, each of us unto ourselves, sorting through the unfairness we feel alone. For a while Mom goes to meetings and marches with a group of mothers who have lost their children to gun violence. I don't have any group like that, so I get closer to Nellie, whose mom is deep in her alcoholism, abusive and erratic, and another friend who lost her father to cancer; I keep them close because we are all grieving. I let my grief consume me.

After the funeral I take a hiatus from eleventh grade. Teachers understand for the most part, although there's one teacher who tells Nellie that I should "be over it by now." She is the same teacher who, later that year, whispers in my ear, "I don't even read your papers, I just give you As," and then winks, as if she's doing me a favor. I am on a mission to get out. I don't even know what I mean yet by *get out*, but

I want to be done with high school, and after that I want to go far away. Away from Oakland. Away from my family. Away from the kids I know. Away from what feels like hopelessness.

I think of Junior as I study and write my essays and struggle through algebra and then trig, and then geometry and chemistry—all classes I'd previously failed when he was still here. I must make them all up if I am to get out of here. I must not let his death be in vain. In my personal life, I am intoxicated and reeling, but in my academic life, I am focused. I feel self-imposed pressure to excel because he is gone and he will never be able to go to college or go to another country or go anywhere at all. I must live in his name. I decorate my bedroom walls with a collage of his photos. I have a special photo album that gives me comfort when I am overwhelmed by life, and create a ritual out of it: I take out the album, flip through pictures of him, light candles, talk to him, and slice little cuts on my thigh with a razor blade. I don't want to forget him. When I see my family doing what feels like moving on—going to work or to school, being in relationships—it makes me even angrier even though I am doing the same. It looks like we are forgetting. Moving on is forgetting, so I hold my grief close.

The next time I see Danielle, it is by accident outside a Safeway near my high school. She is very pregnant, holding the time that's passed in her body. She tells me the baby is his. I will be an aunt. My niece will not have a father.

Right before Christina is born, I have a dream that Junior is smiling and holding up a baby to the sky. Without him as our reason, Danielle and our family force our way into each other's lives so baby Christina can be loved. Our shared trauma was our only connection, but now we have this beautiful baby girl. Christina makes us all feel alive. How could a being be so happy, so vital, so willing to love and be loved? She knows nothing of sadness or death. But she will know what it is to grow up without a father. My love for her is pure and intense, as if he is here again. I keep looking for a feature or a behavior, but she is her own person—optimistic, positive, smart, confident. You're little now, I think as she grows and grows, but soon you will also have collages of him on your bedroom walls, and you'll want to know if you are like him, you'll want to know who he was.

I SIT PARKED outside my gym in my silver Honda Civic—my pride, the only thing I've ever owned—listening to the sounds of my car resting, and I start to feel a familiar heavy feeling. It's a few years after I graduated college in New York, twelve years after Junior's death, and I've just moved back to Oakland. Recently I find myself doing this: sitting in my parked car, in a numb state, trying to muster the energy, the courage to move my limbs and take myself to the place I'm supposed to be going—home, the gym, therapy. Today I'm outside the gym, willing myself to work out, but also willing something more.

I think of Mom and Dad. It is getting close to Thanksgiving and as the family peacemaker still, I am the one to organize holiday meals, plan the menu, keep everyone talking and happy. What a burden. It starts to feel heavy, and then I am reminded: We are together. We still have each other. What a beautiful thing. And then another memory enters: one of us didn't make it.

I know I need to call Mom and Dad to discuss the holiday, yet I know calling them will leave me unsatisfied. They have not grown more emotionally available over the years, but they've gotten sweeter with age. I wish Junior could see how sweet they are. I'm no longer angry, I just want them to be proud of me. Instead of talking about feelings or rehashing old memories, I stand before them, do a little twirl, and let them be proud of me. *Look at me. I grew up. I can take care of myself. I'm happy.* It is our gift to each other, these tiny lies; it is easier than talking, easier than anger.

They live in the same house, and I enter it just as I did as a teenager: heavily. My bedroom is nearly intact, the whole house a symbol of a very hard time in our lives. Whenever I arrive, my legs become lead, but I walk up the stairs leading to the front door anyway. This time, I'm greeted by Dad. Mom is scrambling to clean for me, but she stops when I come in and her smile when she sees me is so big and genuine. Dad opens a bottle of white wine that he bought from the new wine shop on Piedmont Avenue. We drink out of mugs, and he goes back to pretending to read the paper while Mom and I talk. It is not so easy for Dad and I to talk, but he likes to be in the room and hear our cheerful chatter; it makes him happy.

They are absolved, my parents. They did their best, and I know that now—working hard with six kids, navigating their own trauma they came into this world with. I can barely drag myself from place to place some days, let alone attempt to raise six children. I forgive them and love them wholly. I ask them how they are, and Mom says, "Well, just wonderful," and I know she means it. "Chris won us tickets to a concert at this real cool place in San Francisco and we danced last night. Let me tell you, girl! All the young people were amazed that these old people could dance. Right, Chris?" And Dad chuckles, blushes. Just as I twirl and let them be proud of me, they give me a show of their love and I know it is real and I let that ease me.

I sit in the car for a while, my hands over the steering wheel, my forehead resting on one of my arms. I know this position well. I want so badly to fill my sadness, to make it go away. It's always there, lying dormant, ready to activate at any moment. My sadness has an anger to it today: One of us didn't make it. One of us didn't make it. One of us didn't make it.

Eventually, I make myself walk into the gym, eyes red, but proud. I did it again: I faced my sadness and lived anyway. I feel better. I will show up to life. The people in the gym will look at me strangely, wondering if I've been crying, and I will walk past them, feeling victorious because I've shown up for another day.

I AM IN my thirties now, Christina a teenager. On a lunch date one afternoon, she tells me she is being bullied by some girls at her school. She tells me she wants to enroll in independent study so she doesn't have to be in a toxic environment every day. As she speaks, I am in awe of her confidence, her practicality and wisdom, her survival instincts, her intelligence, her resilience. I tell her I support her and that I'll talk to her mom. Our family has learned what can come of bullying, and it is not worth it. We will not let violence touch her life more than it already has. After our lunch, I drop her off at her house and walk inside to say hello to Danielle, but before I find her, Christina invites me to come and see her new room. They haven't lived in this East Oakland apartment long so I follow her into her room and sit on her twin bed with her. Immediately my eyes are met with pictures of my brother, her father, taped in a large cluster to the wall. She hasn't always had her own space or she's been too young, so this is the first time I have seen her trying to create a story around her father. She holds on to that cluster of photos in place of lived memories.

At the end of her senior year, Christina asks me for pictures of her dad. She wants to put them on her graduation gown. I send her all I have and she adorns herself in him. Her robe is a collage of him in all phases of his short life. She is now almost as old as he was when he died. She needs him with her as she walks across the stage and collects her diploma, to support her as she approaches womanhood.

This is what trauma looks like nearly two decades later and how it will look always. It has been passed down and will continue to be passed down. It is in utero. Cellular. It's hers and mine; it's all of ours. It's singular yet collective, shared. It is a collection of photos and memories on walls, in minds, on paper. It is the heart stitched closed as an act of self-preservation, and then it is a wondrous capacity to love that rips you back open. This is life in the aftermath of grief, the tides of oceans breathing in and out against sand and rock, creating such violence, but what is left behind marks us, leaving sometimes beautiful patterns that lead us to each other.

I ANSWER A call from Dad in early summer. I am living in Oakland still—we don't see each other as much as they'd like, but Dad calls often. He is silent for a beat too long, and I wait for him to tell me what's on his mind as I usually do. "Oh," he finally says, surprised I've picked up. "Chris Valentine here."

"Hi, Daddy, I know it's you."

He clears his throat.

"What's up? How are you?"

"Okay," he says. Another pause. "We've been getting some fantastic rain for the past week. It's just pouring down. It's pretty exciting to see." He says this as if we don't live in the same city.

"That's great, Daddy."

"Yeah, the plants are doing well." He speaks through plants still: "They're really happy" (*I* am really happy). And he speaks through my mother still: "I'll put your mother on the phone; she is eager to hear from you" (*I* was eager to hear from you).

"Hi, Mama."

"Hi, Melissa." Her familiar voice has an operatic quality to it; she sounds like she's in a good mood. "We're on our way to Quaker meeting. It's just raining down cats and dogs! My goodness, I wish you could see this." And I know what she means is *I wish you were with us*. "Melissa, you're coming to Alabama, right?"

"I'll see, Mama."

"You have to." She is performing, starts to whine: "Please, Melissa, please, I really need you this time." Unlike Dad, she is sharp, speaking her needs clearly and crisply. "I'm not asking you." Dad won't be going this year because of a new gardening job with the city and she needs someone to drive her to and from the airport. All these years she never learned to drive and so she has developed the expectation that she will be taken care of. It is part of who she is now. I will take care of her. And so, when we hang up, I charge an expensive ticket to Birmingham, Alabama, to my credit card and reserve a rental car for us—because even though I'm in my thirties, I still do what my mom says.

We are a family. We have experienced a trauma together, and so we take care of one another. In these small ways, we give one another space to be our traumatized selves, to give it room to speak sometimes, to have the patience to listen for its hidden language. It sounds like my dad's silence, his shock to hear my voice, his aching for the earth to be okay—his metaphor for life, for us, for himself; it sounds like the desperation in Mom's voice, looks like her dependence on me, her reassurance that she will be okay, that we all will.

I wait in the Birmingham airport for Mom, who's on a later flight. She has a flip phone that she barely knows how to use, and so I stay close to her gate not wanting to miss her. I watch for my mom, five-foot and smiling. I want us to have a good time on our road trip together.

When we're finally in our rental car, I tell her that I want to see the ocean this year. I tell her we will drive to Mobile before we return home and swim. She raises an eyebrow at me from the passenger seat. "I ain't swimming in no ocean," she says. "I'll put my feet in though." She smiles.

Her hairstyle for Alabama is a short curly bob with bangs, courtesy of Danielle, who still does her hair after all these years. It is fresh and too stiff to blow, but if it could it would blow in the wind as we fly to the country in our tiny economy rental. When we arrive, Aunt Bernadette is already there. I announce that we are going to the beach tomorrow. She gives me a look: "You're crazy if you think I'm going to the beach. It's three hours away, Melissa."

"I don't care," I say. "I need to see the ocean." The news has me down. There have been three black deaths at the hands of police in the last week, and it is all I can think about. I need a small joy.

The next day I put my swimsuit, my towel, and a change of clothes into the car. "C'mon, Mama." Aunt Bernadette and Aunt Annie both shake their heads. "We need to be cooking, y'all," Annie says. "The reunion is in two days!"

"I'll cook all day tomorrow, I promise." I walk to the rental and start the engine. Mom labors into the front seat reluctantly.

"Look what she's making me do, Bernie," she says. "I'm a hostage." They both burst out laughing.

"Hold on," Bernadette says reluctantly. "Let me get my purse."

I squeal. "Yay, road trip!"

I am determined to feel lightness in all the heaviness of our lives, the heaviness of memories we carry around, the heaviness of the news. I am determined to have some joy. It is my healing. And sharing it with Mom and Bernadette is so special. I drive fast, eagerly. At first, it is forced fun. "Come on, this is fun!" I say, only so that I might believe it. We have two more hours of driving. I connect to Bluetooth and play some music we might all enjoy. I fumble around and randomly choose Adele so I don't crash. In between ballads, Siri tells us which way to go and Bernadette says each time, "That girl is tellin' you to go the wrong way. Don't listen to that girl." I turn the volume up and sing loud. I peek in the rearview mirror and see that Bernadette is smiling. "I know this song," Bernadette says. "I like this song. Turn it up! That girl can sing, can't she?" Bernadette is singing, I am singing, Mom is happily nodding her head to the rhythm. We pass through a storm and it rains so hard for a few minutes that I can't see what's in front of me and we are all a little terrified. There are huge claps of thunder, lightning all over—some of it appears to hit very close to us. But it passes. And soon our tiny car is approaching the coast.

When we arrive, it is softly raining but still sticky hot. I take off my cover-up and go straight for the water. "Come on," I say to them.

"We'll be right here."

I swim. The water is greenish and warm. When I come up for air, it is raining even harder, large drops falling on my face. This day is such a joke, but I don't care. I'm having the best time. I look for my mom and Aunt Bernadette, and spot them on the shore; they have rolled up their jeans to their shins and are walking along the incoming tide, their hair covered with towels. The sight makes me so happy. I am looking at my lineage. Of all the things I have inherited, let me have the knowing that we will be okay. That we will be better than okay.

We return to Selma and the usual festivities of the reunion go on—the fish fry, relatives coming and going, hours and hours of cooking. This year grief is loud, and it asks me to listen. I have been trying to write. There's been the constant news of death and I am raw from it, from my own memories. For me, the South is where the circle completes, where I can see the origins of our ugly history of slavery up close; but it's also tangled up with so much love, beauty, and resilience that is also here encircling us, making this kind of news deeply personal. Death feels close, as if it could be another member of our family.

As the reunion winds down and we prepare to head back to Oakland, we make a visit to the family cemetery. Now that so many of us have passed, it has become ritual on our last day on the land to go up the dirt road to the cemetery and pay our respects to our ancestors. Grief is the way of our lives, it seems. We must have conversations with ghosts. Aunt Bernadette comes with us, wanting to soak up our final day together.

On our way to the cemetery, they show me their old house. "Right there," Mom says, pointing to a wild patch of weeds and bushes. "Right there, just beyond the road there. See?" I stop the car and look, but all I see is brush and red dirt. All evidence of that tiny one-room house and those days of sharecropping has been grown over. It just looks like the woods and yet I see my mother having real memories of her early life. Once you get out of the wild country parts of Perry County, you can see how the economy of the city of Selma has been hit too. The same structures of the fifties and sixties remain like relics of the past—a library, empty shops, abandoned colonial-style buildings, permanently closed diners—against a backdrop of empty, silent sidewalks, the great Alabama River flowing through town, and the iconic Edmund Pettus Bridge, a beacon of certain progress, a reminder of time passed.

I look into the woods Mom points to, and I try to envision fourteen children and my grandparents and all the other families "back yonder." She points in every direction. "There was a corn field right there. That's where Cousin Sang lived. That's where someone died in a ditch. Up there is where Grandma Inez lived . . ." We continue on the country road, driving very slowly so the dirt-coated rocks don't nick the car. My mom and my aunt each point and remember what used to be here.

At the end of the road is a humble family cemetery. In front is a small Baptist church, and in the backyard is where all of our ancestors are buried. Grandma and Grandpa, aunts and uncles, their names crystal clear, their graves well-kept by remaining relatives in the area and members of the church who still remember them. And beyond them, several other generations rest. It's all fallen leaves and overgrown kudzu. Hardly anyone remembers them now, and so their graves are not often cleaned. No one brings flowers anymore. We speak to the newest ancestors, and then I ask Mom and Bernadette to show me the others. "No, no. Snakes back there," Bernadette says. She gets back into the car to wait for us. Mom and I walk back to the wild part. It's shady, on a slight downward slope. I brush the leaves off graves, one after another. "Who is this?" I ask Mom, and she strains her eyes as if doing so will help her remember. "And what about her?" I ask. "And him?" She knows them all. I uncover the dates. "He was born a slave. So was she. So many," I say.

"I guess so," Mom says.

How close it all is. I think back to my research at the library in Selma just days before: 119 slaves. The plantation couldn't have been more than a few miles away from the place I stand—now either wild woods or converted into quaint inns with sanitized guided tours of slave quarters (described obliquely as "tenants' quarters") and fields that used to grow cotton. How close it all is: to be enslaved, to live, to die, to do it all again, in this small circle. I look around at the trees, the graves, and I think I can see it all. I can see how everything connects from here, and yet my knowing changes nothing.

I feel the same need to look around when I'm standing at Junior's grave in Oakland, to connect every dot and see where it leads me, to see how his lost black life is every lost black life, how my grief is part of a collective sorrow. So much time has passed and no time has passed. Here they are and here we are, all of our histories mixing with the present. We bear witness, and because we do, it is our duty to tell the truth only we know.

Standing on the oldest graves in my lineage, I look around and ask back to the grief, the sorrow, What have I come here to do? Where do I go now? What do I do? And I think I can hear Junior in his joyful boy voice, ahead of me as always, saying, *C'mon*. Motioning me to catch up, motioning me forward.

ACKNOWLEDGMENTS

Thank you, Junior, for sharing your life with me, for giving me this story, and for making such a mark on my life. You taught me about love and grief, and then you taught me about healing. You are still teaching me. I miss you, brother, but at least in this book you will live forever.

Thank you to my family—my parents and my siblings— for trusting me with this story and always being supportive. I truly don't know where I would be without you. Dana Pettus and Terian Valentine, you are so special to me and I am so grateful to be part of each other's stories. I love you all so deeply.

A very special thanks is owed to my parents for understanding my need to write this and for having the generosity and kindness to be proud of me still. I am so grateful for my upbringing and the life you gave me.

Enormous thanks to my mentor and friend Catherine E. McKinley for seeing the seed of this story that needed to be told all those years back at Sarah Lawrence. You saw me at the exact moment I needed to be seen. I learned to love the craft of nonfiction in your class.

Huge gratitude to my agent, Charlotte Sheedy, for believing in this book and in me from the beginning and making sure it got out into the world.

Thank you to Louise Meriwether for paving the way and to the judges of the Louise Meriwether First Book Prize—YZ Chin, Glory Edim, Tyler Ford, Natalia Oberti Noguera, Brontez Purnell, Emily Raboteau, and Melissa R. Sipin—who chose my book and made this dream come true for me. Thank you to the whole Feminist Press team for making this endeavor possible and being so supportive and excited from day one: special thanks to my publisher, Jamia Wilson, to Lauren Rosemary Hook and Nick Whitney for all the editorial support, to Lucia Brown for coordinating the prize, and to Jisu Kim, Drew Stevens, and Dorsa Djalilzadeh.

Thank you to my teachers at Mills College, especially Elmaz Abinader. It was in your classes where I conceived the first chapters of this book.

Special thanks to Sadie Barnette for creating the beautiful image that graces this book's cover; I will be forever grateful for this image and for you.

Thank you to Sasha Phipps, Diana Hickey, and all my childhood friends and their families who helped shape me and who inspired parts of this book.

Thank you to the Brujas—the best writing group ever. You talented women inspire the hell out of me and your support is so powerful even from afar.

I would like to thank all my soul friends who have held me up emotionally and spiritually during this entire journey. I've been writing this book for a long time, and you've been my support system for the long haul.

And lastly, to my loving and supportive partner, Mahader Tesfai, thank you for being my best reader and for your constant belief in me. I couldn't imagine being on this journey without you.

The Feminist Press publishes books that ignite movements and social transformation. Celebrating our legacy, we lift up insurgent and marginalized voices from around the world to build a more just future.

See our complete list of books at
feministpress.org

Founded in 2016, **The Louise Meriwether First Book Prize** is awarded to a debut work by a woman or nonbinary author of color in celebration of the legacy of Louise Meriwether. Presented by the Feminist Press in partnership with *TAYO Literary Magazine*, the prize seeks to uplift much-needed stories that shift culture and inspire a new generation of writers.

**THE LOUISE MERIWETHER
FIRST BOOK PRIZE**

THE FEMINIST PRESS
AT THE CITY UNIVERSITY OF NEW YORK
FEMINISTPRESS.ORG